PROUD

PROUD

MY AUTOBIOGRAPHY

GARETH THOMAS

and MICHAEL CALVIN

EBURY
PRESS

1 3 5 7 9 10 8 6 4 2

Published in 2014 by Ebury Press, an imprint of Ebury Publishing
A Random House Group company

The Random House Group Limited Reg. No. 954009

Addresses for companies within the Random House Group can be found at
www.randomhouse.co.uk

A CIP catalogue record for this book is available from the British Library

The Random House Group Limited supports the Forest Stewardship
Council® (FSC®), the leading international forest-certification organisation.
Our books carrying the FSC label are printed on FSC®-certified paper. FSC
is the only forest-certification scheme supported by the leading environmental
organisations, including Greenpeace. Our paper procurement policy
can be found at www.randomhouse.co.uk/environment

Designed and set by seagulls.net

Printed and bound in Great Britain by Clays Ltd, St Ives PLC

ISBN 9780091958336 (hardback)
ISBN 9780091958404 (trade paperback)

To buy books by your favourite authors and register for offers visit
www.randomhouse.co.uk

CONTENTS

Chapter One

THE SCENT OF A WOMAN

I wanted to be a beautiful corpse. My eyes were red-rimmed, milky and stagnant. They stared accusingly from the mirror as I bathed them with cold water, forcing me to focus on the image of someone I had come to despise. He was weak, deceitful and dangerous. The least he could do for those whose love he had betrayed was to have a decent death.

It was an automatic, numbing process. I moved from the bathroom, into the bedroom. The airy aroma of a fresh white shirt was faintly repellent, because I felt unclean. I chose a dark tie, tightened in a Windsor knot, to wear with one of the well-cut grey suits the Welsh Rugby Union issues to all internationals. A pair of black, patent leather lace-up shoes completed the mask of normality.

I walked around the bungalow I shared with my wife, Jemma, in a quiet cul-de-sac on the outskirts of Toulouse, where I played for one of the great clubs in world rugby. I opened the shutters, and the late-autumn sun flooded in through picture windows. It was one of those crisp, cloudless days on which running around the paddock was a reaffirmation of faith.

The house had Jemma's imprint all over it: she was such a good nest-maker it had no stamp of my personality on it. She had arranged the furniture, selected the fabrics, and ensured there were always fresh flowers on the table. Things had seemed to happen magically: the kitchen was always spotless, the beds always made, and the clothes in the right place. She did everything my mother would do, everything a home-maker does.

But she had gone. She couldn't bear to live my lie any longer.

I had made my confession to her three months previously, in our house in the village of St Brides Major, in the Vale of Glamorgan. Yet we had decided to return to France to work at our marriage in the vague, romantic belief that somehow things could change. All we really had was each other, and we had conspired in the belief that our daydream would be enough.

Everything fell apart when I returned from training to the empty house. I knew, instinctively, that things would never be the same again. I rang her repeatedly, but couldn't get an answer. A better husband would have called her friends, or the police; he would have leapt to the panic-stricken conclusion that she had been run down by a careless driver while out shopping. But, instead of fearing the worst and heading to the local accident and emergency department, I sat there, in oppressive silence.

Her departure was hardly a surprise, and it forced me to confront what I had become. Deep down, I knew I had not been man enough to ask myself two hard questions, with two simple answers: Why are you doing this? Who benefits when you pretend that life is a fairytale – you or Jemma?

In answer to the last, I did – in the short term, at least. The pretence of a normal marriage kept my secret safe. Jemma was getting nothing out of the arrangement. I was being hideously unfair, terribly selfish, yet, at the moment of crisis, I was consumed by self-pity: 'Shit. People are going to know something's wrong now. Everything I have hidden so well for so long is going to be discovered. For the first time in my life, I'm on my own.'

I knew I would have to carry on playing and training. I knew the phone calls would come, and that Jemma's return to Wales would set tongues wagging. So I acted entirely in character, and lied through my teeth: I called my mother, Yvonne, and told her Jemma had walked out because she had discovered me cheating with another woman. I repeated the story to Ian 'Compo' Greenslade, my best friend and best man.

It is only now, when I recall the tone of their voices and the eloquence of their silence, that I understand what they were thinking, what they were too kind, loyal and loving to tell me: 'Come on, Alfie. You can't keep this going much longer.'

I was in too deep. I felt I had no option but to retreat into my delusional world, where I kidded myself that I was able to fool all of the people, all of the time.

I had not dared to be true to myself for so many years. The word 'gay' still made me shudder. It had terrorised me from my late teens, when I first played along with the idea I was one of the lads, out on the pull with a bellyful of beer. I could play the role of macho man to order. It was only when I was alone that I could acknowledge the truth to myself: I was sexually attracted to men.

I could suppress my urges, but they needed to be fulfilled; I could subdue my fears, but they never left me. The rest, the international career, captaining Wales and the Lions, was just window-dressing. Until I was honest, irrespective of the consequences, I didn't deserve the privilege of looking myself in the eye. I wanted my sport to define me, because I wanted to live by its fundamental values of honesty and integrity.

A form of madness gripped me that first night after Jemma left. I needed her presence, so I invented it. I climbed into her wardrobe, and sprayed her favourite perfume, Chanel's Coco Mademoiselle, around the interior. I pulled her clothes off the hangers and shelves, and buried myself in them. In my warped state of mind, it was my only way of getting her back. I sensed her spirit, savoured her scent. I was in her space, her sphere. I missed her so badly, and hated myself for what I had inflicted on her.

I'm a tall guy, 6ft 3in, but cowered in a foetal position until dawn. Cramped and claustrophobic, I stared determinedly into the darkness because I was too scared to go to sleep. Whenever I closed my eyes, even for an instant, I'd see a series of nightmare images, projected onto an imaginary screen. They were slow-motion scenes of the destruction I had caused, the mayhem that was about to engulf me. If I blinked it felt like an eternity.

I saw my friends and family crying because I had killed myself. There was a single word, set into a screaming headline:

'Why?' I was dead, but had still not been spared the ramifications of my death. Jemma, her parents, my parents, my friends, my teammates. Every time I closed my eyes, they would be there. I heard them: 'What a selfish fucker … Everything he's ever told us, everything he's based his life on, has been bullshit … We watched his back, we helped him out …'

It was continual. It reminded me of the sequence in the film of *Charlie and the Chocolate Factory*, where Gene Wilder's group is in the boat on the chocolate river. Images appear on the ceiling of the tunnel along which they are travelling in a trippy, hallucinogenic way. This was identical. The faces of my loved ones were grotesquely distorted, as if they were made of melting candle wax. They were nasty, sneering: 'You should have done this, you shouldn't have done that … You should have been honest, you should have been truthful.'

The solution – the fool's way out – was waiting to be discovered the following morning, in a pantry on the way to the garage. It was where I kept my boots, trainers, kit and the odd bit of exercise equipment. There, on a shelf, were bottles of spirits and liqueurs. We used to store them, along with a few boxes of wine and several slabs of beer, in case we had a party. Friends used to come over regularly to visit in the summer. They'd bring booze, chill by the pool and have a nice holiday. We loved their company.

I never usually drank at home. My parents rarely do. I've never been the sort to go out every night, have two or three pints and stroll back to watch something mindless on the telly. Alcohol was just something to get me obliterated on a night out, when I drank to get pissed with my mates. But that day, I remembered the Heinekens, and I thought, 'Fuck it, I feel like getting pissed.' So that was breakfast taken care of.

One thing led to another. I found the vodka and discovered that by taking a couple of paracetamol tablets with it, I could lapse into a sort of sleep for 20 minutes or so. The witches were still waiting for me when I woke up, but they weren't so cruel and caustic. Everything was a little mellower, a little easier. Then the demons started to befriend me, whispering: 'The more you take, the easier things get, the more chilled life is.' And I began to think to myself, 'There could be a nice little way out here.'

I ventured outside, through the back door, and onto the patio. A set of stairs and a gate led to the swimming pool and a moment of revelation – I would drown myself. I'd never again have to deal with a vision of someone screaming at me. I'd never have to justify myself. I'd do it properly, in the grand manner. I'd dress smartly, for my mother as much as anyone. It would be a beautiful way to go.

Looking back, it was a form of nervous breakdown. Before I knew it, I was poolside, suited and booted. A fresh bottle of vodka was in one hand, a full bottle of pills in the other. I removed my socks and shoes, meticulously rolled my trousers up to the knees, and dangled my legs in the freezing water. The Man had a Plan.

I decided I wouldn't gobble the pills, or chug down the booze like a cartoon drunk. They were, after all, my weapons of choice. Instead, I'd repeatedly take a small swig and a single tablet, propelling drugs and drink into my mouth with what, in my frazzled state, I interpreted as a symbolic stabbing action.

My suicide would be measured, civilised. I would gradually become incapable, and slip gently into the water. My last image, before I eased beneath the surface, would be of my family, in happier times. I'd finally understand one of the eternal truths of the sea: the reason drowning men are invariably discovered with a smile on their face.

So much for the fantasy fatality ... I couldn't follow it through.

I staggered away to be sick. I don't know how close I was to losing consciousness, but survival made me angry. I was consumed by self-loathing, and the internal conversation wasn't pretty: 'You're a shit. If you want to do something, whether it's killing yourself or fucking winning for your country, do it properly. You're weak, a fucking pussy.'

I've asked myself countless times over the years, but have never worked out why I didn't take that final swig, that last tablet. Was I a coward? Was someone watching over me? All I know is that something was stopping me – something wasn't right. Even though I was ready for death, had prepared for it and wanted it, an unseen force was saying, 'Not now. Not now.'

The drink was a means to an end, because I didn't like it. It anaesthetised me, but offered no release. Every time I woke, after dropping off for a couple of minutes, there would be a split-second where I had forgotten my circumstances. Then would come the king hit, the realisation that nothing had changed, and the cycle of self-pity and self-loathing would begin again.

I would have given anything not to worry about waking up to a lonely cold house, to an unmade bed that I once shared with Jemma. I would catch a faint whiff of that perfume, and fantasise about waking up to people who loved me and weren't going to judge me. I made empty promises about finding the right time to do the right thing.

It was weird. Even though, rationally, I knew Jemma had gone, almost certainly for good, I convinced myself she was still there. I'd never lived in this house without her. She'd never been there without me. The eerie feeling that her ghost was still watching over me made things worse. For weeks afterwards, I'd be lying in bed and, though I knew she wasn't around, I'd call out her name. I wanted her to answer, to reassure me all would be well.

I was still utterly alone. The only way I could face a return to training, after two sleepless nights, was to neck three bottles of Stella on the drive to the club. I hadn't eaten, because I wasn't hungry and I had lost weight with alarming speed. I felt listless, desperate, but gave the impression of training well.

All experienced athletes know how to cheat their way through a conditioning session with a minimum of fuss, but I could not fool a friend. Trevor Brennan won 13 caps for Ireland, either in the second row or on the flank, but his playing career was destined to end soon, and controversially, in the aftermath of a tempestuous Heineken Cup match against Ulster in Toulouse. While warming up, as a replacement, he jumped into the crowd to fight with a travelling supporter who had called his mother a whore. I was led away by Serge Lairle, our venerable forwards coach, after flicking the finger to his assailants, who were showering me with abuse and plastic beer glasses. We were blood brothers.

We both faced a hanging jury, formed by tournament organisers who were determined to play to the media gallery. Trevor was banned for life, an over-reaction barely tempered or excused by its subsequent reduction to a five-year suspension. A hard man of the greatest integrity and dignity, he promptly retired. I was banned for three internationals, and was appalled at the vindictiveness and incompetence of the authorities.

But all that was in the future. What he first noticed were the empties in the passenger seat of my car, and he growled through the open window: 'What the fuck is going on with this?'

I did my usual desperate song-and-dance act about drinking to forget that my wife had discovered my imaginary infidelity but he was ahead of me. I learned later that Jemma had spoken to Paula, Trevor's partner, and asked them to keep an eye on me. They knew the truth, but they didn't seek confirmation. It was an unforgettable gesture of tenderness and respect, because they were prepared to wait for as long as necessary for me to tell them, on my own terms.

I was out of control. The beers had been demolished within a few days, so I began working my way through the spirits shelf. I needed oblivion. I was a feral creature, acting absurdly with little or no conscious thought. When Trevor walked through an open front door into the house that evening, shouting my name, he found me under the table. I had heard his knock, but was beyond caring. A burglar could have helped himself.

I still don't know whether it was a child-like attempt to feel safe, or the irrational action of someone beyond redemption, but I had made a camp. The chairs were pulled in tight, so I could only stick my head out between their legs in response to his call. Trevor saw that I was wasted, noticed the bottle in my fist, and gave me an undeserved opportunity to benefit from his tough love.

'If you want me to go, I'll go, but if you want me to stay, I'll stay,' he said. 'I'm not going to force you to do anything – you're a grown man. If you've decided to drink it's your decision. You live by the sword, you die by the sword.'

He didn't get a lot of sense out of me that night, even though I wasn't drunk in the established sense – I wasn't wobbling around, making an idiot of myself, but I was confused. I was destabilised by the knowledge I didn't really want to be alive, or face things I would have preferred to forget.

Trevor said nothing the following day, when he sat next to me on the bus to a game against Montferrand. We made small talk about going home immediately after the match, to start to prepare for the autumn internationals, but our eyes conducted a parallel, unspoken conversation. Eventually, he cracked.

He gave me a quizzical look and said, 'All you need to do is fucking tell me what's wrong. Whatever it is, don't worry, because it's fine with me.' Then I think he gave me a wink.

And I thought, 'OK. I'm not ready to tell you, because I'm not ready to tell anyone, but thank you for caring.' I knew he knew. He knew I knew he knew. But, to be honest, I'm not sure how I would have reacted to him challenging the depth of my duplicity. I needed the conceit of being in control of my destiny. Trevor's silence was simply his way of telling me not to go any lower.

It wasn't as easy as that, of course. Returning to Wales to face the rituals of an international series was a schizophrenic experience. There were rugby issues to address, matches to win, collective ambitions to rationalise; I had coaches to impress, fans to please. I needed to renew the bonds of respect and inter-dependence with my teammates. But, on a personal level, tittle-tattle had to be dealt with. I was on autopilot, sustaining the fiction that Jemma and I had split because I had been unfaithful with another girl. I was happy to perpetuate the myth, but, in my quieter moments, I felt an utter fraud. People knew something was up. The knowledge that Jemma was answering the same questions, and having her private life reduced to a tasty morsel of gossip, haunted me.

For all my faults, my friends regarded me as a loyal, decent sort of guy. I may have had problems remembering names – I have a habit of calling everyone '*butt*', the Welsh equivalent of 'mate' – but they knew me as a good type, who'd help if he could. I was expecting them to ignore their instincts; that there had to be more to the situation than met the eye.

Strangers were a different proposition. I had no idea of what they were gossiping about, but couldn't avoid the suspicion that they had leapt to a plausible conclusion. I couldn't influence them, because I couldn't reach them. It's the modern way to be blissfully ignorant, and make something up about someone in the public eye – what if their Chinese whispers unintentionally hit on the truth that Jemma had left me because I was gay, and spread the word? The prospect was random, but real. It scared me witless.

I cherished the unconditional love of my family, but there was nowhere in the world at that point I would have felt comfortable. Had I been alone, in the middle of the Sahara desert, I would have still been fearful of company at the occasional oasis. I wasn't comfortable with what I'd done, with who I was. I still hadn't accepted there were three people in that wrecked marriage, and that two of them were me. I had a hopelessly split personality.

I had six months left on my contract at Toulouse, which was due to expire in the summer of 2007. I was playing for what I regarded as the Real Madrid of rugby; I had an amazing salary, and they wanted me to stay. It was the fulfilment of a childhood dream – everything for which I'd worked hard as a player. But I wasn't sleeping. I couldn't tell anyone what was troubling me, and I was drinking like a fish. I had to be sober to play and I didn't want to be sober, so I began to fake a back injury.

My mind was blown. I had a panic attack in a toilet at Bristol Airport, after a brief trip back home on the pretence of considering the offer of a new contract with Toulouse. I called my mother, who excused herself from work and flew to France on the first available plane. She sensed I was in big trouble, but loved me too deeply to insist on the details.

Eventually, I sold the French house to one of my team-mates, Omar Hasan, an Argentinian prop, because I just didn't trust myself to live in it. There had been more aborted suicide attempts, and the pool retained its macabre fascination for me.

Due to the imminent move, Jemma returned one day, while she knew I was out training, to retrieve her belongings. Trevor had agreed to take some of our furniture – ornate pieces which we had so enjoyed studying, and buying, at auction. I booked myself into a hotel, which was a disaster. While it wasn't exactly The Ritz, and room service left a lot to be desired, I was incapable of looking after myself.

The club drew their own conclusions about the move, asking, understandably enough, why I wanted to sell up after verbally agreeing a contract extension – one I had no intention of signing. I insisted I was injured; they suggested I play. It was a mess. I became increasingly depressed, and made a conscious decision to flee.

The manner of my departure was inglorious and unbecoming. I booked an afternoon flight, but reported for physiotherapy treatment in the morning. I am ashamed to admit I compromised my mother by asking her to call the club at midday, insisting that she speak to me because of a family problem.

When she did so, I was summoned from the treatment room to the office to call her back. I dialled an incomplete number, and invented a conversation about the death of my grandfather, who had, in truth, passed on some years earlier. I insisted on going home immediately, to support my mother and pay my respects.

It was embarrassing, disrespectful and utterly unprofessional. I didn't bother to retrieve my belongings from the hotel, and flew back to Wales. I had no intention of returning to France.

The people at Toulouse deserved far better. They had welcomed me as one of their own. They sent a huge bouquet of flowers to my mother, to sympathise with her supposed loss. I felt worthless, wretched, wracked by guilt. Another lie: more conniving. How low could I go? I had involved my own mother, and her late father, in my dishonesty. It was unforgivable.

Mum is fiercely protective of her three sons, and her four grandchildren, but is unafraid to tell us our fortune if we have disappointed her. This time, though, she understood the pointlessness of anger, sensing that I had to find my own way through a minefield of destructive emotions. I wasn't thinking straight. I didn't want to be alive. The last thing I wanted was for someone to sit me down and give me a lecture about right and wrong. I needed it, but just not at that juncture in my life.

It was more than enough to know my mother was there for me. I'd catch her out of the corner of my eye, watching me like a hawk. She was reading the signs, assessing her priorities. I never had to tell her I was gay. She just knew. She devoted herself to my welfare, and tried to create an environment where I could be at ease, and feel loved and safe. She wanted to reduce the pressure on me – I couldn't hide the strain from her or my father.

I'd love to say that it was perfect, my return home; that the depression lifted instantly and we were Walt Disney's version of a happy family, but that would be yet another half-truth, at best.

I felt terribly conflicted that first night back in the white-washed, semi-detached house, which had been home for my entire life. Lying in my old single bed, in the front bedroom, I had to contend with the inner voice that sniggered that I was a failure. There I was, a grown man of 33, struggling to sleep in the same room I had occupied as a fretful adolescent of 13. What did I have to show for those 20 years? I refused to give myself the easy way out, by concentrating on my rugby achievements. Instead, I questioned my status as a son, husband and lover. Did I deserve such a great family? What sort of person was I? Why did I devastate a wonderful wife? Why could I not summon the courage to invite the world to accept me for who I was? What did I have, spiritually rather than materially?

Viewed from the outside, I had everything. I was approaching a century of caps for a country that regarded me as a favourite son. I had a form of fame that millions craved. I had a storied career. I played for a fantastic club who looked after me, taking pains to be supportive even when they realised I was faking a bad back. They still wanted me to be a part of their team when I was a hopeless drunk.

How did I repay them? By running away, jumping on a plane and leaving them to pick up the pieces. I felt I lacked any redeeming human qualities. I wasn't even able to do something simple, something I craved, like killing myself. Pathetic.

Lying there in the darkness, I tossed and turned. I gave up trying to assess what was good about my life, because everything seemed irredeemably bad. I had created total chaos, and then brought it back to where I thought I belonged. But, I realised, the old certainties had gone. I felt helpless, trapped. Coming home was almost too much, psychologically, for someone so fragile. It triggered feelings of guilt and despair rather than relief and optimism. Rugby was still there for me, because Cardiff Blues were offering a contract, but the athlete had first to answer to the little boy in the front bedroom.

At my lowest point, I had to come to terms with who I was, and how I intended to make my family proud.

Chapter Two

TEULU (FAMILY)

As entrances into the world go, mine was distinctive. It involved a black Labrador puppy, a privet hedge and a pile of soot. My mother, in trying to catch the dog in our backyard, tripped over a temporary gate, fell through the hedge and landed, head first, in the contents of our recently cleaned chimney.

It was enough to trigger a two-day labour before I was born in Bridgend General Hospital at noon on 25 July 1974. I was a week early but since I weighed in at 9lb 12oz, and filled the cot from head to toe, I had been ready to make my appearance.

My father, Barrie, had been banished from the delivery room, and heard the happy news from a foreman at Costin's Cement Works where he worked, on the far side of town.

'You have a baby,' he was told, in tones that didn't quite do justice to the miracle of childbirth. 'Unfortunately, it's another boy. Sounds like he's a big fella, though.' Dad, one of life's gentle souls – just as well, really, since Mum tends to go off like a Catherine Wheel on Bonfire Night – was content. If he had a premonition of his third son captaining his country and becoming an international cause célèbre, he kept it to himself.

Historically, it was a day of some significance. In Washington, President Nixon was forced to hand over the Watergate tapes, which led to his impeachment. In rugby, the British Lions were completing preparations for the final Test against South Africa in Johannesburg; they had won the previous three but, in keeping with the sour mood of a brutal tour, were denied a chance to do more than draw the last game, which was ended four minutes early with them camping on the Springboks' line.

Sport was big in our household. My parents love their rugby, and Dad claims he was a decent footballer, but they made a point of sacrificing their time to enable us to develop a variety of interests. It was a happy home, in which the front door was always ajar, and to this day I refer to our neighbours as Auntie and Uncle. No one stands on ceremony. I know this sounds corny, but when someone recently asked me to sum up my life in six words, I chose the phrase, 'My family has always loved me.'

That's not strictly true, of course. My brothers, Steve and Richard, five years and sixteen months older than me respectively, used me as a human punch-bag from time to time. Steve is closer in character to me: he is impulsive, entertaining and aggressive when the need arises; Richard is more studious, sensible and precise – virtues with which I have rarely been associated.

We were taught the enduring values of honesty, humility and hard work. We looked after our own. We were expected to be compassionate, combative and principled. We understood the importance of where we came from, the significance of what we represented.

The greatest gift – a strong sense of identity – cost nothing. We weren't British. We were Welsh. That wasn't a political statement – although the English sense of entitlement has been mentioned in many dressing rooms I have occupied – but a simple matter of flesh and blood. My forefathers came from a group of tightly knit communities situated within a four-mile radius of Sarn, a village of 2,500 souls, three miles to the north of Bridgend. Money was scarce; life was hard. One of my great-grandfathers on my mother's side did well enough to run a grocery shop, and then a fish shop, after leaving the mines. His wife, who came from the Wye valley in mid-Wales, was disowned by her family on their wedding day, because of the stigma of having supposedly married beneath her station. They never contacted her again.

I've a greater association with my mum's other grandfather: I was given his mining lamp by my granddad, his son. I became really close to him in the months before he died. He was a man's man, a kindly character whose house was a treasure trove. He had noticed me admiring the lamp, which hung beside the fire, and made sure I got it when he passed away. He'd do anything for anyone. Soon after my rugby career had taken off, I decided I needed a little space and moved into a house with my auntie, Denise. She's 17 years younger than my mother, her sister, and acted as my surrogate sister. My nan and granddad would scour the place, from top to bottom, three times a week. We used to call them the cleaning fairies. His eyesight had almost gone, but he insisted on painting the place. We never had the heart to tell him we repaired his handiwork on the quiet.

His dad was one of those extraordinary, ordinary men. He was sent down the pit when he was nine years old, in the days when it was not unusual for 18-hour shifts to begin at 2 a.m. Boys were invaluable in tight, compressed seams. Some were used as 'putters', pushing trucks along subterranean lines; others were 'trappers', who sat in the dark, opening and shutting a series of wooden doors to allow air to circulate around the mine.

The human cost of coal mining was seared into everyone's consciousness where I lived. To my parents' generation, the 1966 Aberfan tragedy, in which 116 children were killed when a colliery spoil tip collapsed onto a junior school, is the equivalent of the Kennedy assassination: everyone remembers where they were when they heard the news. My mother was ironing in her mother's kitchen. Her father was on nights, but she woke him with the words, 'Something awful has happened.'

Families were so close that a degree of intermingling was almost inevitable. On the day of my parents' marriage, my maternal great-grandfather and my paternal grandfather recognised each other immediately. They were the same age, despite representing different generations, and had not seen each other for decades. They had grown up together in adjacent houses in Cuckoo Street, and had fought bare-knuckled on the pavements for pennies. Understandably enough, they were driven by social injustice. They had joined the Hunger March to London, staged by South Wales's miners in 1927. Poverty in the Great Depression had stripped them of everything but their pride and their belligerence. They had railed against means testing, and considered strike-breakers to be the lowest form of life.

My nan and granddad lived at the bottom end of Sarn in a terraced house with an outside toilet, and a small bathroom that adjoined the kitchen. They moved into the new council estate at the top end of the village when it was built in 1951. They lived there, on the corner, opposite our current house, until they died. So much for 'social mobility' – one of those airy phrases used by public-school educated officials in Westminster who don't generally have a good grasp of the real world.

People were conditioned to staying where they were. They tended to be born, live and die in a small area. Dad hailed from Ogmore Vale, just along the valley, where the shale mines provided steady employment, and took entire families underground. It was hardly less bleak on the surface; Mum refused to move from Sarn when they decided to get married, because she wasn't prepared for the culture shock of 'living in a place where the clouds descend to street level and you can get lost in the fog'.

His brothers worked down the mine, but he was prevented from joining them because he failed the necessary medical, at the age of 17, due to an irregular heartbeat. He did his apprenticeship as a stone mason, but went to work in the Avon rubber factory when Steve arrived on the scene. The money was good, but he hated the noise, heat and foul air.

He moved to the cement factory, which gave him the chance to feed a growing family, but couldn't afford the insecurity of his next job, as a central-heating engineer reliant on seasonal contracts. He finally found his niche as a postman, where he walked the walk in Bridgend and the surrounding villages for 28 years before his retirement in the summer of 2014.

He's happy with his lot, and I understand why. In a spiritual sense, I've never moved away from Sarn. I'll never call anywhere else home, even though I have a place in London. I've grown up there: I've won Wimbledon on the road, where it straightens, a few yards after our house on the bend; I've scored World Cup-winning tries and Test match centuries on the semi-circular patch of grass a little further along, past the house in which Richard now lives with his young family.

I can walk to my infant school, where I screamed the place down on my first day – Mum had literally to prise my grip from the front gate. I obviously got the hang of school, however, as by the time I was in junior classes, I had started playing pick-up rugby on a pitch that could have staged a downhill skiing race in winter.

I got sucked into sport for no other reason than the fact that I loved it. You don't need a reason to exist, but every kid at six or seven needs a reason to feel like they can be part of a group, or that they have something rather than have nothing.

Sarn is nothing special to look at, but it represents stability. I'm the real Gareth Thomas when I'm there. I've no role to play.

People know me as the naughty kid, or the tearaway teenager, rather than the rugby player, or the only gay in the village. They knew me as a kid when I wanted to be Monkey, star of the cult Japanese martial arts TV series. They accepted me as the boy who'd always accept a dare, always get caught, and always take his punishment.

In that spirit, I dared my mum to share some of the secrets of my childhood. They say the woman who brought you into the world is the one who knows you best, don't they? That can be a double-edged sword, but this is her version of living with her youngest son. It is unexpurgated, although God knows I've wanted to edit it …

'Gareth has never changed. Honestly. He's absolutely never changed. As a boy he was just a walking disaster at times. There's one holiday story that sticks in my mind. It absolutely typifies him. We were in Malta. It was lovely, chilled and relaxing. One evening, the hotel put on a poolside barbeque, with the food piled on trestle tables.

'We were all sitting down eating when Gareth suddenly got up. I asked him, "Where do you think you're going?" He turned to answer me, caught his foot on the trestle table, and the whole lot went down like dominoes. Everything collapsed – plates, food, candles in bottles, well, they all went in the pool. He just looked at me and said, "I've told you before, Mammy. I can't walk and talk at the same time!"

'Not a thought in his head. When he started playing rugby, he used to lose so much stuff it drove me mad. I had a word with Matthew Harry, who was the captain of the youth team at Pencoed. He used to make Gareth stand in his kit bag to undress so that it would all go straight in. He still managed to mislay something or other, though. You always know where Gareth has been because there's a trail of shoes, socks, training gear. He's so untidy. And he'll never change.

'He was a lovely lad, but no angel. At school he was a waster, especially when he went up to Ogmore Comprehensive. I was working part-time in a children's home at the time, and it was pure coincidence that I knew the head of the middle school, Mr Evans. He had done his year's teacher training at what was the local secondary modern, when I was a pupil there.

'He kept on sending for me to talk about Gareth's behaviour. I was busy bringing up three children, and one day he asked to see me at nine o'clock. He didn't turn up until quarter past nine. I'd had to change my shift to get there, so I was furious by the time he came in through the door. I just went for him. I said, "The next time you send for me, Gareth's either been physically or verbally abusive to the staff or another child, or he's been truanting. Other than that, I don't want to know."

'I'm not a fan of teachers, to be honest. Richard had this gift in school, where he always did well. Poor old Gareth was coming up behind, in the year below. Teachers would say, "Gareth is nothing like Richard." They just couldn't help themselves. They have a sense of expectation, which is usually misplaced. They lose patience.

'They used to say Gareth had a poor concentration level. I told them to teach him in a way that kept him interested. They said that when they took a ruler off him because he was tapping the desk with it, he began tapping the floor with his foot. What was I supposed to do about that? Tie his legs together? Once I was sent for because he'd broken a fire alarm. His story was that someone had pushed him, and a tennis racket had gone into the alarm. Oh, and he'd smashed a lampshade, with a rugby ball ...'

In my defence, they did give me the rugby ball. Eventually, the teachers just sent me out to the playing field to make my own amusement.

I went back there recently. The school closed in 2010, and it has basically been abandoned. Returning was a strange, eerie experience. The rugby posts remain upright, but they are rusting; the long-jump runway and pit is only marked by an indentation in the overgrown grass. My favourite unofficial classroom, the black hole – a tunnel between teaching blocks where the bad boys and girls used to go for a cigarette and other forbidden, extra-curricular activities at break-time – has been filled in. There were poignant reminders of normality; a long-forgotten box of pencils on a broken grey cabinet – and the classrooms are generally a wreck. The fire alarm by the door had been repaired, mind ...

To be honest, I hated school. I've a natural aversion to authority. That's why I had a lot of problems with coaches, especially when I first started playing. Most were ex-teachers. It wasn't a question of a lack of respect, but I was conditioned to rebel against anyone who spoke down to me. I just couldn't handle that, even later in my career. It explains why I learned nothing from any of my international coaches, until Steve Hansen became Wales coach.

The most illustrious example of the teacher-coach is Graham Henry. He has done everything in the game. He led the British Lions and the All Blacks. He was even knighted for services to rugby. Yet when he was in charge of Wales between 1998 and 2002, the so-called Great Redeemer and I never got on. I found him arrogant and ignorant; he found me chippy and unpredictable. He had his teacher's pets – senior pros and top blokes like Rob Howley, Scott Gibbs and Scott Quinnell. The rest, even those of us with 50 or so caps, were treated like second-class citizens. Henry used to annoy me by comparing me unfavourably to other players in front of the group, for no apparent reason. His knowledge was immense, but the tone of his voice and the self-importance of his body language meant it never got across to me.

I have a simple philosophy, in rugby and in life: treat others in the manner you'd be expected to be treated yourself. I believe coach and player, teacher and pupil, are engaged in a 50-50 partnership. That's why school never got the best out of me. They never worked out that, suitably inspired, I loved learning. The boy they dismissed as feckless and unruly has grown into a man who loves being challenged. Set me a task, and I will do everything I can to master it.

Most people know me as Alfie, after Alf, the Alien Life Form, the central character of an American kids' TV programme that was popular in my early teens. The series charted the misadventures of a loveable rogue from the planet Melmac, who follows a ham radio signal to Earth and crash-lands on the garage of the Tanners, a suburban middle-class family in the San Fernando Valley in California.

It was daft escapism. We loved his capacity for chaos, especially his constant attempts to eat the family cat, the ironically named Lucky. We were watching one day after school when Stephen Hughes, one of my mates from the estate, suddenly exclaimed, 'You look exactly like him.' Since Alf was huge, with pronounced ears, a pig's snout and a gorilla's torso, it wasn't meant as a compliment.

I won the retaliatory wrestle on the carpet, but the name stuck, along with its derivatives: Alfonso and Alfredo. I still have a miniature version of the puppet, which takes pride of place on one of my sofas at home. Apart from some trophies, awarded during long-forgotten school sports days, it represents the most enduring legacy of my time in the state education system.

I find I can communicate easily, and was pretty decent at English at school. The problem with the subject, though, was where the classroom was situated, at the end of a block. It meant I looked out over a steep grass bank, down which the younger boys were rolled in one of the school's initiation ceremonies. Tennis courts and a playground littered with old tractor tyres were on a plateau above this bank, while our three rugby pitches lay beyond. The open space teased me, beckoned to me. It was where I was accepted and admired.

Sport gave me status. As soon as the bell went for playtime or the lunch break, I'd come alive. I'd be the first selection in the pick-up matches. That validated me. So, when we were herded back into the classrooms, I preferred fantasy to facts. You wouldn't believe how many matches my imaginary teams won out there, though the teachers who recognised my glassy-eyed reveries for what they were probably had a decent idea.

I understand why they decided to cut their losses with me and devote more time to those who wanted to learn. As a captain, I've made the same choice. Concentrate on those who are on your wavelength, prioritise the ones who care. Those who don't want to engage, or become a distraction because they think only of themselves, are energy sappers. Fight the battles that are worth winning, with the troops you can trust.

I would fantasise about getting home, getting out of the classroom – occasionally, I didn't bother arriving. We used to walk to school across the common and dive into the sheds, which contained winter hay for the horses that gnawed the meagre grassland. We were rebels without a clue, really. Bunking off seemed a great idea, but sitting there at ten in the morning, real-ising we had nothing to do until half past four, was pretty daft.

I preferred to be bored at school, or make better use of my illicit time. One of my mates had a table-tennis table in his garage, which we used for six-hour marathons if his parents were away. We built camps, went bird nesting. I was good at climbing trees to steal the eggs, because I was reasonably athletic, but I wasn't so clever at getting down. My school trousers were mended so often they resembled a patchwork quilt. Organised adventure, in something like the Cubs or Boy Scouts, never appealed. I loved climbing trees because it was a physical act that got the adrenaline flowing, but sport, specifically rugby, was my preoccupation.

I was quick and wiry, surprisingly strong, but judged to be nothing special as a rugby player in my first couple of seasons at Pencoed, my first junior club, where I did my time as a replacement for age-group teams. I had difficulty coming to terms with the competition – I might have been notable in the District Schools team, but this was a team of all the talents. I wore a furrow in the mud behind the touchline, sprinting to get noticed in the hope I would be summoned to action. Rejection wasn't an option.

I used to spend hours alone at Pandy Park, home of Tondu, a junior club who played in the village of Aberkenfig, just down the road. I had a rugby ball and my dreams. It didn't matter how hard the rain fell, or how painfully the hailstones stung; I would try to make penalties successfully from a variety of angles and distances. I was oblivious to everyone, and everything. I'd kick the ball, run, collect it, run back to my mark, and kick it again. I'd sprint down the wing, shrugging off imaginary defenders with feints and sidesteps. I'd test the accuracy of my passing, short and long, by aiming for a particular muddy mark on the outside of a post. It didn't make me unique – I remember reading how Don Bradman practised alone, hitting a golf ball with a cricket stump in his backyard – but it made me feel alive.

I'm naturally self-reliant. Training on your own for a team sport may be counter-intuitive, but I've always done it, because the ends justify the means. I've been a secret trainer all my life. When I played for Wales I was the fittest in the squad. Nobody could understand why, until they realised I used to push myself to the limits when no one else was watching. I thought nothing of committing my time to maximising my talent. Gary Player's insistence that, 'The harder I practice, the luckier I get' may be a hoary old sporting cliché, but it has the ring of truth.

I'd do running, weights, sit-ups. Set the goal, achieve it, set another target. Beat yourself before you can beat others. Solitary confinement was liberating, which is something that I can't adequately explain, given that I love the team environment, where I spark off the personalities and problems of others. Maybe I really am two people, who are conditioned to compete against each other.

I often wonder whether my life could have been a lot easier had I taken up an individual sport. I was good at athletics, karate, judo and swimming. They suited someone of my character, because I was naturally dedicated, and pathologically determined. Michael Jordan's athleticism is central to his basketball legend, but I loved his attitude: 'Obstacles don't have to stop you. If you run into a wall, don't turn around and give up. Figure out how to climb it, go through it or work around it.'

The irony, of course, is that switching sports would have denied me something that ultimately saved my life: the understanding and support of my teammates. It could not have been a lonelier existence, but I would have been isolated from my clan, my own. They were the first to recognise my potential as a rugby player. Big men with bigger bellies watched me improve and began to whisper, 'This kid could be the one.'

Things changed when I broke into the youth team at Pencoed. It was a really good side. Matthew Harry, my long-suffering captain, went on to play for Bridgend, as did our fly-half, Lyndon Griffiths. My mate, Gareth Jones, played in the centre for Bridgend and Wales. That was no coincidence, because bloodlines were as important on the pitch as they were down the pit.

Pencoed is an inconspicuous place, a small town with a population of around 11,000 that once had a Norman castle, and which can trace its origins back to the Bronze Age. Its identity is based on the mines, which flourished in the late 19th century. Like so many communities that expanded and contracted with the coal industry, it takes great pride in being represented by a rugby club that is imbued with the spirit of the game.

The clubhouse is basic, and the concrete beer garden is run-down, but it has its holy relics, presented by former players like Scott Gibbs and Gavin Henson. I'm particularly proud of the wooden cabinet in the corner of the bar, which contains my Wales shirts.

None of us would have achieved anything without youth coaches of the stature of Viv Thomas and Gareth Jones. They gave us standards. We won the league in our first year but were never allowed to foster what the sages on the touchline referred to as a, 'Fur coat, no knickers' attitude. We were ordered to act in an appropriate manner: never gloat, never glory in your superiority; be humble in victory and graceful in defeat. Respect the opponent, because without an opponent there is no game.

They were invaluable life lessons, which are overlooked far too easily in these days of pre-try celebrations and choreographed showmanship. It's attention-seeking, 'Look-at-me-Ma' rugby. Junior clubs like Pencoed, left to fend for themselves like pit-head orphans by the regional giants, are victims of perceived progress. The game has changed, massively. Professionalism, and the cult of personality, has cheapened it, stripping it of deeper meaning.

When I started off, the ethical code of the game was the most precious thing for a player. Now it is almost an afterthought. Rugby's comradeship will never be lost, but it has been diluted. As money has come in, the game has mutated. Pressures build and burst, so selfishness is expected and excused.

Everything is focused on the individual. There are defined targets for levels of fitness and strength. There are personalised diets and conditioning programmes. So help me, there are computer-generated key performance indicators. In such an environment, it is only natural that a player should think of himself before his team, especially when he has a mortgage to pay. I get that, but we have lost so much of what attracted me to the sport.

When I began in the amateur era, so much was about how you interacted socially. Lads worked for a living and played for the love of the game. You'd develop great friendships off the field, which would come into play on it. Of course, you still had to perform, but you were expected to watch your buddy's back. You'd do anything for a mate. If you were big enough to hand out punishment, you were big enough to take it. Now, it is about the result, the win bonus. It is almost entirely driven by personality, which is ironic given that the game has consequently lost its true characters.

I could have gone down that path. Bigger clubs began to take notice of this scrawny back with long, blond hair. Pencoed were determined to invoke the rule in operation at that time, which insisted that a player should play a year of senior rugby at the junior club that had nurtured him, before moving up the pyramid. I, however, had had enough of the queue for the brown envelope with £10 beer money in it if we won – I wanted to take the opportunity to move to Neath, and started to sulk when I didn't get it.

I got what I deserved: a monstering from some of the old boys and a stint in the second team before I saw the error of my ways. I was no different. I had to take my punishment, learn my lessons. If I did that with sufficient courage and class, I would earn the right to pursue my ultimate dream – a move to Bridgend, the local club which, to me, represented the pinnacle of achievement.

That final season at Pencoed, playing against men in valley rugby, was an education. Some of the matches were psychotic. It was always pissing down, and they were beasts. Even the young ones were brutes. It taught me to respect what rugby is about: the code of the changing room, the ethics of looking after your mates. It told me how tough you have to be to play it.

Rugby is not like football, where a lot of the violence is verbal. In our games, if someone said, 'I'm going to fucking kill you,' he'd be laughed at, because he'd never get the chance. Instead, he'd be told, 'Don't tell me what you're going to do – just do it. I don't want to hear what you're going to do, just show me.' I was taught to say nothing if I wanted to hurt someone, because then they would know I was coming for them. Stay schtum, and then hit them. That's payback, for all the bleating.

I grew up fast in a good team. I learned respect. Everyone wanted to intimidate us, to find that crack or flaw. We stuck together and looked after our own. I was an innocent, who literally didn't know where the next punch was coming from. Yet I survived and thrived, because I had good people around me. I'd turn around, see someone writhing in the mud, and realise an unseen ally had taken out an aggressor who'd been intent on doing me harm.

I had discovered my extended family, and I loved them dearly.

Chapter Three

LOCAL HERO

It was the end of innocence. I had left school at 15 without taking my GCSEs, and found myself in a factory making car filters. Rolls of steel were fed through ten giant presses, and it was my job to ensure the production line never stopped. That meant hauling heavy metal across the factory floor in ridiculous heat, and watering the machines through a cloud of steam.

The careers teacher hadn't mentioned I would stink of sweat and feel as though my very soul had been singed. All I could do, on getting home after my first shift, was go to bed, immediately. I awoke the following morning, convinced that I had taken an hour's nap and was ready for tea. The realisation I'd been asleep for 11 unbroken hours, and was about to do it all again after a rushed breakfast, was horrendous.

It wasn't manual labour; it was a life sentence. As so often in my life, Dad came to the rescue. He had a quiet word in the right ear about his son the rugby starlet, and persuaded the Post Office I was worth an apprenticeship. That meant us getting up at 4 a.m. to walk to the sorting office, but after my misadventure in the manufacturing industry, being out in God's fresh air was a blessing.

It's my kind of town, Bridgend. It's blue collar, true to itself. It has taken its fair share of hard knocks, but bounced back for more. A postman takes the pulse of his community; he's one of the first to notice the empty shop, the boarded-up house, or the over-eager pensioner who craves company. He's a cross between a workhorse and a dog handler – those Bonio biscuits came in handy around the council estates, and on the darkened stairwells of shabby blocks of flats.

There was a comforting simplicity to the rhythm of my day. I'd cram in a weights session between deliveries, and train in the evening after grabbing a quick nap. Although I had the occasional brain fade in my early days at Bridgend – inexplicably heading one up-and-under instead of catching it in textbook fashion during a notorious pre-season friendly against South Wales Police – I largely justified the faith of Compo Greenslade, my mentor.

Yet all was not as it seemed. I was physically weak, mentally fragile. I was barely 18, a confused kid thrown into an overtly male environment. I didn't sign up for the banter, the casual brutality dealt out to the new boys. The initiation rituals were savage, and refusal to participate was not an option. Ceremonial conformity resulted in survival and eventual acceptance.

The humiliation was systematic, and accompanied by the manic laughter of teammates who knew what was coming. On a bonding trip to Warrington, I was stripped to my underpants and forced to wear a pillow over my head. Liniment and a vile cocktail of bodily products was smeared across my face. Relay races in which we had to eat cat food or raw offal were common.

At a sevens tournament in France, Tabasco sauce was rubbed into my eyes, genitals, and up my backside. I was forced out onto a tiny, second-floor balcony, and ordered to sing 'Land of My Fathers' to bemused passers-by. Since I couldn't see, I stumbled forwards, and was only prevented from falling 25 feet by Compo's firm grip on the waistband of my pants.

Madness, but it was my duty to take it, without a murmur. Alcoholic oblivion eased the pain, but the fear remained. It was a tough school, barbaric but somehow acceptable, because it was standard practice. The code was clearly defined: work hard, play even harder. Pay your dues. I went along with it, on the basis that everyone suffered at some stage. My split personality became even more pronounced, though I kept that to myself.

The Public Me – let's call him Alfie – loved the *craic*. He drank to excess, picked fights in pubs, and played to the gallery by rampaging around town in a range of fancy-dress masks. Jar Jar Binks, the bumbling *Star Wars* character, was a particular favourite. He was the one who began to spin the web of lies, telling anyone who cared to listen of his imaginary conquests.

The Private Me – plain old Gareth – understood it was nothing but a façade. Big boys *do* cry, when no one else can see. They have a conscience when they treat childhood mates as stooges. Since I was not being honest, I was betraying their trust. Deception is neither big, nor clever. It strips self-esteem. Not for the first time, I suppressed my fears and used rugby as my release.

Playing for Bridgend was all I ever wanted to do, and strangers were starting to tell me I was pretty good at it. The boot money, £20 a week, helped me stretch my wages as a postie, but it was incidental: for all the hypocrisy of the amateur era, which I was quite happy to play along with, I would have turned out for nothing. I never expected fame or fortune. Playing for my town, my people, was a source of priceless pride.

Naïvely, I never saw myself as playing that well. I was still a wide-eyed kid, who would think to himself, 'Oh, we won! That's cool. I scored a try and we won. And we played again and I scored two tries. That's cool as well.' I was really enjoying it, so I never really stood back and appreciated the bigger picture. It never occurred to me that things were starting to happen for me.

I made my Bridgend debut in a home friendly against Birchgrove in October 1993, but my first competitive appearance was against Cardiff, at the Arms Park. I could have been playing on the Moon: my country's capital city is only 21 miles from my birthplace, but I had only ever been there occasionally on the train. That may seem strange in this day and age, but I felt no need to stray beyond familiar boundaries. The rivalry between the working-class town and cosmopolitan city has a social, as well as a sporting context. It was to provide one of the defining memories of my career. Though the tribal nature of the contest is timeless, one derby game stands out, as being special. 'Jiffy', Jonathan Davies, had returned from rugby league in 1995. He had helped Cardiff win the Welsh Cup, despite struggling to readjust because he was consistently played out of his best position, outside-half. They were the number-one club, and not averse to loose talk about dynasties. They signified wealth and privilege. Bridgend's ground, the Brewery Field, was heaving when they came to town. Historic resentment at Cardiff's habit of stealing our best players simmered, and spilled over onto the pitch.

We basically beat them up, and won by seventeen points to zero. The reaction was extraordinary. There was a primitive howl from the terraces, and the pitch was invaded. The first person to reach me was Auntie Denise. She sprinted from beside the dugout, enveloped me in a bear hug, and wasn't about to let go in a hurry.

There were hundreds of people milling around the entrance to the dressing room. I didn't know their names, I only recognised some of their faces. I had no insight into their private lives, but they were inviting me to share their joy. It was a moment of epiphany, because it revealed one of rugby's hidden truths. Sceptics can dismiss it as a game for muddied oafs, but I know it matters. It lightens the load, addresses the inequalities of everyday existence; it can justify prejudices, right wrongs and put things on an even keel. That's amazing, if you stop to consider it.

These, literally, are home truths. I rapidly understood what playing for Bridgend meant. Your town is deemed to represent who you are as a person. It represents your family, because your family comes from the same place. It represents your friends, your friends' families. All of a sudden, I found myself representing this area, these people, this mass of humanity.

It was of no consequence that the vast majority were strangers, to whom I had never spoken. I knew we had common goals. I knew they, like me, saw the rugby club as the heartbeat of the town. When we lost, when we failed them, the heartbeat would slow down; when we won, when we made life good, or even tolerable, the place would thrive. It was all about giving people pride, encouraging them to identify with who they were and where they came from.

Players have to keep their side of a sacred bargain. Doing everything to the best of your ability is the least that is expected. That day on the Brewery Field taught me that if a group of people who are of average ability work their bollocks off, they can beat a team of stars who are not allowed to impose their natural advantages. That Bridgend team realised it was involved in something bigger than itself – we didn't do it for ourselves, but for the jersey we wore and the people we enthused. In return, we were elevated to the status of local heroes. It was a unique form of appreciation, because it was given by those who understand the concept of struggle. It had nothing to do with the privilege of being put on a pedestal, or the perception of fame. It was a reward for making the town a better, happier place.

What other job gives you the chance to put those sorts of smiles on people's faces? How many of us have individuals we have never met tapping us on the back to thank us for doing that job? What does it feel like to be congratulated on behalf of an entire town? To be told that you are inspirational to people's brothers, mothers, fathers, sisters, grandparents?

It's bonkers, to be honest. While some of my school friends were preparing for their A levels, I was being treated as some sort of a surrogate father, brother and son. I was 'Our Alfie'. It's no wonder I felt so close to my community: I'd been delivering mail to those supporters that morning, yet there they were, hollering my name.

I never wanted to be an individual because I felt comfortable in the collective. I felt safe, protected. The team looked after me, because they saw I was ready to give everything back to it. Had I been a selfish bastard, and sponged off them, or turned my back when it all got a little testy, I would never have made it.

Of course, I never gave everything of myself. I was becoming increasingly aware of my difference, sexually. It was an inner torment, a private struggle. I convinced myself I was giving my teammates more by not telling them the truth about my deepest, most intimate feelings. I didn't think anyone in the town or the game was ready to handle the truth. I felt I was being almost the bigger man by pretending that nothing was wrong.

I can understand, but cannot accept, such reluctance being portrayed as a cop-out. I was brought up to be judged on telling the truth, but I was trying to protect a definitive truth. I was proud of what I was giving my town. Had I come out at that stage of my life, I would not have been judged on the pride and passion I gave to the jersey I wore, and the commitment I shared with my teammates.

And I was scared. I was afraid of losing my people, my town, my game. The inner voice of Private Me, plain old Gareth, begged Public Me, Alfie, to keep quiet: 'Don't tell them, it's not about you. It's about everyone else, it's about the environment. People don't want to know your problems, your fears. They're losing jobs, struggling to make ends meet. Don't spoil things for them.'

I needed inspiration, and found it in three men who are true local heroes. In their own distinctive ways, Glen Webbe, Compo Greenslade and Rob Howley helped me through the first of many crises. Without knowing it, they taught me how to deal with intolerance, aggression and disappointment. Almost through a form of emotional osmosis, they made me believe in myself.

They gave me such strength, through what they stood for as rugby players and as hard, honest men. I would stand back, watching them, and try to learn from their example. Sure, they took the piss, constantly. I tried to be as macho as they were, but it went deeper than that. They were sharp, but never cruel. I wanted to live up to their belief in me.

They taught me the rules and regulations of rugby that never make the textbook. They taught me how to hold my head up high as a man. They taught me about leadership, passion and pride in who I am, and what I represent. Most of all, they taught me to trust my instincts, and relate my life to the lessons of my sport.

I would want them in a team that played for my life.

They have an uncanny ability to seize on people's traits. I think they saw me as a good player and a good person, who was probably holding something back. But they never intruded.

They gave me time and space. I've always suspected that they knew more than they let on, as I felt so comfortable with them that I let my guard down, but they were never nosy.

Glen was a pioneer, though he will hate that term. He became the first black man to represent Wales, and won ten caps on the wing between 1986 and 1988. He was a one-club man with Bridgend, but he dared to be different. He was the first player to wear gloves, sourced from American football – he'd conform when he needed to conform, but he was a lateral thinker who had immense physical and moral courage.

He was a great player and is a great person. He was muscular and resilient, hard and fast. The prejudice he experienced, and overcame, was astounding. He would laugh at bigots from opposing clubs who threw bananas at him. He didn't consider the simple option, the easy route to praise, because he is a take-it-or-leave-it person. If he felt he needed to do something, no matter how unorthodox, challenging or potentially harmful, he did it.

I drew such strength from Glen. I sensed nothing was beyond him, because he had the mental capacity to do whatever he wished. What he perceived other people thought of him was utterly irrelevant to him. He set an example I was too weak to follow, but I never forgot his lead, or these words: 'I'll tell you what you need to know, the rest you can figure out. If you're wrong, you're wrong, if you're right, you're right. Figure it out. If you get to know yourself, you'll find out a lot more about life.'

Glen quickly made himself known when I began to train with Bridgend during my senior year at Pencoed. He was proud of his speed, and made a point of telling me, 'I can chase eggs,' when we were on the running track at Newbridge Fields. Sessions dominated by the dreaded ritual of 150-metre repetitions were a rite of passage. He had issued a challenge, designed to coax me to my physical and mental limits: how was my character? Would I cheat when I thought no one was looking? Did I dig deep when I needed to?

I must have passed the audition because he sat me down in the clubhouse at Llanelli, after a good Welsh Cup win in my first season, and told me my fortune: 'You're at that age where you just can't see your capabilities. All you want to do is play. You play and play and play. Your natural exuberance just takes you through it all. I'll tell you something. You're head and shoulders above the rest. You're going to play for Wales in the next year.'

I swear I blushed. 'Oh, no, give over!' I protested, hoping that such praise had been lost in the hubbub of a crowded bar. 'I won't. Of course I won't. You're on the wind-up.'

Glen looked at me so hard he barely blinked. He was deadly serious. 'OK. Let's put the money down. One hundred quid says you will.' I accepted the bet, and wondered what fate had in store.

Glen stimulated my sensitivity, and shared his people skills. He knows what to do when a group is on edge and how to react if there is a sudden need to impose itself. He gives the impression of being laidback, but I've heard he's still a beast in the gym.

Please don't even think of considering me a hero in this man's company. When Glen was diagnosed with cancer, he didn't tell a single person: he fought it and beat it, on his own. He was reaching the twilight of his career when we played together, yet he still trained by himself, to give himself an indefinable edge. He was ripped physically, and remorseless mentally. I'd trust him with my life. He has such insight, power and grace. He's a magical person.

Compo is rough and ready, a loveable rogue who has the wisdom of a whiskey priest. He was my early captain, a hooker who proved to be a formidable tutor in the dark arts of the scrum, ruck and maul. When you are diving head-first at a wall of vengeful opponents, putting yourself into harm's way, there's something uniquely comforting about feeling him at your shoulder. He's my Fairy Godfather.

When he was around, I knew I'd be safe, whether the situation called for playing within the laws, or being strategically naughty and taking a walk on the wild side. Compo's specialist subject was fighting his way out of trouble, though I did once foolishly put him in mortal peril when he was sufficiently rash to select me for his sevens team, The Welshmen.

Those tournaments were traditionally staged on a Sunday, when everyone tended to pile into the minibus still pissed from the night before. I'll spare you the more gory details of the consequences of playing with a hangover and loose bowels, but the resultant mayhem became part of Bridgend folklore.

On this particular day we played Fiji, the sevens specialists. They were big boys, proud of their culture. They ran like gazelles but fought like tigers, and they didn't take kindly to anyone taking liberties. Which, of course, I did. I high-tackled one of them just as he was about to cruise through the gears and he went down as if he had been hit by a rubber bullet.

Cue chaos. I managed to stagger away from the advance guard, who piled onto me with malicious intent, but my obituary was probably being written as the rest of the squad advanced, murder in their eyes. Compo appeared from nowhere, stood between me and them, and started talking, urgently yet soothingly. He somehow calmed them down and persuaded them to forgive a silly kid.

I was naïve, and slow to learn the rules of engagement. My habit of starting fights I was in no position to win must have been wearing. Compo watched my back, whether I knew about it or not, on countless occasions. He also introduced me to the light and shade of captaincy, how to read the mood. He knows when to have fun, and when to get serious. He understands when a situation needs a cool head, and when it requires a screaming skull.

Rob is one of the rugby greats, a former Wales captain who has developed into a key coach for both the British and Irish Lions and the national team. He's a little less than four years older than me, and was already a Bridgend legend by the time I arrived at the Brewery Field, as a scraggy, silly ingénu. The self-appointed experts were already urging Rob to leave his home-town club, but he was having none of it.

His gifts, as a scrum-half, were obvious. He was a sinuous runner, a clever and quick thinker, and had a flinty character. He was also supremely fit. I latched on to him immediately, because he was everything I wanted to be. We trained together, and competed instinctively, whether it involved sprinting or lifting weights. I knew I was nowhere near him in terms of talent or achievement, but he was my marker in the sand. His example told me how hard I needed to train, how single-minded I had to be, if I was to make something of myself.

Bridgend had given Compo and Rob jobs as development officers. I didn't know it at the time, but they scouted me while I was at Pencoed. Compo dug around, discovered I had just started at the Post Office, and suggested Bridgend pursue me after I scored a hat-trick of tries in a youth match. His report – 'The ginger kid in the centre is a big, tall lad, with pace and good touch. He's setting it alive' – may not be a classic of its kind, but it set me up for life.

I still thought of myself as just a link in a sturdy chain, but others were starting to make contingency plans. People marked me more tightly, spoke about me more extravagantly. They were saying I was flash, fast, and I felt no shame or embarrassment in that. However daft or distracted I have occasionally appeared to be, I have always worked myself to the bone. I wasn't surprised by the attention, but I was scared by its implications.

Everything happened so fast, I had no time to think through the opportunities which were starting to open up for me.

That Rob Howley had to wait a year longer than me for his international debut remains a mystery. I was still working as a postman when I received a letter, informing me I was in the training squad for the 1995 World Cup squad. The prospect of playing for my country was no longer a fuzzy fantasy, shared and savoured by those around me; it was all too real. I should have been ecstatic; privately I wasn't even indifferent: I was actively hostile.

As a 20-minute drive to Cardiff held the same terrors for me as a trek to the centre of the earth, the realisation my career had reached another level prompted panic. Illogically and in theory, unforgivably, I decided to make such a spectacle of myself I would effectively sabotage my call-up, by taking a detour en route to my first training session so that I would fail to report for duty.

When the day came, I got off the M4 two junctions before I should have, meandered along a country lane, and then disappeared into the maze of a so-called executive estate on the western outskirts of Cardiff. I calmly parked, bought a bar of chocolate and sat listening to the radio for a couple of hours before I turned around and headed home.

Terminally stupid, and terribly insecure, I even tried to fool my parents that everything had gone well. That particular ploy lasted for as long as it took for the telephone to ring. Surprise, surprise, I had been missed by the coach, Alec Evans. I claimed to have got lost, and played the village idiot which, under the circumstances, was appropriate. Quite why I wasn't told to stay away as a result of my foolishness, I have never worked out. Instead of the sack, they invited me back, 48 hours later.

The welcome at my first training session at Sophia Gardens, the National Sports Centre in Cardiff, was understandably apathetic.

No one really knew me, but Mike Hall, another Bridgend boy, offered a measure of assurance. I've never forgotten his supportive gesture, because it takes time to understand that the rhythms and rituals of an international squad are little different from those which dictate life at club level. The fitness drills are similar, if not identical. The skills are transferable.

Gradually, it began to dawn on me I was not naturally inferior: I could run at the front of the group; technically, I felt as if I belonged. There was even the odd sneaky smile when I put a move on an exalted colleague. Playing in a World Cup still seemed an idle fantasy, but I surprised myself. It felt nice, very nice. It felt right. My days of playing truant from the national team were over.

Confirmation came just before dawn a couple of weeks later, as I was sorting my mail for the first delivery. My father arrived in my section clutching an envelope embossed with the Welsh Rugby Union logo. It was addressed to me. He stood there, breathlessly telling me to, 'Open it, open it.'

Deep down, I knew what was coming. Time became compressed as I read confirmation of my selection for South Africa.

Dad began break-dancing, and I started to do a soft-shoe shuffle. I did my best to maintain the pretence of being delighted, but I dared not share my deeper feelings. I knew it was going to complicate things. I feared unprecedented scrutiny and separation from everything I held dear. It was a dangerous time, and I felt trapped by the joy of those who knew me best.

Dad phoned my mum immediately. Mum phoned the town crier, Auntie Denise, who threatened to hang out the bunting.

My brothers, uncles, cousins and neighbours congregated at the family home in Sarn. It didn't take long to understand I was a passenger on this rocket ship, and that my job was to make the journey as memorable as possible for those who had supported me through thick and thin.

I had to ignore the inner voice telling me to turn down the invitation. I had to re-adjust my view of what was acceptable, what represented right and wrong. I could no longer play by my own rules. I didn't have the excuse of not being good enough. This was huge, life-defining, and it triggered a tsunami of joy in my family. They were proud, I was petrified. Welcome to my nightmare.

Alcohol provided its customary distraction. This was not – yet – a world in which Welsh squads staged a scientific search for fractional advantage. We ran about a bit, and then headed into the bars of central Cardiff to let off steam. Such concessions were the hallmarks of a sport lingering between eras; no professional contracts had been signed, so the coaches had limited control over amateur players. We worried about our livers, rather than the WRU's lawyers.

At no point during the preparations had I even considered the possibility of making the starting XV in South Africa, yet the next thing I knew, I was standing there, singing the national anthem before our opening group game against Japan in Bloemfontein.

Ironically, my fate was to be inextricably linked with that of Steve Ford, who had more reason than most to be resentful of the system. The Cardiff wing was briefly banned by the Welsh

Rugby Union in the mid-1980s for the heinous sin of playing two trial matches for Leeds' rugby league club. It was absurd, since he never played an official game, yet he was expected to carry the stigma throughout a fine union career.

Steve, recalled to the World Cup squad four years after winning the last of his eight caps, tipped me off the night before the team announcement. 'Congratulations,' he said, when he spotted me in the hotel lobby.

'What do you mean?' I responded, a little dimly.

'They've told me I'm not playing,' he continued, matter-of-factly. 'That means you're in.'

My reply was hardly erudite. 'Fuck off!' I exclaimed. 'Don't be stupid, man. That can't be right.' I scuttled away to seek out my roommate, Robert Jones, my new best friend.

Rob had been there, seen it, done it and swapped the T-shirt. I joined the squad after hiding during an impromptu tour of suburbia; he came in as one of the Originals, a member of the Wales team that had finished third in the inaugural World Cup in 1987. He spoke with the authority of a two-time Lion, and was the nicest man you could wish to meet. I was a gawky, over-grown schoolboy with a dubious taste in music.

The room we shared was a sanctuary. He sensed my discomfort: I was 20, and didn't know what to do or say in such pressurised surroundings; he was 29, going on nine, a big kid who just happened to be the smoothest, most accurate passer in world rugby. He put me at ease because we did nothing but play silly, childhood games.

It sounds weird, in an age in which athletes are expected to be teeth-grindingly serious, but those games would start the moment the lights went out and we were in bed. Neither of us were instant sleepers. 'Sing a song starting with A,' came the disembodied order. I tried, and failed, to get away with something by Abba. The charades continued until we exhausted the alphabet.

The game was usually decided on the letter X, my speciality. If you ever see me in a karaoke bar, advancing on the stage with a glint in my eye, run if you don't want to be subjected to me massacring 'Xanadu' in a manner that would make Olivia Newton-John weep tears of solid silver. The Electric Light Orchestra, her collaborators, would be within their rights to sue.

Rob, a former Wales captain, never realised how fundamental he was to me staying sane, never mind succeeding. He advised me on how to respond when the media got a little excited when I scored a hat-trick of tries in a 57–10 win on my debut. It was a version of Glen's sage advice, which he dispensed regularly as I bedded into the first team at Bridgend: 'If you're going to read the good things they say about you, never avoid reading the bad things.'

Glen, who was playing in a sevens tournament at Porthcawl that day, hadn't forgotten our little heart-to-heart at Llanelli. This was in the era before texts and Twitter, so he resorted to a telegram: 'You owe me one hundred quid.' I resolved to pay him as soon as I was home.

Unfortunately, Alec Evans lacked authority as a coach, mainly due to his perceived bias towards Cardiff players. He was merely obeying the conventions of his trade, in entrusting responsibility to those in whom he had faith because of personal experience, but that didn't sit well with sections of the press and public. Committee-room opportunists and marginalised players added to the pressure, so it was no real surprise when he refused the job as Wales coach on a full-time basis after the tournament.

Rob wasn't in the side for the second game, against the All Blacks, but he warned me to expect some harsh life lessons. I had little idea of how tough – and rewarding – they would be. As a kid, I had no real sense of the social significance of the tournament due to Nelson Mandela's historic endorsement of the Springboks, but I knew my game was changing, fast. Jonah Lomu took me to school during that 34–9 defeat.

He was in his prime in 1995, though New Zealand would be beaten in extra time by South Africa in that fabled final. He was the ultimate opponent, who lived up to his billing as a cross between Mike Tyson and Godzilla. The fact that he didn't use me as a doormat – as he did the entire England team in scoring four tries in the semi-final in Cape Town – made me realise I did have something to offer at the highest level. His being scoreless when he was taken off against us in the second half, was a huge badge of honour.

I studied him intently throughout the tournament. The only other player who made a comparable impression on me was Josh Kronfeld, the All Blacks' openside flanker. His speed to the breakdown, and his sheer intensity, was another indication that international rugby was rapidly evolving into a fast, physically shattering sport. The irony that Lomu, a force of nature, would ultimately succumb to mortality in the form of serious kidney problems is overlooked too easily.

Rob's humility taught me that though you can do things on your own, you should never take all the credit. We shared the bittersweet experience of his last Wales game, a stomach-churning, easily avoidable 24–23 loss to Ireland in Johannesburg that resulted in an early flight home. We never recovered after shipping 14 points in the opening 12 minutes, but the specifics of the game are muddled memories.

That confusion is probably a self-defence mechanism, since we were awful, but something really special to me was forged on that trip. My friendship with Rob has lasted beyond retirement, and our mutual respect will, I hope, persist. He set up my international career by persuading me to go out there and simply play. It was a gift in a plain package – heartfelt advice that any young player should heed.

New horizons were opening. I signed my first professional contract with Bridgend, worth £18,000 a year, on my return from the World Cup, turning down £50,000 offers to sign for Bradford or Salford in rugby league. But, deep within me, nothing had changed; I was still struggling with that which made me different.

Had I confessed quietly to Rob, during one of our games of 'I Spy', it might have been different. But there was no way that could happen. The Rob of 1995 would have probably been OK with it, but the Gareth of 1995 couldn't tell him. He wasn't ready, and playing for Wales was pushing him even further into the closet.

Chapter Four

THE FEAR

No one would hear me cry: my tears were muffled by a pillow out of respect to my parents, who slept next door. I lingered in a small black and white bedroom, with a portable TV in the corner and a shelf on which sat gilt and plastic trophies that marked half-remembered victories. The single bed, set to the left of a window illuminated by a streetlight, was a sanctuary that also felt like a cell.

It had been a homecoming fit for a hero. They had all wanted to tap me on the back, clasp me in a firm handshake or swallow me in one of those clumsy man-hugs which are rarely, well, manly.

Everyone told me I was great, that my mum and dad were the best mum and dad since Mary and Joseph. People wanted to give me awards. It was wonderful, warm and kind.

But then I'd climb the stairs by the front door in that house I knew so well, turn left at the top, take four strides along the landing, and close the bedroom door. I would be alone, and those familiar, taunting questions would begin to rattle around my brain once again. Why? Why me? What is it all about? What am I going to do? Acid would scour my stomach; my throat would be lined with sandpaper. And I would cry a river.

I was so scared. Really, really lonely. I was sick of pretending to laugh, pretending to be proud of who I was and what I had done. I was being pulled left, right and centre, like a rag doll, but realised I just had to go with it. I didn't want to be the perfect human being they were making me out to be. I didn't know what I was, I didn't know who I was, but I knew what I wanted to be and who I wasn't.

The problem was that everyone had invested so much time and emotional energy in me: I was the one who made their lives just a little more manageable. I didn't want that responsibility. I hadn't lived myself, for goodness' sake! But I went along with it. I went their way, because I didn't know my own way. I didn't know where to go, or what to do. So I went down their yellow brick road.

I felt ugly. I felt guilty, because I absolutely hated the talent that appeared to be my greatest gift – it would be the thing which exposed me, revealed my secret. I knew rugby wasn't ready for someone like me. I didn't want to play well half the time. I know that might sound shocking, a betrayal of those who had such great expectations of me and for me, but I knew that if my life followed their script, I'd be lost.

That's your lot, *butt*. Face it, there's no way you're getting married and playing happy families, is there? You will be competing in the game of hide and seek from Hell. Ready or not, here they come. Getting caught isn't an option. That simply cannot be allowed to happen. You will have to find more elaborate ways to hide, better pieces of camouflage. You will become paranoid about the furtive glance or the casual change in body language that betrays your sexual interest. You will become more solitary, and oh so desolate, because, ultimately, there is nowhere to hide.

I was living my life for other people because I knew no other way. I followed those in whom I trusted; those I believed had my best interests at heart. I listened to my parents, coaches and close friends. I began to invest more faith in my teammates. I had no choice, because the brotherhood demanded loyalty and fealty. I followed their example on the field, where we put our bodies on the line for one another, and I followed their example off it, even though that meant being someone I was not. I couldn't bear the prospect of letting them down, or losing their respect.

Deep down, I'd always wanted to play for Wales, despite my stupidity in deliberately missing that first training session, but I didn't realise it would come at such a price. I began to doubt not just my ambition, but my mind. I was a piece of blotting paper. I would study people in the dressing room, and follow what they were doing instead of instinctively being myself. I began to live their lives by proxy. It was tiring, because the self-imposed pressure to measure myself against them was so constant.

I was tall for a back in those days – I could run, but my size made me conspicuous. I was so paranoid about standing out that I would do stupid things, like trying to squeeze into boots that were one size too small. I'm not sure whether I'd been reading about the Chinese court dancers who bound their feet tightly to remain dainty, but I was determined to stunt the growth of my feet. Ridiculous I know, but I wanted to be Mr Average.

I'd copy everything, from how to sink a pint to how to lace up my boots. I'd take notice of how people looked, what they wore and what they were talking about. If they liked the Eagles, I'd discuss the deeper meaning of the lyrics of 'Hotel California'. I dared not offer even a hint that I was different. It was a form of self-induced brainwashing. I became 15 parts of other people instead of one part me. No wonder I cried so bitterly, so often.

As I people-watched, trying to read their mannerisms, I would try to imagine their thoughts. On the dark days I'd just sit and look at someone and think, 'Fucking hell, how good must it be to be you. How special must it be to have an opinion, and not have to justify it, or not to feel afraid to justify it.' I'd hope he wouldn't notice me staring intently, and wonder what was going on.

The only thing I really had going for me – my rugby career – was simultaneously the best and worst thing for me. My ego was caught at the bottom of a ruck, and taking a comprehensive shoeing, so big wins and performances should have helped. The problem was, I couldn't take those successes at face value.

There were times, though, when I lost myself in the game. In those moments, during the frenzy of a relentlessly physical contest, I could almost be myself unconsciously. But the TV viewers, tuning in for *Scrum V* in Wales, or the Six Nations on the BBC, would actually be watching a version of *Catch 22*, the film in which everything is contradictory and nothing is as it seems.

The greater the freedom with which I played, the more stringent my imaginary jailers became. The better I played, the more the pressure built. That inner voice became more insistent: 'There's going to come a time when you can't get out of this. If you carry on this way, you're going to be doing what other people think you should do, and acting how other people think you should act, for the rest of your life. It's a long fucking time to be alive, or to think you're going to be alive.'

I had started to feel the pressure to conform between the ages of 16 and 17. My mind and body was telling me I was different, and that was dangerous. I couldn't be different, because I had to be the same. I loved the physical release rugby gave me as a kid, but now I loathed the attention it generated. I wanted to be the secret rugby player. I wanted to be a link in the chain, rather than the garish gold medallion that catches people's eye.

Those links can be replaced, but they make the whole thing work. As far as I was concerned, people began to be dazzled by the decoration. They started coming to watch me, rather than the team. I was desperate not to stand out, but became known for doing stupid things, like scoring match-winning tries. I was boy bling.

That's scary because, at that age, it is natural that a boy should be awkward, socially. He's not quite sure of his communal status, uncertain of what defines him. His body image is distorted. By definition, he's immature, incomplete. His hormones are in ferment. He's tiptoeing through puberty with a sideways glance to check if others are going through the same experiences.

Inevitably, given the aggressive nature of the game, rugby rears alpha males. They're the ones who race through adolescence, and are ready to pounce on any weakness. They're the scourge of teenage acne, the peaks and troughs of a half-broken voice or – let's be honest, boys – that acorn in a pig's blanket between the legs.

I developed at an average rate, but still felt vulnerable. I didn't want to be derided, because that would have meant I'd been noticed. I was conscious of my spots and felt compelled to go along with that daft obsession with developing a bum-fluff moustache. I was mortified by the plastic boots Mum bought from Woolworths when I played at Pencoed, but I got away with that because we weren't the only family obliged to count the pennies.

The woodpecker banging away on the inside of my head couldn't be ignored, however. One loose word, one incautious action, and I'd be fair game. Kids are cruel, and if they discovered how lonely I felt, and how different I was, they would have picked my carcass bare.

It wasn't a question of sticking up for myself physically, though I wasn't that great a scrapper in the playground, and nor was it a question of being hurt, because pain is rugby's great leveller. It was more subtle than that. Threaten my family or friends, and I would fight you to my last drop of blood; menace my teammates, or try to take my shirt, and there will be a reckoning. But blindside me with a cruel word when my guard is down, and I'm in real trouble. I'm massively vulnerable. I was back then, anyway – I probably still am now.

My secret crush, growing up, was the actor Lee Majors. He played Colt Seavers, a Hollywood stunt man in *The Fall Guy*, a long-forgotten action series, after appearing as Colonel Steve Austin in *The Six Million Dollar Man*. Yet, for appearance's sake, I had a girlfriend throughout school.

Debbie Davies was a lovely girl, and we were on the same wavelength. We shared a questionable taste in music – our song was 'The Final Countdown' by Europe – and a dubious dress sense. I was a fashion disaster, excelling myself at one school disco by turning up in a pair of shoes that had Grolsch bottle tops pinned on the toe caps. I tried to explain that since Bros wore something similar I was uber-cool, but all the boys from the rugby team could blurt out was, 'What the fuck have you come as?'

Since they were wearing ripped jeans, black shoes, 'Frankie Says' T-shirts and white bandanas, they were not, perhaps, in the best position to prompt a debate. But I let them off. I was determined to enjoy what would be a brief interlude, in which covering my tracks wasn't so obsessional a pursuit. I knew there was still something wrong, something different, but I was getting by.

Debbie was such a sweet girl. It was too soon, too fleeting, for us to have any real depth of emotional intimacy, but she offered me companionship, and simplicity. We would hold hands and walk around the school like any other clueless, supposedly loved-up couple. She'd be watching at break time as I went onto the field and played football with the boys, and I'd puff out my pigeon chest and feel like I'd done my masculine duty.

How could I feel so unsure when appearances suggested Barry White would struggle to match me in the lurve stakes?

Debbie now works in the pub where my parents drink. She is still a lot of fun, as survivors of her 40th birthday celebrations, in the spring of 2014, can attest. She's a little like my Auntie Denise – she spreads joy, but has the odd screw loose. They each, in their own way, make me feel like a million dollars.

Auntie Denise claims she is my biggest fan. She started compiling a scrapbook of my rugby exploits even before I'd got those plastic boots out of the carrier bag at Pencoed. She collected every article, each programme, all the photographs. There's a library of them at home, even though she – mercifully – got a bit bored with it when I went to Toulouse.

She also has a video collection that deserves a place in the Science Museum, or the London Dungeon. It goes back to the days when matches were rarely shown live. Denise would pore over the highlights, which tended only to show the tries. She'd sit in front of the TV with the remote, hitting the record button whenever I appeared. The pictures are grainy and resemble those of the early Moon landings. It's like seeing my life on speed. Hairstyles come and go, until the hair disappears.

I signed up for rugby: I didn't sign up for the ceaseless sexual innuendo, but that's what I got, courtesy of the bravado culture. Homophobia wasn't an issue, as such, because an alien from the Planet Zorg was more likely to turn up for scrummaging practice than an openly gay man. I knew no one who shared my preferences. I was, literally, the only gay in the village.

A lot of things were said in the dressing room which would probably have made my teammates think twice had they had an insight into my true feelings. You'll be able to guess the standard of conversation: 'Don't worry about him, he's a fucking bender and he can't tackle to save his life.' They might be small examples of ignorance, uttered without any malice, but they upset me because they referred to fellow human beings. Cut them, and they will bleed. Insult them, and they will recoil.

Those throwaway lines didn't make a whole lot of sense. Take the classic: 'Just put the ball up in the air for the full-back. He's a right fucking bender, can't catch a ball to save his life.' I know it sounds like an obvious point to make, but since when did someone's sexuality involve their hand-eye coordination? Or how about that other favourite: 'That centre won't tackle, he's a poof, scared of his own shadow.'

I know, intimately, how much strength is involved in coming out. I hated it, because I became increasingly introverted every time I'd hear the word 'gay', or a similar term used in a derogatory fashion. I would retreat deeper into myself, and use my discomfort to justify my lies. How could I tell the truth when such casual 'banter' was so widespread? It was all part and parcel of the laddish vocabulary of the game.

Somewhere, my logic would run, on any given Saturday there will be a married guy with three kids in a changing room with his mates. There's every chance he likes to play full-back. The opposing team, preparing next door, will be clearing their throats and hawking out the traditional rubbish: 'We'll have him, lads. He can't catch a ball because he's bent.'

If they were saying that about him, through random, inexplicable labelling, what would they say about me if they *knew*?

They'd throw the lot at me, every puerile insult in the book. And if the players were allowed to say those things, imagine what the fans would be tempted to say …

Now, I think more of my sport, and the people in it, than to believe that such things would go unchallenged, but testing that belief was beyond me, for so many years. I had to wait for my time to come.

Waiting wasn't easy. I tried to shut some of my component parts down. I didn't think about girls, although I had, by now, started a relationship with Jemma. And I didn't think about boys. I didn't think about anything but rugby. The secret trainer put in overtime – I worked on my skills and analysed my game.

The transition to the professional era was anything but smooth. The Wales squad, under a new coach in Kevin Bowring, who was promoted from the A team in the autumn of 1995, was drifting. Everyone involved – coaches, players and fitness staff – was making it up as they went along. The public knew we were being paid, and the media, understandably, demanded we offer value for money. We were expected to work hard instead of working smart, and levels of motivation were diluted.

There was no sense that the team bus carried valuable cargo. New players were not nurtured properly. It was almost as if they tossed that sacred scarlet shirt at you, and expected you to get on with it. Sink or swim, kid. It is up to you. There are plenty more where you came from. The result was unnecessary in-fighting, and a culture that encouraged no one to care. There's a fine line between insecurity and indolence.

I often examine the photograph of me that is hung in the so-called Hall of Fame in the chairman's room at Bridgend, which features portraits of all the club's full internationals. Mine was taken on my return from South Africa. It was posed with a brown sheet as a backcloth, and it is an exaggeration to suggest I looked comfortable in front of the camera.

My first Welsh cap was a size too small although, mercifully, it did cover the worst of an inadvisable haircut. My face is creased by an approximation of a smile although, to be fair, it could have been stage fright, or a case of indigestion. What I'm interested in is the eyes. They're distant, a little glassy. There is a lot going on behind those eyes, not all of it good.

I awoke one morning to find that I was the great hope of Welsh rugby. I was trapped. I had been able to intermittently subdue feelings of insecurity and loneliness when my horizons were limited to my home town, because it was reassuringly small and intimate. As soon as I played for Wales, though, the world seemed a big place. I would walk through the streets of Cardiff and sense I was being followed by countless pairs of eyes. I'm thinking, 'Fuck. Oh my God. This is scary.'

I was in a world I neither knew nor trusted; a world populated by people I didn't understand, and I didn't think would understand me. I felt I'd finally reached the point where I'd have to explain myself, and I couldn't. I just couldn't. I just loved playing rugby. I couldn't explain how I came to be playing for Wales. I trained hard and I loved the game, but I didn't think I was special. I didn't dare to explain why I was different to everyone else.

My sexual awakening was painful, traumatic and a source of enduring regret. It was inevitable I would succumb to temptation at some stage, but I expected more of myself. I felt so dirty and disgusted with my behaviour. There was no tenderness or consideration in my first homosexual encounter. It was as far from a loving relationship as it is possible to be.

My response to it was extreme. It occurred in Bridgend, of all places. My turf, my territory. My actions had defiled my tribe. I felt physically ill as I made my way home. It was late, and the streets were silent, but the voices inside my head were accusing, mocking, screaming: 'Why now? Why here? Why him? Why, why, *why*?'

When I got home I spent a long time in the shower, scrubbing myself until my skin was red-raw. I felt so violated and in the wrong. I was convinced everyone would see through me, condemn me for what I had become, for what I had done. I might as well have tattooed my shame across my forehead. I was wanton, foolish, reckless.

I was consumed with desperation to avoid the consequences of my actions. My logic – wash the stain away down the plughole, and people will never discover the truth – was distorted. I couldn't get rid of it, toss it away like a rotten apple. I wouldn't walk out of the bathroom as a clean, new-model Gareth Thomas. I had crossed the line, and in my home town.

The threat of being discovered was now huge, ever-present. I had reached a tipping point under cover of darkness. When I look back, and consider how I reached a certain stage of denial, I realise that was the moment I concluded I couldn't go through life feeling so disgusted. I was driven to create a parallel universe, in which doing everything wrong, cheating on people, could be excused. My biggest lie, which set the time bomb ticking, was to myself.

It was easier to reinvent myself as a chameleon creature rather than having to keep sluicing my past down the drain. Such callousness doesn't make me proud, but it helped me survive. I saw the advantages in a false, multi-layered existence, because multiple personalities enabled me to share the blame. I didn't foresee how much damage that would do to people around me, but at that moment I was too selfish to care.

Life went on, ostensibly as normal. Publicly, Alfie was still cutting a fictional swathe through South Wales; privately, Gareth, his alter ego, was licking his wounds. Both versions of me needed friends who would not be judgemental. I was lucky to have Glen Webbe and Compo Greenslade on call, even if I underestimated just how perceptive they were.

Glen rang me at my parents' house one day, about a year after I'd come back from the World Cup. We swapped small talk and rugby gossip before he said, with an artfulness I failed to detect, 'Oh, by the way, I just want to ask you a question.'

I was an innocent at large: 'Sure, what's up?'

Without any warning, he came right out and said the unsay-able: 'Are you gay?'

We had been out on the lash in Cardiff. His sister, who is a fantastic singer, was appearing at a place called Minsky's. It was a showbar that staged regular drag shows. Let's just say the audience was colourful, excitable and appeared to contain several Village People tribute acts. I had been entranced to see others more confident in their sexuality than I could ever be – some of them couldn't wait to get up on stage to join the acts. I hadn't been able to take my eyes off them, and hadn't wanted to leave. I had obviously given away more, much more, than I intended.

'What are you on about?' I asked, with as much insouciance as I could muster, which was very little indeed.

Glen wouldn't let go: 'Oh, I was just wondering. I just asked a question, are you gay?'

I was only 21. I wasn't ready for my life to flash before my eyes. I had the sudden sweats, but tried to think clearly. Can my parents overhear this conversation? No. Am I giving the impres-sion of being alarmed? Probably not, though, to be honest, anything is possible. Is Glen being Glen, and taking the mick? I gambled that was the case. 'Aw, shut up,' I said. 'What are you on about?'

'Nothing,' he said. 'Just wondering …'

I can still hear that split-second's silence, and the unspoken accusation I feared it contained. It terrified me. When I put the handset down, all I can remember is thinking, 'Where the fuck did he get that from? How the fuck did he know that?' I knew that Glen was a very special person – he sees people, understands them intuitively. He just gets it. *Had he got me?*

Maybe, deep down, I realised Glen and Compo, my two best friends, did know. The signs were there. Compo was a cross between my second father and my minder. He took it upon himself to protect me in anything and everything I did. He would lie for me if he thought people were on to a scent.

Larger-than-life Alfie would be in his element on a boys' night out, clearing a tray of shots and indulging in empty banter about the delights in store for the female population of the principality. But he'd slip away when he thought the coast was clear. If anyone missed him, Compo would come up with an instant alibi: 'Oh, didn't you see? Alfie's sloped off with that bird.'

I rewarded him by driving him mad. A typical example was when he called one morning, asking me to do him a favour by marking out the pitch for the following day's home game. He took me into his confidence, and explained he was double-booked because of a private job. It was to be our little secret.

He took me down to the Brewery Field, showed me the line-painting equipment, and left me to it. Big, big mistake.

Compo took a call that night from Steve Fenwick, his boss at the club. It was a short, sharp conversation: 'What the fuck have you done?' Steve demanded.

'What's the matter?' Compo gabbled, knowing he had no answer to the predictable follow-up: 'You fucking know. Get down here and sort it out.'

It was perhaps as well he couldn't find me for 24 hours, because the sight that greeted him at the club wasn't pretty. I had painted the word ALFIE in huge letters in the dead-ball area, almost across the width of the pitch. I had an NFL thing going on at the time, and had figured it would look great on the overhead TV camera shot.

It was a strange, confused time. Alcohol brought out the darker side of my character, and Compo sat me down when he recognised I was out of control. I was playing the hard man, throwing alcopop bottles around and offering to settle differences out in the street. 'Calm it down, Alf,' he ordered. 'I see what you're at. You're trying to be one of the wild boys, and overdoing it a little bit. Trying to be one of the boys instead of trying to be yourself.' I had no idea who I was at that time, so I told him, unforgivably, to fuck off.

I didn't discover the extent of his honourable dissembling on my behalf until years later, and I will never forget what he did for me. I felt the same warmth from Glen, despite his unwelcome wake-up call. He is bigger than the rugby bubble. He has this way about him which is worldly wise. He is Yoda, with a mean sidestep and a killer sense of timing.

Sometimes, when your world is tiny, and revolves around an oval ball, you need the perspective someone like him can offer. The way he has lived his life gives me the courage of my convictions. My life doesn't have to be a stereotypical version of what others think it should be. He gave me the vision and insight to make more informed choices.

We'd not discussed that telephone call, apart from a brief conversation when I came out, until we met in the process of compiling this book to put things on the record. I had lied to him, blatantly, and maintained the pretence, even though he saw through me so easily I could have been made of plate glass.

If I ever receive an accolade, or am asked about the goodness that's masked by rugby's blood, sweat and tears, I will give Glen and Compo due deference. A vulnerable kid, like me, feels lonely, confused and utterly exposed. He needs support on his terms, to work through potentially devastating issues. He needs true friends to keep their eyes and ears open, and be primed to repel predators. Above all, he needs someone to put his arm around him and say: 'It will be OK.'

Chapter Five

RISKING
IT ALL

It wasn't OK. It wasn't that simple. I wanted more, like a gambler whose first instinct on winning a large bet is to go double or quits. I didn't consider what I had to lose: loyal friends, a fabulous family and a fantastic life. I was prepared to risk it all. There was no logic to the process, however hard I tried to rationalise my foolishness.

Drip, drip, drip. That was the soundtrack of my secret life. Mentally, I had this vision of a cup, sitting at the core of my being. It was empty during adolescence, but slowly, an unseen tap had begun to loosen, and leak. Drop by drop, the cup began to fill. It was no problem at first; the flow was minimal. But inevitably, inexorably, the cup began to overflow.

I had no option but to metaphorically throw away the contents, and start the cycle again. I shudder to think what a psychoanalyst would make of this, but I recognised the contents of that cup as my sexual needs. They were negligible initially, manageable generally, but ultimately impossible to ignore. Emptying the cup, as I had that fateful night in Bridgend, represented the release of sexual tension.

The drip became a trickle as time passed, and I entered my twenties. It was never a torrent, but it changed the cadence of my life. I knew I could not seek partners close to home. Instead I manipulated those around me, so that I had scope to travel to London. Rugby gave me all the cover I needed.

It was an introduction to a world of temptation and opportunity that is simultaneously both seductive and destructive.

Soho's reputation preceded it. My first port of call, after a match against Wasps, was Comptons Bar, on Old Compton Street. I gathered myself at the door and entered, pausing by the stairwell on the right.

I was transfixed by the bar, which was bathed in light. How I envied those who had the confidence to stand there with their drinks and their companions, to laugh, talk, see and be seen. Newcomers like me gravitated towards the shadows. The darkness was the initiate's friend. It was straightforward to melt into the background, and you were never alone. There was a constant stream of people, circulating slowly. Some were singles, well versed in the ways of a hidden world; others were like me, reticent and unsure of the conventions of the scene. Everyone focused on the door, to see who was coming and who was going.

The Haves are comfortable with who they are – they have active social lives, and an easy manner; the Have-nots are isolated and unsure – they have melancholy histories, and are perpetually on the back foot. It was the latter group who set the tone that night. Some had come to London in search of companionship and a better life after being rejected at home; others were experimenting, tentatively and fearfully.

Gay bars are lonely places for lonely, lonely men. They stand in corners or alcoves and calculate the percentages. Some may be married. Others may be curious. Very few are open, with themselves or with those they meet. I'm not talking about those lucky men in the light, with relationships and opportunities; I'm referring to those who are standing there, alone, because they feel they have nothing better to do. They are friendless, and mute.

I want to make an important point here. I have no wish to disrespect London's gay community. I am massively in its debt. It protected me, embraced me long before I came out. I love the diversity and vivacity you can find in Soho. These are not sordid pick-up joints; instead, they are suffused with sadness, because of the emotional baggage which many of the clientele carry with them, over the threshold.

I was no different. I looked for a friend, but talking to a stranger honestly involved an unrealistic degree of trust. I lied, shamelessly and systematically, because I had something precious to protect. I wasn't about to abandon Gareth Thomas, the dutiful son, firm friend and international rugby player. I merely parked him, replacing him with a bewildering cast of characters who had the life expectancy of a mayfly.

I used so many false names I was in danger of losing track, but had to make that alternative reality compelling and believable. I became a method actor, living and breathing the role I had created for myself. If that involved adopting a different personality, and losing myself in the deceit so completely I was able to look everyone in the eye, unblinking and defiant, that was fine by me.

The strange thing was that, despite that level of aloofness and cynicism, my characters were never pre-planned. Whenever I walked into a gay club I was a blank canvas. I'd invent a name and occupation for myself instantly, instinctively. The details were decided by the nature of the guy to whom I was speaking.

The charade depended on what he did for a living. Let's say he was a farmer. I'd be a worker in a coffee shop. If he worked in a coffee shop, I'd be a policeman. If he was a policeman, I'd be a banker. The idea was that I would be a diametrically opposed character, to throw him off the scent. I didn't want to make the first move, just in case I told the farmer I was, say, a grain merchant, before he revealed his hand. That would have given him a chance to expose my ignorance and, consequently, my dishonesty.

As ridiculous as it sounds, I used to hope they were telling me the truth. If they weren't, we would be in a weird, parallel universe in which nothing was at it seemed. I didn't want to get my head around that, but I had to have a degree of mental versatility to commit myself to the scorpion dance in the first place. And it worried me how comfortable I was with the process.

A favourite ploy was to order a drink in a French accent, or even in French itself. I was passable with the language, and made a great play of trying to speak halting English to anyone who tried to strike up a conversation. There literally would be a language barrier, which, following my logic, was a shield. How could they possibly make a connection between say, a French wine merchant, and a Welsh rugby player?

There's a theory in sport and business which suggests that to find a solution to a problem, and impose order, you have first to create chaos. I certainly did that. That was my survival mechanism. The more elaborate the ruse, the better.

This might be difficult to understand, because it is so unorthodox a concept, but I realise now that my thought patterns were similar to those of when I felt suicidal. Just as I had to go through the process of trying to kill myself to want to survive, so I had to create a cast of strangers to want to be myself.

Fate almost gave me no get-out. I was at home in Wales just before the 1999 World Cup, watching television, when a news-flash made my blood run cold. A nail bomb had detonated in the Admiral Duncan pub, one of the landmarks of Soho's gay scene. Three people had been killed and more than 70 injured in an outrage carried out by a neo-Nazi sympathiser who hoped to stir up homophobic and ethnic tensions.

It was shocking and horrific. I couldn't react to the grainy CCTV images, other than to express disgust at the carnage. I had been in that pub the previous weekend, en route to Comptons bar. My brain was racing. Had that bomb been planted a week earlier, I could have lost my legs. I looked at the victims and thought, 'Holy shit. That could have been me.' Even had I been relatively unscathed, I would have been unable to explain my presence there.

I was playing a foolish, dangerous game. There were things I couldn't control, however clever I thought I was being. But I had urges to satisfy, and I couldn't do that at home. I had to take considered risks.

It was acceptable to resist being drawn into a deep and meaningful conversation in the bars. There was the occasional frisson of fear, when someone did a double-take as if trying to put a name to a half-known face, but in general I felt secure. They understand. They acknowledge the privacy and discretion required. Their lives also revolve around risk and reward.

In fact I began to realise, quite quickly, that there were those who knew my real identity. They gave me space, because they knew the complexity of the situation. I, in turn, was fortunate because social media was not as all-encompassing as it has become. There were telephones and cameras around, of course, and since greed, malice and opportunism cross the boundaries of sexuality, someone could easily have sold the story of me supposedly on the prowl.

Had any images been distributed, or such stories seen the light of day, the consequences would have been fatal. I would have killed myself, without a shadow of a doubt. I wasn't ready to confess. I wasn't ready to beg the forgiveness of those I was deceiving. I could not have handled the shame or remorse.

That's terrifying, and explains, I hope, the respect I have for the community, which I mentioned earlier. Like Compo in the bars of Bridgend, they were looking out for me. The word had gone out: let him live his life.

Rugby at this time was not without its worries and complications, either. Kevin Bowring's tenure as Wales coach was going from bad to worse. I didn't mind him as a man, but given that his approach was shaped by his background in teaching, he was never going to get the best out of me. Too many of the squad, including myself, were just going through the motions.

Occasional highlight-reel incidents, such as my interception try from inside our 22 in a 28–19 defeat by Australia in the autumn of 1996, couldn't disguise a downward trend. Our inconsistency that season, when we avoided finishing bottom of the Six Nations table only on points difference, smacked of poor preparation and excessive self-regard – newspaper ratings had become a greater source of debate amongst the group than the post-match debrief. I was counting caps, instead of earning them.

We conceded 60 points against England at Twickenham in 1998, in an infamous match that began with me setting up a length-of-the-field Allan Bateman try by running 40 metres from behind our goal line, and ended with Lawrence Dallaglio banging on our dressing room door and informing us, 'You've been dicked.' I wasn't aware of it, at the time, but he had a point. It was harsh but fair, in the circumstances.

Bowring was never going to survive a 51–0 thrashing by France, at Wembley of all places, later that year. Graham Henry was announced as his replacement, and the Millennium Stadium, in the final stages of construction for the following year's World Cup, was earmarked as his palace. The players, the great unwashed, had yet to be convinced, however.

By that time, I had gone over to the dark side: I had left Bridgend, after a tearful session with chairman, Derrick King, to join arch rivals, Cardiff. I knew what I was getting into. It wasn't a case of taking the traitor's shilling. It was a professional necessity, because I needed to play in the European Cup, which was beyond the means of my home-town club.

It was a natural transition, and I was following a well-trodden path, but it went against the tenets of the tribe. Earning my freedom was a pretty demeaning process for all concerned. I was obliged to argue my case before the club committee, in a room above the main stand. I felt for Derrick, a warm-hearted man with rugby in his bones, but had lost respect for those around him, who had all the empathy of the speaking clock. When they insisted they needed better reasons to let me go, I lost it and stormed out.

Derrick, to his credit, was also distressed. He persuaded John Phillips, an abrasive Kiwi who had been our coach for a year, to drop his opposition to my departure, provided I played in a showpiece match against the touring Tongans.

The vast majority of former teammates and supporters wished me well, and understood the concept of playing at the highest possible level to complement my international career. They knew my time at my home-town club had been a labour of love. But it would make me an easy target. Without exaggerating, it could have wrecked, or even ended, my life.

I didn't expect rose petals to be thrown at my feet the first time I returned to the Brewery Field in Cardiff colours; I was ready to take my knocks. These, after all, were fierce contests, and a sly dig invited due retaliation. The crowd were not going to be inquiring after my welfare. Yet the abuse I received, from one spectator on the far terrace, has never left me.

I was on the wing, and in the direct line of fire: 'Eh, Thomas! You're a fucking bender!'

I convulsed as the words hit me, and was immediately beyond conscious thought. The insult had barely left his mouth before I had hurtled across the boundary to the fence. I steadied myself with my right hand, and threw my left leg onto the top rail.

It was extraordinary – time was smooth, slow and dangerous. The word stretched to infinity. I turned on the B; by the time I registered the E, N and D, I had made eye contact; on the E and the R, the 80 or so people in his cluster had begun to scatter. I was there. My plan was to strangle him until his eyeballs popped out.

In that endless second, I realised I knew him. He had black hair, glasses and was wearing a Bridgend shirt over a slight pot belly. He was one of my own. He had been watching me play since I was a kid. We had fought the same fight, for our town and our people.

He was frozen to the spot, his eyes widening. I didn't think about what I was doing, because had I paused to think I wouldn't have done it. I was breaking every rule I had ever made. My mantra was: 'Never react.' No matter how hurtful the word – gay, bender, homo, faggot, or anything else sufficiently vile to make the blood boil – don't make a scene. Never do anything that suggests guilt by association. Walk away. If you're in a pub and someone brings up a conversation about some guy who is gay, get up, walk away and buy a bag of crisps. Don't be associated with that word.

Everyone in the vicinity was in shock. The game was still going on. No one on the field had noticed, because I had spent large spells of the game isolated, waiting for a decent pass. I dimly remember saying, 'What the fuck is going on here?'

Thank God, Wayne, the Bridgend water carrier, grabbed me and pulled me back on the right side of the barrier. He saved me. There would have been no way back if I had done the guy harm. A long suspension, perhaps even a life ban, would have been the least of my worries.

The obvious inference, that the guy was the voice of the silent majority, was chilling. My abuser took his chance, slipping away to his right, and melted into the crowd. The media noticed some sort of commotion, but I bluffed my way through their questions, insisting it had simply been a fan with a Judas complex. I managed to twist it by saying that, as a Bridgend boy, I couldn't handle the resentment. It was the perfect alibi.

He knows who he is, so there is little point in giving him his 15 minutes of fame, and I still see him when I'm back in

Bridgend. He's a massive Bridgend fan. He's even been to watch me playing for the various other teams I've represented. Time, I suppose, is a healer. I hold no grudge against him. It was insensitive, and the first time I realised how easy it is to be hurt by an insult, but I've rationalised it. I learned to understand that fans sometimes say things they don't actually mean, because in their eyes they are supporting the team. They aren't really having a go at you – you are just some strange sort of symbol, a figurehead.

So while it is so, so wrong, I do kind of get it. I can still hear what he said, and can still see him saying it, clear as day, but I have forgiven him. He taught me a fantastic life lesson that day. He reminded me that it only takes a second to ruin everything. I was petrified for weeks afterwards, because I feared the fallout.

Thankfully, the eternal soap opera of Welsh rugby is never short of distractions, and our home World Cup in 1999 was a time for hosannas and hysteria.

I loved Steve Black, our fitness coach and New Age guru, to bits – his belief in the power of the mind has been central to his long-term relationship with Jonny Wilkinson – but what he was doing taking us to the Brecon Beacons in the build-up to the tournament is still beyond me.

Picture the scene. We are playing imaginary games of rugby, in small groups, with an orange for a ball. We stop to acknowledge the occasional hiker, or dog walker. Blackie then insists on us visualising scoring a match-winning try in the last minute of the World Cup final. He calls us onto the balcony of a cricket pavilion to receive a nondescript trophy, which Rob Howley lifts exultantly to the heavens. We're then expected to make a lap of honour, whooping and hollering.

You couldn't make it up. And we didn't need to: a ten-match unbeaten run was ended when we lost to Samoa 38–31 in the group, and 24–9 to Australia in the quarter-final.

My relationship with Henry, never serene, splintered completely when I marked my 50th cap by drunkenly singing Cardiff City football songs during the official speeches at the dinner which followed a 33–23 win against Italy in Rome, in April 2001.

To be fair, I was undisciplined. Not to put too fine a point on it, I was a piss-head. I still had the amateur's love of getting leathered on boozy nights out with running mates like Leigh Davies, a free spirit who made my three years at Cardiff an enjoyable blur, off the field at least. I was courting Jemma strongly, but had simultaneously become more accomplished at slipping away to London, especially if we had a training camp or a Friday night away game.

I was an effective, almost compulsive liar. It helped me retain control, as I was increasingly drawn to the gay scene. I began to be more cunning in my forward planning. Spacing my visits to London by several months minimised the risk of meeting the same guy. It was unlikely, given the nature of London life, but an avoidable risk. As awful as it sounds, I didn't need the complication of an emotional commitment at that time. My visits were for one-off encounters. Familiarity and fidelity didn't go together.

*

Any smugness or complacency I may have slipped into disappeared one winter afternoon, when I tackled my opposing wing, an English player, in a South Wales derby game. It's a surprisingly intimate, *mano-a-mano* activity, tackling. The ball had gone, but our bodies remained locked together. In what was probably a misguided attempt to gain a psychological advantage, he fixed me with a stare and hissed, 'You're bent.'

As in that Bridgend incident, I was electrified. He rolled away and rose to his feet in the fraction of the second it took me to realise that I had to restate my macho credentials. I had to convince him I was not some limp-wristed victim.

Mine wasn't a subtle strategy – I basically beat him up whenever I had the opportunity. I spent the entire game chasing him around the field, promising heinous retribution. The code of the alpha male meant I had to impose my dominance on him physically, so that he would begin to doubt the wisdom, and the truth, of his slur. I tried not to be too obvious, but in the second half, even my teammates began asking questions: 'What's your problem with him?' and 'Why are you going after him so much?' or 'Why are you so wound up?'

Every time he had the ball, I would hit him as hard as I could, while remaining on the outer edge of the laws. If he struggled and attempted to get up, I would put my hand on his face and push it into the mud. There are age-old ways and means to inflict punishment when you are set on operating just within the limits of legitimacy.

I know how to hurt someone. Let's say you are so angry with what an opponent has done to you or, more likely, one of your teammates, that you want to kick them in the ribs and break those ribs. If you're a good enough rugby player and you really have a problem that you feel compelled to sort out there and then, you can do so subtly and legally.

When a ruck is formed and somebody has their back to you, the trick is to run in as hard as possible and plant a shoulder into their ribs or kidneys. You can also wrestle the wind out of a victim on the ground and tackle into the solar plexus to achieve the same effect. I went through the card that afternoon. My intention was to demoralise him.

It was the first and only time a player has used a homosexual reference to wind me up. It was cheap, and I was determined that he would pay a heavy price. Controlled aggression is the optimal state of mind for any rugby player; my aggression was out of control. I remember catching sight of my opposite number, in the centre. He was an Aussie lad who had just been brought over. I could see him thinking, 'Jeez, this is a tough old school.'

I didn't speak to my victim afterwards. There was really no point, because he never apologised. I'm not sure, even now, he comprehends quite what he did. He understands the consequences, though, because I tried to hurt him, every time we played, for years afterwards. It was a vendetta. Eventually, after his umpteenth battering, he turned to me and said: 'Oh, for fuck's sake. Please, just stop it. Whatever I've done to you, just fucking leave me alone.'

There was a part of me that really wanted to reply, 'You shouldn't have said it,' but I had made my point. I don't believe the guy is homophobic, or has a problem with me; it was just a heat of the moment idea which blew up in his face. He was subjected to my anger and fear, which is a pretty toxic mix.

I needed to recalibrate. Bridgend, under the new ownership of a garrulous local businessman named Leighton Samuel, were set on paying silly money in an attempt to win the Welsh National League. It was a no-brainer to return, so I spent the last two years in the old club system in reassuring surroundings. We took the title at the last available opportunity before regional rugby was introduced in 2003.

The decisive victory over Neath on a balmy May evening was a bittersweet occasion. It was Bridgend's first major honour for 23 years, but unfortunately Samuel felt the need to remind everyone the club was his personal fiefdom. He brandished the cut glass trophy and came up with the crass line, 'That's the most expensive vase I've ever bought.'

It wasn't the classiest comment, but it typified an era. Players were becoming more mercenary, and it started at the top. The bonus system introduced by Graham Henry meant we were on £5,000 a win for Wales. We purposely ran to the cameras, flaunting five fingers. It was a private joke which, in retrospect, wasn't funny.

The sudden show of wealth at Bridgend was at odds with a town that was struggling economically. I returned principally for the money – denying that is beyond even someone with my ability to be economical with the truth – but I also felt for the place. Its vital signs were worrying. It was dying, slowly.

It's funny. I'm long since retired, and have a body that goes into meltdown if it is asked to run for more than a couple of miles, but I would love to play for Bridgend just one more time. The Ravens, as they have been rechristened by the marketing men who consider themselves indispensable in the modern game, are not that desperate, but they have hit on hard times.

At low moments, I have returned to the Brewery Field to commune with the ghosts. My car takes me there on automatic pilot. I sit in the empty stands, or on the halfway line, and imagine it as it was: alive with conjecture and caustic wit, humming with hope and expectation. Our teams were never the most naturally talented, but they understood the honour of wearing the shirt.

That's not the case these days. The pride has been stripped away. Regional rugby cares nothing for tradition, for the ridiculous number of internationals and British Lions produced by an unfashionable club supported by folk who work hard for their money. Those people are not going to put their hands in their pockets on a Saturday afternoon to watch second-class rugby. That's no disrespect to the current players, but a fact of life.

I still view the town with a postman's eyes. So many shops and pubs have closed. Business has drained away. There are charity shops and drop-in centres, rather than butchers and bakers. The town is on a life-support machine. It used to be a happy, thriving place; now, the young people can't wait to get out and find a life.

I did a session at the local college recently. The kids couldn't believe it when I told them all I wanted to be known as was a Bridgend boy. They felt no connection with the place. None of them watched rugby, and only a couple played it. They were becoming detached from the game that once defined their country. I was saddened, but unsurprised.

Rugby tells us how our landscape has changed. It is no longer a constant factor in villages and towns. My mum has been involved with the Tondu club since she was a child. The heartbeat of the community has not stilled – they recently staged a sevens tournament in aid of the family of a former player, taken too young – but the pulse is getting weaker. Hardly anyone drinks in the clubhouse bar after matches. The players come from outside the village and have no incentive to stay.

Further along the valley, the villages around my father's birthplace in Ogmore Vale are in more acute distress. Places like Wyndham, Lewistown, Pant-yr-awel, Blackmill and Evanstown once produced good rugby players and teams that reflected the hardness of their upbringing. They have been contracting since the last deep coal pit closed 30 years ago. Residents are marooned, amidst tanning salons and estate agents who are grateful to get £50,000 for a house.

I used to play school rugby there, taking a decrepit double-decker bus which we tried to tip over by running from side to side on the top deck as it negotiated the corners on the Blackwood Bends. Our pitch, the Planca, was a former quarry, filled in when the local slate mine closed. It is now used by Nant-y-moel, whose clubhouse is a terraced house. They're struggling for players, because the youngsters move away as soon as possible.

There's a pattern. The village has a charity shop, a chip shop, a pub and a struggling rugby club, kept alive by hidden heroes. So much talent goes to waste, because there is nowhere for it to be developed. Local kids go wild when they're 15 because there's nothing to do. They would be ideal rugby players, because you've got to take a knock to live in a place like that.

You can occasionally see them throwing a rugby ball around in the street. The area is still classed as Bridgend. They once could have played top professional rugby, ten, 15 minutes away, in front of their own people. Now they're probably dreaming they're Jonny Wilkinson, playing in the sun in Toulon. What's that going to give back to the area?

It is easy to think villages like Ogmore Vale and Nant-y-moel are on the road to nowhere, but they are not. They lead to a special place that made me understand what it means to represent my country.

Not quite *Baywatch*, is it? My brother Richard and I braving the
cruel sea during a summer caravan holiday at Porthcawl.
I learned to swim a couple of years later, aged seven.

'No Mam. We don't want our picture taken, thanks.'
Dad and his three sons pull faces for the camera on holiday in
Benidorm. My bodybuilder's pose needs some work.

Do not feed the animals. The Thomas brothers in a more
co-operative mood on a trip to Bristol Zoo.

Ogmore Comprehensive rugby team. A ball and a bunch of mates.
Who needs lessons?

A trophy and a hat trick of tries for Pencoed Youth. The word was starting to spread...

Life lessons learned playing for Pencoed Youth: 'Never gloat, never glory in your superiority. Be humble in victory, graceful in defeat. Respect the opponent, because without an opponent there is no game.'

Image from a lost world: Valley rugby was fierce, emotional and elemental. Here I'm being tackled by Gavin Owen of Treorchy, one of the top clubs in the Rhondda.

Suits you, sir. Doing a bit of freelance modelling in the Cardiff club shop, after joining the Blues from my beloved Bridgend.

My town, my people, my team. Celebrating Bridgend's Welsh Premier League title in 2003: we were unbeaten at home that season.

With my long-suffering roommate, Martyn Williams. 'Nugget', a real man's man, was one of the first to know my secret: 'Bud, don't worry about it. Let's have a beer'.

Glen Webbe bet me £100 this would happen. My Wales debut, aged 19, against Japan in the 1995 World Cup.

Don't look behind you. My interception from inside our 22 in a 28–19 defeat to Australia in 1996 led to the longest solo try at Cardiff Arms Park.

Top of the world, Mam. Celebrating a Rhys Williams try against
Scotland at the Millennium Stadium in 2004. A special place,
where I asked my team to 'stand tall with me'.

Wales's Grand Slam, 2005. Great day, great occasion,
great memories, but bittersweet. I was a one-armed warrior
at the time – just wish I could have done more to help.

Want to know how much it hurts to captain a losing Lions team in
New Zealand? Look at my face after the 48–18 mauling by the
All Blacks in the second Test in Wellington in 2005.

Chapter Six

WIND OF CHANGE

My summer of love was in 1992. Man, I was chocolate. I wore a Lacoste polo shirt, cream trousers and brown Timberland deck shoes. The killer fashion statement – a Pringle v-neck sweater – was green with yellow diamonds. It cost £90, nearly two weeks' wages, from the only cool clothes shop in Bridgend. My mullet didn't exactly cascade onto my shoulders, but it managed to highlight the ring in my right ear.

How could I fail? The lights were dimmed in the front room at James Bunyan's 18th birthday party. The DJ teed up 'Wind of Change', the power ballad by the Scorpions which remains one of the biggest-selling singles of all time. Jemma Cooling was swept along by the tsunami of adolescent hormones, and agreed to a slow dance.

We smooched, sharing our first kiss to the anthemic excesses of a German heavy metal band. Eat your heart out, Tom Selleck.

Up until that moment, watching Magnum PI, the moustachioed detective, on TV was as romantic as it got. But there, with other entwined couples silhouetted against the sofas, something strange and wonderful occurred.

I'll be delicate here, because my mum will read this. Let's just say that as we danced, I became aware of a stirring down below. I thought to myself, 'Oh my God, I'm not different.' I was so excited, really chuffed. It was a natural process. I didn't have to concentrate, or think of super-hot Tom on the mean streets of Hawaii. I know this sounds pathetic, but it was a real eureka moment.

Maybe Jemma was The One? It was a confusing time, because it made me wonder whether I was in fact doomed to be as lonely as I feared I would be. I was fiercely attracted to her. We were easy together. She was among a group of girls from Pencoed who would come down to watch the youth team play. I was the hot-shot rugby player, giving it the big 'un. Beneath the bogus seen-it-all bravado, I felt flattered that such an attractive girl was evidently smitten by me.

Apart from Debbie, at Ogmore Comp, Jemma was the first girl to take an interest in me. I was never that out-going with girls, for obvious reasons, but she made it easy. I didn't have to do the chatting or the chasing. She made things less complicated. I really liked her, and selfishly it meant I could integrate more effectively into the rugby team, because I'd have a girl-friend to take out on dates with other couples. It made me feel less isolated.

I was still completely screwed up, mind. I began to play games with her, in the pretence of being a big shot. I stood her up. I behaved badly, because it offered me yet another easy escape route. Following my pattern of thought can be perplexing, but I had realised that nothing had fundamentally changed. Therefore, since Jemma had instigated the relationship, only she could end it. If she finished it, I was off the hook. I know, I know. Ridiculous. Almost cowardly, isn't it?

We were happy, and that was putting me under more pressure. I was stressed out, because I was conditioned to regard contentment as a temporary condition. I sensed I was falling in love with her, and knew how difficult that would make both our lives. I couldn't finish with her – deep down, I didn't want to – but I needed her to make the call because I didn't want to tell her the hidden truth. Her walking away, because I was such a bastard, would solve everything.

It was a complete cop-out, but I reckoned without Jemma's resilience. She just kept at it, continued to deal with everything I could throw at her. Our love blossomed slowly, gradually and naturally. I became entranced by her femininity and humanity, because she is such a sensitive, caring person. That led, against all my initial expectations, to intimacy.

Jemma remains the only woman to whom I have made love. I make that distinction, because I did have drunken sex with a stranger on a solitary one-night stand which we both immediately obliterated from our memory banks. My life with Jemma evolved at its own pace. It was a long courtship, since we were together for nine years before we got married. We set up home together first, because we decided, sensibly enough, to see how it worked.

Again, I appreciate that this may sound cold, but we started to live together for the same reason I've done a lot of things: I felt that's what I had to do. People may never understand how a gay man can love a woman, but society pushed us together and society kept us together. The stereotype about a rugby player needing to settle down, sharpish, meant that after a certain time we felt under external pressure to get married. Society ushered me towards Jemma, politely but firmly.

Life doesn't feature too many breathless, lilac-scented Mills & Boon fantasies. We clashed occasionally, because we are each strong characters. I even proposed during a row at the house we were doing up on the outskirts of St Bride's Major. It was an inconsequential tiff that came to a juddering halt when I said: 'OK then, let's just do it. Let's get married.'

Not quite the Knight Gallant getting down on one knee, but I meant what I said. Jemma had never really raised the subject directly, but I wanted to make a commitment to her. She made me feel safe, secure and loved when I most needed reassurance. Selfishly, I craved the shelter of her affection, because so much of my everyday existence felt so wrong. Being loved and valued by her felt so, so right.

She was the nicest, most caring, girl I had ever met. I don't believe in judging people by their looks, but she was strikingly pretty. You could not fail to love her. She took such pride in her appearance. I cherished the softness of her skin, and the warmth in her eyes. She accepted me for who she thought I was. I wanted to make love to her because of the strength of my feelings for her. I desired her.

Yet, deep down, I remained confused and conflicted. I was very difficult to live with. I feel remorseful about that, because I denied Jemma the respect of allowing her truly to know the person to whom she had committed. That was the least she was entitled to expect of us as a couple.

When you are under the same roof, you go to bed together, you're intimate together, you wake up together, you eat together, you fight together.

I could never imagine living with me, as I was then. That's why Jemma is the heroine of this story. She deserved a medal, not the booby prize of being lumbered with whatever, or whoever, passed as me on a particular day. I became a hologram of contrived normality, rather than a grown-up human being. I was a bad character actor, who lied and hid and connived. I was never nasty towards her in a physical sense, but I reverted to type and became emotionally barren.

I never contemplated sharing my deepest feelings. It was the same old story, with a twist: I wasn't ready to break her heart, and the lie had mutated. It now involved Jemma's family. Another set of parents, siblings, grandparents and relatives were drawn into the web. The wider the web, the more adhesive the lie, the harder it became to free us both from it.

The London scene continued to exert a fatal attraction. I was playing a game of Russian roulette. On one occasion I called

Jemma, pretending that I was in Newcastle, for a stag do. I was just about to turn into Old Compton Street when I saw a mutual friend on the other side of the street. I stopped and stooped, in a panic-stricken reflex action. I must have looked bizarre, but all I cared about was her walking past, oblivious to my presence. The crisis passed agonisingly slowly, step by step.

That little psycho-drama scared me, but didn't deter me. I was perpetually on edge, living in fear of the consequences of being a cheat. Jemma had earned the right to honesty and clarity. She should have known everything of the man she married, the person she promised to spend the rest of her life with.

The church in which we married in 2001, St Bridget's in our home village, dates back to the 12th century, but has been a holy site for even longer. It is small, with nine rows of pews, five seats on each side of the aisle. The pulpit is set on the left; the chancel, which lies behind the altar, features a stone tomb-chest from the 16th century. John Butler lies next to his wife Jane, in full armour, with their children shown as so-called 'weepers' on the side.

I had surprised my parents, who are not particularly religious, by arranging to be baptised at the age of 18. It was a deeply-felt decision. I had no particular connection to any branch of Christianity; I was baptised in an Anglican church because it was closest. I simply wanted to establish a connection with God, because I never felt I could speak to anyone else about my troubles. I had this vision of Him as a benign being, able to hear my thoughts and entreaties.

Like most lonely kids, I had created an imaginary friend. God would provide answers to my unspoken questions. He was bigger than me. I could tell him my problems and receive magical guidance. The innocence of that initial devotion soured, however, when I left my teenage years behind. Now, as a man preparing for marriage, I expected it to be a simple bargaining process: in return for not going up to London during the six weeks our banns were read at St Bridget's, I expected to be given peace of mind.

Whenever I walked into the church, past the stone font in which so many had started their spiritual journey, I was struck by a deceptive sense of calmness. My prayers were constant and, truth be told, pretty pathetic: 'Dear Lord. Please make this work. If I stand in front of you at the altar, and make these vows, I say them because I mean them, but I need your help to make them meaningful. Cure me.'

That's an awful, degrading concept, because I wasn't suffering from a disease; I was begging Him to end my frustration, curtail my confusion and ease my anger. Predictably, my feelings remained the same. I continued to live a double life. Lying to everyone about everything was still second nature. I was consumed by self-pity. It was as if I couldn't do right for doing wrong.

I was on the edge, and could have done without a classic, thought-provoking coincidence during the wedding ceremony, when it seemed as if He had decided to make a point. We'd reached the juncture in the service where the vicar challenges the congregation '… to show any just cause or impediment' why the couple '… may not lawfully be joined together'.

It's that Mrs Robinson moment. There's usually a brief theatrical silence, before the vows are taken. In our case, at that precise point, Curtis Greenslade, Compo's two-year-old son, decided to scream for no apparent reason. Cue uneasy giggles, the odd belly laugh, and a sudden increase in my pulse rate. It was really weird. As Catherine, Compo's wife, has said on several occasions since, perhaps we should have heeded Curtis's warning.

But it was a wonderful occasion. We surrounded ourselves with friends and family, and switched off from reality. I can still see the smile on Jemma's face. She was radiant. I can also remember her making a formidable tag team with my mother, when they heard I had agreed to get married in the morning so that I could play for Bridgend against Pontypridd in the afternoon. Dennis John, the coach at the time, was fortunate to escape with a full set of front teeth, because you do not mess with Mum.

We wanted children, and Jemma fell pregnant after about a year. It was a joyous, nervous time, which ended in the nightmare of a miscarriage in the early weeks of her second trimester, between 12 and 16 weeks. The sequence of euphoria and despair deepened six months later, when Jemma lost a second baby at the same stage.

People talk about heartache a little too easily. The word does no justice to the indescribable pain and enduring grief which united us in what was still, deep down, a divisive situation. People were kind and considerate, but they naturally sought simple solutions to a complex problem. Everyone asked the one-word question: 'Why?'

I struggled to suppress the inner demon who cackled: 'You're the only one who knows why.'

Chapter Seven

THE DEVIL'S CHAIR

You have to be alone to understand what it means to play for your country in front of millions. You must climb the mountain to appreciate the depths of despair. You need to feel the ground beneath your feet to let your imagination take flight. You have a duty to open your eyes before you open your heart …

Don't panic, *butt*! I've not gone all hippy-trippy on you. There's no need to dig out Grateful Dead CDs, light joss sticks or search the local second-hand shop for a spare set of saffron robes. In the probable event of you not knowing what on earth I am going on about, I'd better explain.

I never truly valued the Wales shirt until it was almost too late. I knew what it was worth, in terms of my take-home pay, but didn't really understand what it signified. In fact, by 2002, I had reached a point where, in Graham Henry's last match as Wales coach, I cheered every Irish try in a 50-point thrashing at Lansdowne Road.

I had been relegated to the A team the previous day, and didn't care who shared my resentment. I got settled into a good session at the Swan pub in the village of Aberkenfig, but would have happily gone to Cardiff airport and conducted the Wales fans who greeted the returning heroes with a chorus of, 'We've got the worst team in the world.'

It was a mess. We had gone through the 'Grannygate' scandal, when they had been trying to give caps to players whose only association with Wales was a fondness for an occasional pint of Brains best bitter. There were poorly thought-through signings from the Southern Hemisphere and the northern code, rugby league. I was as guilty as anyone of feeling stale and indifferent.

It took the appointment of Steve Hansen as Henry's replacement – he was Wales' ninth coach in 13 years – to change attitudes. In the process he effectively saved my international career.

We didn't like each other initially but his assistant, Scott Johnson, who was to play a pivotal part in my life, and not just my career, acted as mediator. He took me out for a cup of tea and squared me up. I was a newly married man and needed to accept responsibility. That meant succumbing to the rigours of a new regime. If that involved being monstered during 6.30 a.m. training sessions, so be it.

Hansen followed up. I was going through the motions – I had won plenty of caps, but had achieved nothing; I was popular within the squad, but lacked authority. My leadership qualities as a senior player were suspect. He challenged me to respect my talent and my teammates. I resented his forcefulness, and suspected his motives because of his closeness to Henry, but he was right.

He did what all exceptional coaches do: planted a seed in fertile soil and waited to see if it germinated. He had got into my head, provoking me to look deep into myself and visualise a life without international rugby. It was a long-overdue wake-up call, which led to a resolution that playing for Wales would define me.

I spent my last 50 caps making up for the complacency that characterised the first 50.

Carl Jung, the celebrated Swiss psychiatrist who might have found me an interesting case study, summed up the episode perfectly: 'Your vision will become clear only when you can look into your own heart. Who looks outside, dreams; who looks inside, awakes.' I paid my penance, acknowledged I was selling myself short, and tried to make amends.

Hansen's first full season, in which we lost every Six Nations match, was a revelation. It was madness: a poll in a local paper to find the nation's most hated man placed our captain, Colin Charvis, in second place – between Osama Bin Laden and Saddam Hussein – but I found myself fronting up on behalf of the troops.

I captained my country for the first time when Colin was rested after yet another defeat, by 35–12 in a World Cup warm-up match against Ireland in Dublin, in the summer of 2003. It would be more than a year before I was given the job on a full-time basis, but something just clicked. The shirt began to speak to me. It told me tales of who and what had come before, and launched me on a voyage of discovery, which ended with me on the Devil's Chair.

The Chair can be found on the Bwlch, 'the mountain pathway', at the head of the Ogmore Valley, where the road leads over the summit and down into the Rhondda. It is at once bleak and beautiful. Waterfalls seep down ancient gullies; fir forests, planted by English immigrants who sought to supplement mining income by providing timber for the paper industry, decorate the hillsides. It can be a brutal place in winter, but it is where I found myself.

It became my place of pilgrimage, somewhere I could come before international matches, to renew myself as a Welshman. I appreciate that sounds a bit daft, a little trite, in cold print on a page, but it worked for me. I understand now, the Aboriginal concept of the land being part of their spirit. This was where I started the process of coming to terms with myself. In a perverse way, the more emotionally drained I became, the better I responded.

When I am on the Bwlch, and feel the slate beneath my feet, I am, literally, a more grounded human being. I realise that my family and true friends are the reason I live and breathe. At my lowest points, I was confused, spiritually bereft. I would walk slowly, scanning the landscape, asking myself: 'Why are you trying to leave this? What are you fucking running away from?'

Sometimes we lose sight of what is in front of our eyes. I'd bring a Welsh mate to the Chair, and all he'd see would be the grimness of the setting, the hardness of local life. Yet I'd bring an

American friend, and he would regard it as one of the prettiest sights in the world. I think we undervalue what created us, the history hidden in the landscape. It takes a turning point in your life to make you appreciate it.

Sport is a funny thing. It means nothing, and everything. The slightest incident is dramatised and magnified on television. I didn't need a reason to be proud to play for Wales, but it was a really powerful experience to look across the patchwork quilt of fields, and think about the generations of families there, who worked themselves to the bone to put bread on the table. I could see my Uncle Stuart's house in the distance, close to where men once burrowed beneath the earth for a pittance.

I know this will seem over-sensitive and spiritual, but representing your country is beyond the now. It has greater significance than making your parents or your partner proud. It is mind-blowing to stand and look down through the clouds, at the carpet of villages on the valley floor, and realise that, in those miniature houses, there are people whose mood will be influenced by the result of a rugby match.

I was just passing through, I realised, a speck in the timeframe of history. I didn't matter. My insignificance gave me humility and freedom. I was used to praise, but had never felt such awe. That gave me strength and perspective, the thinking time that players are denied in a professional era, where money naturally sets the agenda.

When I moved away from Wales, briefly, later in life, I thought I'd escape the everyday, mundane stuff – in the city, life is ever-changing. But I quickly realised the one thing I loved about my life was the one thing I had abandoned: the comfort associated with tradition. I missed knowing who would be sitting in the corner of the pub every day, or who would make a point of standing on the sideline, in the same place, to watch me play. Here, I felt at ease, because I had so much in common with these people.

International sport is a much bigger picture than most players appreciate. Psychologically, I needed to find my own place to work things out. If you don't understand what you embody, you are not fully engaged. When I played for Wales in the latter half of my career, I was representing every drop of water in those waterfalls, every blade of grass struggling to retain a grip on the mountainside.

It isn't cool to be so emotionally driven. Players who speak openly about how they feel tend to get the piss taken out of them. It gets me through the day, though. You need to be alone to put your achievements into perspective. So many people say good and bad things about you as an athlete and as a man, that there is a premium on being able to listen to yourself. It helps to be somewhere where you become dwarfed, so your petty problems are irrelevant.

That's why the First World War was my other source of inspiration as captain. When we won the Grand Slam in 2005, I was asked to feature in a television programme linked to the Grand Slam team of 1911. It was an eerie, unforgettable experience, which created a link with Johnnie Williams, one of my predecessors, and led to an acutely personal discovery.

Williams was a wing with Cardiff, whose signature move was 'a side step and inward swerve'. He made his debut in 1906 against the touring South Africans, losing only twice in a Wales jersey and scoring 17 tries in his 17 international appearances.

During the 1911 season, the usual skipper, Billy Trew, asked him to stand in for him as captain against France in the Parc des Princes. Wales, held scoreless in the first half, ran in three tries in torrential rain after the interval to win 13–0. Williams, given the captaincy because of his ability to speak fluent French, played a key role in deciphering their opponents' tactical instructions. The Grand Slam was clinched with a 16–0 win over Ireland behind locked gates at the Arms Park, where mounted police were deployed to disperse thousands of disappointed fans outside the ground.

Born in Llwyncelyn, a village in the Rhondda with a single shop and a church, Williams married Mabel and died on 12 July 1916, serving as a captain in the 38th (Welsh) Infantry Division. He was one of around 4,000 men lost, killed or wounded over five days in the taking of Mametz Wood during the first Battle of the Somme.

There, troops were hopelessly exposed as they attacked in a northerly direction over a ridge. They were slaughtered by machine-gun fire, and became involved in bloody hand-to-hand fighting with bayonets.

The wood still stands today. It is possible to make out bomb craters and trenches in overgrown grassland. A commemorative statue, a red Welsh dragon tearing at barbed wire, overlooks the battleground.

I visited Mametz Wood in search of Williams and another Welsh international, Dick Thomas, who was killed on the first day of the engagement, 7 July 1916. He captained Mountain Ash after playing for Ferndale and Penygraig, junior clubs in the Rhondda. A durable back, he featured in the Grand Slam-winning team of 1909, and became a company sergeant major in the 16th Battalion of the Welsh Infantry after enlisting.

Unlike Williams, who is buried in an extension to a communal cemetery near Amiens, his body was never found. Instead, he is commemorated at the Thiepval Memorial to the Missing of the Somme. It was there that I made the discovery that stunned my family, and made the concept of sacrifice more vivid and personal. There, among the names of 72,191 British and South African men with no known graves, I found my great-uncle, William.

It was a surreal, spine-tingling sensation to trace the letters of his name with my finger. Unreal, since here was someone, a relation, who had died for his country and disappeared into the ether. It seemed so inappropriate, so sad, that he had needed to wait for so long for one of his kith and kin to find him, and pay tribute to what he had done.

It was a fragment of family folklore, come to life. After I traced him, one of my uncles sorted through long-forgotten heirlooms and unearthed two sepia postcards. One features William, posing in profile on a chair. He sits, straight-backed, with an officer's cane across his lap. It is a portrait of quiet pride and heartbreakingly misplaced confidence, which speaks from beyond the grave. The other is a photograph of his younger brother, Eddie. This is, if anything, a more haunting image. He looks directly into the camera with an air of implacable resolution. When William was posted as missing, Eddie lied about his age and immediately enlisted, in the naïve notion he would be able to find his brother in France. In one of those small tragedies that punctuate a war of unimaginable scale, he too died. No record of him remains.

I have often wondered where Eddie lies. My imagination was stimulated by a tour of Mametz Wood, when the guide spoke of bits of bodies being regularly unearthed during the ploughing season. Some mass graves appear to have involved the burial of casualties with their arms linked together, elbows overlapping. Calcified fragments of bone are also being discovered, intertwined, with victims fused together in what was obviously an explosive, body-shredding death.

The concept of long-dead comrades coming up for air, decades after the War had ended, was explored in a poem inspired by the battle. It was written by Welsh poet, Owen Sheers, who, in one of those strange coincidences, spent a year working as a writer-in-residence at the Welsh Rugby Union for the 2011 season. The following, entitled 'Mametz Wood', forms part of his prize-winning *Skirrid Hill* collection:

For years afterwards the farmers found them –
the wasted young, turning up under their plough blades
as they tended the land back into itself.

A chit of bone, the china plate of a shoulder blade,
the relic of a finger, the blown
and broken bird's egg of a skull,

all mimicked now in flint, breaking blue in white
across this field where they were told to walk, not run,
towards the wood and its nesting machine guns.

And even now the earth stands sentinel,
reaching back into itself for reminders of what happened
like a wound working a foreign body to the surface of the skin.

This morning, twenty men buried in one long grave,
a broken mosaic of bone linked arm in arm,
their skeletons paused mid dance-macabre

in boots that outlasted them,
their socketed heads tilted back at an angle
and their jaws, those that have them, dropped open.

As if the notes they had sung
have only now, with this unearthing,
slipped from their absent tongues.

When I re-read that poem, and study those two postcards, I am incredibly moved. I am so proud of those two strangers, who are so close to me, but so obviously of their time. Of course I've not known them in life, but feel I know them in death. They will never know me, but I feel blessed, privileged, that I was in some way chosen to tell their story.

William has his monument. Eddie's sacrifice has, finally, been recognised. Was that an accident of fate, or something that was somehow pre-ordained? Do we have something in common? Will I find strength from them, because I come from another branch of the same family tree? There are no answers, inevitably. It is a really, really strange sensation, but a nice, very nice, feeling.

It all comes down to identity. When I saw William's name, and subsequently visited the graveyards, where an honour guard of white headstones stands to attention above nameless graves, I thought of all the times I spoke of rugby as a battle. OK, I gave my all for my sport and my nation, but, my God, to have such bravery in my bloodline makes my entreaties sound so empty.

I'd give my life for my country, without question or pause for thought, but William and Eddie didn't really have a choice. I get the same feeling when I am on the Bwlch: the past, present and future are interlinked, interdependent. Those two missing men are where I come from. They help to map out who I am.

Johnnie Williams is also, in some ghostly fashion, alive in my mind. One of the great rituals about becoming a full international is the award of the cap, and the reminder that you are merely the custodian of the jersey. When you represent your country, you are signing up to a journey that can never really be completed, because it will carry on long after you are gone.

The boys laugh at that sort of stuff, to be honest, but it struck home when I visited Williams's grave. The cemetery was in the middle of a housing estate in the suburbs of a rebuilt city. There was nothing distinctive about his resting place, nothing to mark him as someone special. Yet he was as glorified a player, in his time, as I was in mine. He's now lying in Northern France, and 99.9 per cent of the Welsh public have no idea of who he ever was.

I tried, but failed, to find out how he died. It must have been savage, as illustrated by that annual harvest of bones and bullet cartridges. The guide gave an indication of the suicidal nature of the confrontation. Apparently, such was the desperation to take the wood that troops were ordered back over the top after running short of ammunition. Those inclined to stay in the trenches were told to ship out, or be shot.

What I can't get out of my mind is the image the guide created of mates linking arms, and instead of walking slowly towards the machine-gun nests, as ordered, sprinting towards a certain death. Others are said to have played recorders as they advanced, in an attempt to keep their spirits up. Senseless, disturbing, but unbelievably inspiring.

I suppose it all comes down to duty, loyalty and other old-fashioned values. Just because it is the old way doesn't mean it is the wrong way. Those values were passed down, from my great-grandparents, through my parents, to me. I am massively proud of being a Welshman, and of the traditions that have been instilled in me.

*

In retrospect, the best piece of advice I received in the process of becoming Wales captain in 2004 was from Jemma. She simply told me: 'Don't give them the answers you think they want to hear. Give them the answers you want to give them. Be yourself. Don't try to be someone you are not.'

It was a bizarre process, in which senior players were invited to apply for a role that was usually seen as the gift of the coach or, in less enlightened times, the powerbrokers at the WRU. It felt a bit like undergoing an interview to be king.

It might have been the first formal interview I'd had since my visits to the job centre, seeking an escape from the car filter factory, but it was successful. Mike Ruddock, who had succeeded Hansen as coach, gave me the job as successor to Colin Charvis.

I was playing for Toulouse at the time, after a shambolic season at Celtic Warriors, a regional franchise that expired because of a lack of strategic support from the WRU. They felt it was not financially viable – hardly a surprise to me, given that Jemma and I had to take out a loan to cover our mortgage payments when pay cheques bounced. Less fortunate teammates were treated disgracefully – like cattle at an auction.

The compensation for such indignities comes in the deeper satisfaction of being engaged in surrogate combat on behalf of others. In moments of self-doubt, I often referred to the legendary speech made by Theodore Roosevelt, the former US president, author, historian and explorer. It is worth reproducing in full, because it made me want to be a better man, and a better player:

It's not the critic who counts. It's not the man who points out how the strong man stumbled. Credit belongs to the man who really was in the arena, his face marred by dust, sweat, and blood, who strives valiantly, who errs to come short and short again, because there is no effort without error and shortcoming.

It is the man who actually strives to do the deeds, who knows the great enthusiasm and knows the great devotion, who spends himself on a worthy cause, who at best, knows in the end the triumph of great achievement. And, who at worst, if he fails, at least fails while daring greatly, so that his place shall never be with those cold and cruel souls who know neither victory nor defeat.

Rugby is about being there. The last time those words filtered through my brain was in 2013, when England came to Cardiff in the mistaken belief the Grand Slam was their birthright. That game was the essence of nationhood, expressed through sport. I did a talk beforehand to a group of mainly English supporters; I didn't see the score of 30–3 coming, but I warned them of an impending emotional firestorm.

Everything was in its rightful place at the Millennium Stadium. I popped down, pitch-side, with about 45 minutes to go to kick-off. The stands had started to fill much earlier than usual. The male voice choir was systematically inspiring the home fans, winding them up so tightly they couldn't wait to unravel. Theirs was such a lyrical call to arms, I just thought, 'Hang on, this is going to be something else.' I felt invincible, and I was a non-combatant. There was nowhere on God's earth I would rather have been that evening – there was no way Wales were going to lose.

During the warm-up, I looked at England's so-called match winners, like Owen Farrell, and saw a bunch of boys. Their routines were polished and their game faces were on, but I saw something else in their eyes: they were unprepared for a unique atmosphere.

As a Welshman it was a special day. Though it was England's worst defeat by Wales in 132 years, the occasion somehow transcended the record books. At the end I looked at the Wales players, ready to play all weekend if required, and realised my time had gone, but I identified with them so strongly it was almost painful.

I saw them, straight-backed and exultant, and remembered my first team talk as official Wales captain before a narrow 38–36 defeat to South Africa in an autumn international. All I ever asked of my teams was crystallised by my final four words as we left the dressing room: 'Stand tall with me.'

Chapter Eight

A HOLY PLACE

It is match day. Welcome to the home dressing room at the Millennium Stadium. It's large and unprepossessing, with bare piping which forms a latticework across the ceiling. The team bus has been parked underground, and you have filed in, past security and up a steep stairway, after wandering through a room that commemorates the greats of the Welsh game.

I've got the corner peg: captain's prerogative – I promise it's not due to its position next to the long, rectangular mirror that's seen more than its fair share of would-be rock stars suffering a crisis of confidence. It is because I can sit back in the alcove and see every one of my players without catching their eye.

My mind is alive. I've become an obsessive reader of body language. Is anyone subdued, morose or withdrawn? Are they laughing a little too loudly, smiling a little too readily? Is there a gleam in those eyes, or is no one at home? I'm searching for signs of nerves, indications of human weakness that need to be worked on, subtly, but urgently.

Fine margins define international sport. A player's mindset must be right. The way he speaks, something he lets slip without knowing, might offer a clue about how we could win or lose. Once you are confident the group is switched on as a unit, you can then focus on individuals. It is a case of delivering a quiet reminder here or there. Experience teaches a captain the buzz-words that make his team tick.

It's a precious time. Collectively, the spirit will rise nearer the game but, individually, it can be either inspiring or intimidating in those first few minutes. A changing room can sometimes be a lonely place. The temptation is to become too introspective, to disappear into your own world without concentrating on what the guys on whom you will rely are feeling.

It's a strange mix. There is a delicate balance to be struck between the needs of the team and the individual. It is vital to create and sustain the right atmosphere because, left to their own devices, some players can bubble over far too soon. Preparations need a perfect tempo, so that there is an explosion of energy, mental and physical, when the whistle blows.

The game doesn't start in here, where the pegs are arranged in team order: backs change down one wall, forwards down the other. It is not unusual to have to calm people down. Whoever said the eyes are the window to the soul understood the human condition. You can tell so much from examining them. Are they slightly downcast? Do they blaze a little too brightly for comfort?

There are other telltale signs to watch out for. Be alert for the player who is a little too active. He's obviously trying to expel nervous energy. As a captain you have to be sensitive to his inner being, but an under-stated chat helps: nothing too overbearing, but a gentle reminder that the moment he will be judged is when the game is underway, not when those around him are settling into the rhythm of the day.

It's not judgement time, but people can lose focus if they get too worked up too early. It can get really heated. When people start to punch or head-butt the walls – which is fairly common – I tend to act like an indulgent dad. I'll say something with a light touch but serious intent, like, 'Boys, if you're going to punch anyone, do it out on the field. Use your aggression out there, not in here.'

Dressing rooms are special. They are churches, holy places: what goes on in them is intimate to the people who are in there. They are the ones who are privy to the inner struggle that precedes the public trial. They deserve full rank and privileges. Deep and meaningful relationships are formed here, in victory and defeat.

You enter the room together, you leave it as one, and return as a unit, a band of brothers. The nation shares only what it can see; this is where you celebrate or mourn as a group of players. This is where you steady yourself before you face the wrath or the joy of the nation. This is a place of insight, where the understanding of what you achieved or what you failed to accomplish is at its most acute.

No matter how plush or how grim a changing room is, the sensations are the same. It's irrelevant whether it is in the Millennium Stadium before a Grand Slam decider, or whether it is a glorified shed in the local park, with Bridgend Post Office playing the Royal Mail Strollers. If the boys are at it, electricity is in the air.

Great stadiums have a spiritual dimension, because they are regularly doused in sentiment. Hopes and fears seep into the brickwork. There's something mystical about this inner sanctum, because that is where you see people as they are, and not necessarily how they want to be seen. There is no place to hide – although some seek to do so, in the toilets or the warm-up area.

It's a melting pot of emotions: joy, agony, fear, anticipation, love, hate. They are contradictory but complementary. Eventually, when those emotions are worked through, the layers have been peeled away and you are stripped bare, it is you, uncut. There's no point trying to wear a mask. This is a place of hard truths, because it is where everything is subservient to substance.

A word of warning: if you are a fake, you will be exposed. You can fool most of the people, most of the time out there on the pitch but, in here, surrounded by those who have come to know you so well, you're fooling no one. The false bravado of the pre-match press conference is already being recycled as fish and chip paper. It's time to put up, or shut up.

Share your anxieties, if you feel you must. The homespun belief that a problem shared is a problem halved isn't as silly as it seems. You will be surprised how much can be sorted out by working individual issues through collectively. I'm captain, but I like to see leaders throughout my team. Ultimately, that's why I love rugby. It is a true team sport that can be broken down into constituent parts. Nothing beats that feeling of unity when the mood is right.

The strange thing about the Millennium is that it is still a little too new to be a shrine. I played in the first match there, on 26 June 1999, when we beat South Africa 29–19 in a test event watched by a shadow crowd of only 29,000. It hasn't created its ghosts yet. It's not like playing at the old Arms Park. There, you could feel the presence of those legends who had sat beneath your peg. I played the last ever international there, a 34–13 defeat by England on 15 March 1997. It felt like attending a close friend's funeral.

I don't like to arrive too early at a ground. Others prefer to be there an hour and three quarters before kick-off, so they can be deliberate in their arrangements. That's too long for me, because it is hard to remain balanced, emotionally. Anticipation can be uniquely draining. It saps energy, and dulls thought processes.

If you are in my team, I'll start stoking the fire slowly, with between 30 and 45 minutes to go. I want you at your maximum when that dressing room door opens, not when you have 20 minutes to twiddle your thumbs, or get wrapped up in idle fantasies of what can go wrong if fate has decreed it is not to be your day.

That half hour or so is why I love being captain. That's when people really connect. Guards are down. Trust is total. I can't deny part of the attraction is the awareness that my players depend on me, to a certain extent. That realisation is thrilling. I visualise snippets of what is to come; the surge of pride of being the one to lead this team out, followed by the orchestrated madness of the first few passages of play.

The warm-ups on the field whet the appetite. Most of the crowd are still in the bars, but you can hear a buzz of humanity. You know they are talking about you, doubting you, hailing you, wondering whether you are what you say you are. Then the band strikes up. The male voice choir begins to circulate. I can't bear to listen, because it is so difficult to refocus after doing so.

You can see people listening, drifting off into another place. It is time to get them back into the changing room – I don't want them worrying about whether their mum has got to her seat. And I know that this sounds daft, but I also make a point of checking everyone has their phone switched off.

I tell you, *butt*, you'd be amazed by how many players will be checking their texts and messages with a few minutes to go, if you give them a chance. It's hard to tell whether it's a sign of self-worth, or self-doubt. I suppose it must be a basic human need, to know there is someone out there, rooting for you. I turn my phone off on the bus, soon after we leave the hotel. If we lose, I don't turn it on again for three days. There's so much to think about and, occasionally, escape from.

There is usually a momentary lull when we come in after the warm-up. It is a personal time. Out of the corner of my eye I am aware of people pausing. Putting the jersey on is a moment of truth. It doesn't matter whether it is their first or 50th appearance, you can still see them thinking, 'Fucking hell, this is something special. This is actually going to happen. I'm going to play for my country and I want to do a fucking good job.'

That's why you get the odd banshee, the crazy shouter. Others put their headphones on, and try and lose themselves in the music. I love 80s pop which, to most of the boys, makes me a museum piece. Some of the modern stuff that's played on the communal iPod deck is dreck, but I put up with it because it sustains the mood. The last thing a team needs is a flat spot in the final countdown.

It's about justifying the clichés, which can slip so easily from the tongue. When we speak as a team about putting our bodies on the line for each other, we are not exaggerating. As your captain I will do anything within my power to ensure the group succeeds. If I can stop a match-winning try by breaking my arm I'll take the hit and live with the consequences. There is something noble about the act of feeling pain so that others can share a rare moment of euphoria.

People who are willing to do that are the ultimate team players. It makes them exceptional rugby players. They are the ones you gravitate towards in those sacred two or three minutes before the buzzer goes, summoning you to the pitch. That's when you call the team to arms. There is a crescendo of emotion. Some like to circulate as individuals; others, like the front row or the half-backs, are usually joined at the hip. There's a special type of unanimity in the air. It's just us against the world.

The fitness guys have been hovering with isotonic drinks and carbohydrate gels. The physios have finished their last-minute checks. Strapping is secure. Smelling salts have cleared the sinuses and blitzed the brain. The coaches have completed their checklists. Everyone knows the game plan, and the calls. The room clears and in those final few seconds, the team is left to its own devices.

I prefer to have all 22 players around me: the replacements have a critical part to play, given the intensity and physicality of the modern game. Other captains opt to hunker down with the starting 15. Their replacements join the support staff outside the changing room, and form an honour guard on the way down to the pitch.

What is said between the players will stay between the players. And that's when the dressing room becomes a powerful place, because it's just about us. Some will struggle to control their emotions. As captain, I cannot afford to surrender to my feelings, even though I will be able to hear my heart beating in a snatched moment of contemplation.

This is far from a universal view, but I believe the best way to get a team to gel is to concentrate on the individual. A team is an imprecise entity, because it changes from week to week, in terms of personnel and mood. The essence of captaincy is stripping away everything so that a player's needs and priorities are isolated.

If I see someone weeping silently, I have to make a risk assessment. Is it pride or fear? If it is a positive emotion there is no problem; if it is negative, it could become contagious. I have to get behind the eyes of everyone around me. If someone cries and I understand they can handle it, I will make eye contact to reassure him. If he has broken down, and his performance is jeopardised, I will be less subtle. An arm on a shoulder, or a word of encouragement, tends to recalibrate the worrier or the wobbler.

José Torres, the former world light heavyweight boxing champion who was one of many who tried to tame Mike Tyson, had a wonderful philosophy, which attempted to define the importance of fear. He likened it to fire: control it, cherish it and it can warm you; underestimate it, be careless and it can burn. Anxiety must be handled properly and professionally.

People are physically ill quite often. It is an obvious symptom of nerves. Hearing a player retching in the toilet block as time ticks down is, in a perverse way, rather reassuring when you know it is as much a part of his pre-match preparation as taping his ankles. Get the nerves out of the system, even if it means losing a little of your lunch.

The final team talk is rarely Shakespearian. I tend to be direct. I remind my team that there's a job of work to be done. I assure them of my confidence in their ability to do that job. I have played with them, in internationals, and played with or against them at club level. I have seen them train on good days and bad. We are not strangers. We are not fair-weather friends.

Do not let your emotions run away with you, because the purest emotion is the mixture of exultation and relief which floods over you here, in this changing room, when we return with our ears ringing and our hearts singing. Then you can cry like a baby, or laugh like a hyena. You have earned that right, and no one, least of all me, will take that away from you.

I know the pitfalls. Players listen so intently to a team talk you have to watch not just what you say but how you say it. The tone and tempo has to be right. That's why I never pre-plan them. I want to respond to the emotion, finesse it. The tribal nature of international rugby means that, in many cases, the script is pre-ordained.

If it is Wales playing England, I'll transport myself back to the Devil's Chair. This is history, our battle against repression. It is about going out there like a banshee, ready to run through a brick wall.

You are also on edge against the French, but you have to have that mental pause button, to give you a split-second's thinking time, because they are nuts. They get so carried away with the moment, they will do the craziest things. They might have a brain fade, and run from their own line. They're not bred like the English, who tend to be more regimented. They're wired differently. They can become so fixated by attempting to dominate you physically they forget to play the game. Wind them up, and they can hurtle out of control. Switch off for a second, and give them scope to be creative, and they can kill you.

If the Scots could paint their faces with woad, and carry your heads on the end of a stick, they'd be in their element. The Irish are similarly driven by chippiness, though they rationalise their violent intent by making it sound poetic.

The week building up to a game is spent attempting to get inside the heads of your opponents. There's rarely time to breathe during an international, let alone rationalise things calmly and meticulously. You have to have trigger points. If A happens, you do B. If they surprise you by doing C, instinct suggests D is the only way out of trouble. A team that gets swept up in the moment, and forgets the ingrained lessons of the previous week, tends to lose.

Fatigue washes over you as the match seeps away. The worst thing you can do is allow yourself a glance at the clock. Once is never enough. Time either passes excruciatingly slowly, as a form of neon-lit water torture, or it speeds by, like a river in flood. The adrenaline flow shifts accordingly. You have to be pumped up to deal with the physical stresses of a combative situation, but you have also got to have an inch in your brain where you're still actually able to think logically. Experience allows you to flick back, through that mental filing cabinet, and remember what worked before.

You play New Zealand and you know exactly what they're going to throw at you. They are shape shifters. They have traits like no other. They can play like the French. They can play like the English. They can play like the Irish. They can play like the South Africans, with a confidence bordering on contempt. Then they ambush you, and play like New Zealanders. That, basically, arises from a cocktail of natural talent and a national culture that regards an All Black as a universal warrior.

Game plans are increasingly analytical. Performance has become a science, but the best players are still artists. All you can do is familiarise yourself with them. Take Dan Carter, for instance. He's the All Black outside-half, the highest points scorer in Test match rugby. You know he's got a left foot. You know he's got a step. Make sure that you work him into positions where he can't put his left boot to work, where he can't hand you off with his favourite left hand, or he can't step off his favourite left foot. That's far from being a guarantee of success, because the guy is touched with genius, but it isn't a bad starting point. It's certainly better than kidding yourself that you are invincible, and assured of imposing yourself on him. Self-delusion is an easy trap in which to stumble when you've just bellowed your national anthem and are seized with an overwhelming desire to rip holes in anyone sufficiently imprudent to stand in your way.

There are times for the grand, dramatic gesture. People still talk of the slow walk David Sole's Scotland team took out onto the Murrayfield pitch in 1990, which set the tempo of a defiant performance that denied England the Grand Slam everyone, including themselves, assumed was there for the taking.

Fair play, but that's not my style. I'm not big on superficialities. I'm not attempting to disrespect the Haka, which has sacred significance to the All Blacks, but its supposed mystique has got a little out of hand. Whenever I faced it, I just stood there and enjoyed it. Hooray for Hollywood. That's cool, guys. But can we do what we came here to do, now? Play rugby, like? Chuck a ball into the mix?

I have a high regard for history, and defer to the depth of emotion the Haka is capable of generating. But it all became a little silly when a form of political correctness took over, and it was obligatory to overstate its importance. Let's get real, here. It is irrelevant to how the game is going to pan out.

I sigh when players can't wait to tell the world: 'We won because we faced up to the Haka. We made a statement by walking forward, towards it.' I'm sorry, but you didn't win because of a pantomime. You won because you had the luck of the bounce, or a moment of individual inspiration. Maybe you were just the better team.

While I'm in Victor Meldrew mode, here's another thing. Pre-match huddles: get a grip, people. They might occasionally help to settle down an inexperienced team but, in general, they're a ploy to set the mood and get a crowd reaction. Again, it is ridiculous how much is read into what is a pretty simple situation. It is extremely rare for anything worthwhile to be said in that gently swaying circle.

A captain does his work in the changing room. The final few seconds before the game gets underway are not the time for a brainwave, or a mixed message. You should be sorted, secure in what you are about to do. It is neither the time nor the place to indulge in amateur psychology, however tempting it is for outsiders to exaggerate the natural drama of the setting.

My role model, as captain, is Compo Greenslade. He just understood people. He got it. He formed individual bonds but assessed us collectively, not just as players but as part of a wider team, including coaches and support staff. I was lucky to play under some natural leaders, but no one taught me more.

Without the team, none of us matter. The ghosted newspaper columns, golden boots and the grandiose contract wouldn't exist. I'm captain, but I'm never blasé. If you play for me, I will give you my oath to do everything I can for you. I know I can pull off all the tricks in the book, and play the PR game so that the commentators love me, but unless my players love me, or at the very least respect me, I am nothing.

Absolutely nothing.

Chapter Nine

TOOTHLESS LIONS

It began with a 'Power of Four' wristband, sent by special delivery to our house in Toulouse. Postcards then started to flutter onto the doormat. 'They'll be ready,' they proclaimed. 'Are you?' The telephone calls from Clive Woodward, asking for my preferred options when playing blindside wing, conformed to the pattern.

The British and Irish Lions tour of New Zealand in 2005 was certainly different. I liked Clive, and understood his anxiety to leave nothing to chance, though when the flip charts came out in the team room I often yearned for the compensatory clarity of the dressing room.

We know now, as players, why the tour subsequently went down in history as 'a calamitous circus'. Everyone associates it with the obsessive approach of our head coach, and an entourage that included political spin doctor, Alistair Campbell. But we also realise we simply weren't good enough.

There's no shame in that admission, no hiding from its implications. The All Blacks were close to superhuman. They never gave us a sniff in the three Test matches. But there were times when perspective was lost. Our failure hinted at the fundamental fault of the Lions, the enforced identity of a team created from four nations and four different rugby cultures. I spent my time as captain trying, not altogether successfully, to get back to basics.

I can trace my bloodline as a Lions captain back to Bill Maclagan, a Scottish three-quarter who led a Great Britain team to South Africa in 1891. The mystique of the Lions shirt is sufficiently powerful to leave a wonderful rugby man like Ian McGeechan sobbing breathlessly and helplessly because he is overwhelmed by its symbolism.

Yet I am almost indifferent to what it represents.

I don't feel British. I am Welsh, first and foremost. I never grew up dreaming of playing for the Lions. The fantasy of playing for Wales consumed me. I never imagined myself as Willie John McBride in the pick-up games down the street, which punctuated my childhood. I wanted to be Gareth Edwards or Gareth Davies. To be honest, I pretty much blocked out the fact that the Lions even existed. Before Billy Beaumont, the former England captain, became my Lions manager, I only knew him as a contestant on *A Question of Sport*.

I officially became the 35th man to captain them, after being called to Clive Woodward's room in our Christchurch hotel the day after a traumatic defeat in the first Test, in which injury ended Brian O'Driscoll's tour. I acknowledged the honour in the spirit in which it was offered: 'Holy shit,' was my acceptance speech, as I recall. I was genuinely happy when I called my parents with the news, but had expected Ireland's Paul O'Connell, who would lead the 2009 tour, to get the nod.

I was proud, but in the bigger picture it didn't mean that much to me. The way I saw it, I had just fulfilled my ultimate ambition – that of leading Wales to a Grand Slam. I had won the European Cup with Toulouse, with a group of players who had shown me a respect I ultimately didn't deserve. In fact, my solitary game as skipper of the Wales rugby league team, near the end of my career, would be more professionally satisfying. Nothing could match the emotional intensity of captaining Bridgend. I learned more about myself, and the world around me, playing for Pencoed. I'm fully aware some will see that as heretical. I'm merely being honest.

The response to our winning the Grand Slam, earlier in the year, was a profound experience. The madness lasted for weeks. I was treated as an insane amalgam of rock star and war hero, because I was one of the boys who made going to work on Monday morning a survivable experience.

Everyone was dumbfounded. The streets were crazy. One guy was so out of it he head-butted the team bus in homage. As ever, I knew it wasn't about us. It was about making others feel better about themselves. The Lions can't recreate that experience. There are few reality checks when you play for Wales: it is either a total disaster or a stratospheric high. On the good days, the most memorable occasions, you breathe life into a small nation.

We did so in some style. That Wales team played a high-tempo version of total rugby. People were starting to get a little giddy, making comparisons with the great teams of the 1970s. We were fast and fluid; brains were more important than brawn. We ran intelligently, linked intuitively. The cult of personality, so often a weakness, was deemed counter-productive. We were as strong as the weakest link in the chain, and were big enough not to care who received the credit.

I had experienced more lows than highs playing for my country up to that point, so it was appropriate I was in a plaster cast as, together with my deputy Michael Owen, I lifted the Six Nations trophy after that final 32–20 win against Ireland at the Millennium Stadium on 19 March 2005. I had broken my right thumb in five places making a tackle towards the end of the first half of the 24–18 win in France, and had been reduced to the role of reluctant cheerleader.

I had almost lost it in front of the boys in Paris, before I left the dressing room to head for the hospital, but Scott Johnson, our coach, wanted me to remain with the group. I used my chameleon qualities to hide my disappointment and detachment. Though I did all I could to lift the mood, and contribute the occasional insight, I was dying inside.

There is something completely bloodless about sitting in a suit, watching others ensure you achieve by association. I doubt whether Dickens was a rugby man, but his 'best of times, worst of times' line summed up the occasion. I felt embarrassed to be there, and had suggested we send Steve 'Jabba' Jones, the

Newport Gwent Dragons hooker, to collect the Cup on our behalf. Steve epitomised the unconsidered selflessness that so often underpins success. He was in the training squad of 30 throughout the season, but never made the match-day 22. His commitment was no less complete than that of those selected to play. He put the work in. He sacrificed his time, and shared the dream. He was our unknown warrior, who deserved recognition. I was overruled, because the gesture was a little too left-field for some of the blazers.

Once you make the leap of faith that even the spear-carriers deserve to be treated as stars, you begin to understand one of sport's eternal truths. Though teams are initially artificial, a disparate collection of characters, they have the traits of any other human relationship. They take time to gel and require trust to flourish. Intimacy isn't immediate; it develops as individuals let their guards down, and allow people into their lives. Bonds strengthen, usually in adversity, but occasionally break. There are no guarantees, and there can be no half measures.

The Lions are thrown together every four years. The selection policy of the squad becomes a saloon-bar guessing game for months beforehand. It's fantasy rugby. I thought I had a shout in 2001, when my old friend Graham Henry, who was to coach the All Blacks four years later, was in charge of the Lions. In hindsight, it was probably better for both of us that he didn't pick me. He was the smouldering ember next to me, a box of fireworks.

Clive's attention to detail was remorseless. Some accused him of trying to reshape us in the image of his England team, which won the World Cup in 2003. I am so over that night in Sydney. That final against Australia has been remorselessly romanticised, like England winning the football equivalent in 1966. I admired Jonny Wilkinson's nerve in kicking the winning points, and have massive respect for the leadership qualities of Martin Johnson, but the rest is just endless, sentimental tosh.

The Lions at least taught me to differentiate between the player and the person. I'm not proud to admit I hated Matt Dawson, Will Greenwood, Richard Hill and Lawrence Dallaglio when they wore the white shirt of England. They epitomised the arrogance of Empire. We'd spent what seemed a lifetime bashing each other up, but when I got to know them as people, we had a disconcerting amount in common.

They were strong characters, who quietly kept Clive at arm's length. I detected, in those early phone calls, that Clive was a man with a plan, who understood he didn't have to worry about whether we could kick or catch. He gave us respect as experienced internationals, and tried to sweat the small stuff to make the environment conducive to peak performance.

It wasn't ideal. I arrived on tour late, only 18 days before the Test series began, because of my commitment to Toulouse. Our defeat to Stade Français in the semi-final of the French League play-offs freed me to make a six-plane, seven-city journey from Toulouse to Wellington, via Paris, London, Bangkok, Sydney and Auckland. I suffered from jet leg for a week and had a single game, a 23–6 win over Wellington, in which to acclimatise.

Clive knew time was of the essence, but didn't fully understand the human dimension to the challenge. He could be aloof
and awkward with those who didn't buy into his philosophy.
I made some great friends on the tour, but we were innately
competitive and had pre-ordained, conflicting loyalties. The
history between us wasn't always pretty, because we had given
our all against one another for our individual nations.

A small case in point: the first game of our Grand Slam
season had been against England in Cardiff. We had felt they
were robotic, and more vulnerable than they had been for some
time. They had a new coach, Andy Robinson, and an ageing
squad missing key components through injury. It was a tight,
edgy game, which boiled over when Danny Grewcock, the
England lock, raked his studs down the face of Dwayne Peel, our
scrum-half.

It was a cheap shot, and Dwayne was my mate. As captain
I led from the front, and let myself down. I was sent to the sin
bin, along with Danny, for slapping him across the face. Not only
was it conduct unbecoming – it would have been laughed at in
a secondary school playground – it cost us a potentially decisive
chance to take numerical advantage of the situation. We were not
at our best, and I was guilty of craven stupidity. As it was, we had
won the match in memorable fashion, 11–9.

I got to know Danny beyond the hard-man stereotype as a
teammate in New Zealand, before he lived down to his reputation and received a two-month suspension for biting Keven
Mealamu. The identity of our match-winner, Gavin Henson,

merely emphasised the recklessness of taking players at face value. His fabled late penalty from 48 metres out, after our normal kicker Stephen Jones had decided it was outside his range, made him but almost broke him.

The pressure on us in that game was immense. That day's edition of the *Western Mail*, Wales's national newspaper, carried the slogan 'Just Do It' in a banner headline on the front page, while a single word – 'Believe' – dominated the back page. Gavin was cat nip to the marketing types, who saw a good-looking lad with shaven legs, silver boots and celebrity crossover potential. But he was also a complex character, who kept his distance.

He regards his experience on the subsequent Lions tour as 'a nightmare'. I can understand why. Campbell, our media guru, distributed misleading quotes from him after his controversial omission from the first Test. He also arranged to have a hidden photographer take shots of Clive and Gav, without their knowledge, to give the errant impression that all was well. Gav was, in fact, angry and resentful at his treatment. Clive's decision to change the lineout codes in the build-up to the match because he was convinced they had been discovered by the All Blacks added to an unnecessary sense of intrigue.

I liked Campbell, a fascinating and often funny guy. He let me down badly by making up some quotes from me before the second Test which were so naïve, they gave the All Blacks a free shot at us. I ripped into him but respected him for accepting he was in the wrong when challenged. He had been parachuted in from a world with different parameters and principles. He might have been comfortable with the internal dynamics of the Cabinet Room at 10 Downing Street, but he struggled with the nuances of a rugby dressing room.

His presence also helped to inflame Brian O'Driscoll's tour-ending injury into an international incident. It has become one of rugby's moments of infamy: the first Test had barely begun when Brian was lifted up at the breakdown by Tana Umaga, his opposite number as captain, and Mealamu, and dumped, head first. They claimed to have been clearing the ruck; they broke his collarbone, but could easily have broken his neck.

I was close to it, out on the wing, but had defensive priorities before the ball went dead and 'Drico' could be treated. I chased the linesman, who had walked onto the pitch during the preceding passage of play and simply ordered the pair to, 'Leave him alone.' I screamed at him to get involved, but there was panic in his eyes. He knew the implications of the Lions losing their leader. He saw Drico was badly hurt. His nerve had gone.

It was awful, unforgivable, and duly swept under the carpet. It was one of the worst home-town decisions I have seen. Yet it was done. We had a Test match to play. Rage had to be channelled into our performance. I felt for Brian as he was carted off on a stretcher, but someone had to take control. I took on the job of captain without being asked and tried to make the best of a very bad job. It was a demoralising experience, the damage limitation exercise from Hell.

Christchurch is known as the gateway to the Antarctic, with good reason. The hailstones that fell that day were the size of golf balls, and the wind was lacerating. By the end, when our only compensation in a 21–3 defeat was a Jonny Wilkinson penalty, I was as cold as I have ever been on a rugby field. My hands were numb and my brain was frozen into a single thought: 'Let's get off here and assess where we are.'

We were in a war waged by proxy, through the media. I felt the Drico incident was a spear tackle, but refused to believe the conspiracy theory that the All Blacks' assault had been pre-meditated. Stripped of emotion, it didn't make sense. Why would New Zealand take the risk of having two key players, including their skipper, dismissed in the opening exchange of the series? They were hard men who saw their chance to do what we all do if the opportunity arises – play fast and loose with the laws.

I accepted the role as Drico's replacement the instant it was offered by Clive, with the proviso I did it my way. There was less than a week to the next Test. My priority was rebuilding a tour that was quickly falling apart. Before I could do so, I had to deal with the media feeding-frenzy. The fallout hadn't been pretty: we were being derided as a bunch of spineless whingers. Clive's thoroughness, which had resulted in a referee and a legal adviser being assigned to the entourage, spawned accusations of arrogance.

Sport is about the here and now. I have immense respect for Brian as one of the legends of my game. He retired from international rugby in March 2014 as the holder of 141 caps for Ireland and the Lions and, in fitting circumstances, as winner of the Six Nations Championship. He is one of only three players with whom I have swapped shirts after an international. The others, incidentally, were Stirling Mortlock, the former Australia captain, and England's Will Greenwood. I had a lot in common with Stirling, a Wallaby legend who spent almost 15 years in the trenches before retiring in 2012; Will is a nice guy who caught me at a weak moment.

I didn't like giving away my Wales shirt, but when Brian asked I did so, as a mark of the esteem in which I held him. It is a measure of him as a professional, and as a man, that for all his natural talent and ability, he was a team player. He played rugby in the right way, for the right reasons. He was dignified and durable. He never lost his hunger, and deserved the hosannas in his honour. Yet, on that tour, he was history. That may sound callous, but we are all expendable. When one falls in battle, another takes his place.

Brian knew I had to find my own way. He left the tour with some quiet words of encouragement: 'Good luck. I will be with you in spirit.' There was nothing much more to say. His bandwagon may have been careering out of control, but I couldn't worry about those who wanted to sift through the wreckage. When the media tried to drag the story out, I was blunt: 'If you want to keep writing about it, boys, don't bring it to me. I've forgotten about it. It should not have happened, and I wish it had not happened, but I have to move on.'

The unique nature of a Lions dressing room, which contains natural cracks and fissures, was the overriding problem. It was a short tour with a large squad, and inevitably players gravitated towards their international teammates. We suffered, initially at least, from the first-day-of-term syndrome, where long-standing friends find comfort in familiarity. I tried to break down such barriers by appointing Steve Thompson as my deputy.

Steve, England's most capped hooker when he retired for the second time in 2011 after the recurrence of a serious neck injury, was on my wavelength. He believed in working hard but having a laugh. You only have to take a look at his medical records to appreciate his willingness to put his body on the line. There was no room for anyone whose first thought was for himself.

I've never been able to quite live down my team talk on the eve of the second Test. It's a classic of its kind, for all the wrong reasons. 'It's all about effort,' I told the players, huddled in a tight little circle around me on the training pitch. 'So many words have been said this week. It's about actions now. I've just got two words to sum up our situation at present: "Don't fucking panic."'

There was a split second's silence before I realised my mistake. 'Shit, that's three isn't it?' I said, as the circle exploded. The legend of Alfie, the mathematics professor, had been born.

Unfortunately, I also lost count of the score the following day. The All Blacks pummelled us 48–18 after I had triggered false hope by scoring under the posts in the second minute. The series had gone, and I spiralled out of control in a post-match bender which resulted in a two-day hangover.

I had managed to bluff my way through the post-match speeches with some lager-fuelled Bridgend blarney and an honest appreciation of New Zealand's rugby culture. Then I went postal. At one point, in the early hours, Tom Shanklin, the Welsh centre, made the mistake of turning up with a tray of a dozen shots. I cleared the lot before storming the stage, where I tried rapping, scratching the hosts' vinyl collection in hazy homage to hip hop. Give it up, ladies and gentlemen, for DJ Clueless ... When I took to dancing in shades and a comedy headband with incandescent antennae, Richie McCaw, the All Black icon, pronounced me a nutter. He was not far wrong.

When I sobered up, the problems were acute. A losing dressing room is an emotional minefield, at any level. Clive's decision to differentiate between the midweek and Test squads had inevitably created a divide. No one approached me directly, but the word was out: the midweek boys were resentful. They felt they deserved to be promoted, en masse. I had no problem with that. Anyone burbling about lack of loyalty doesn't understand the reality of professional sport.

Tension, created by unfulfilled ambition, is a positive force if handled sensitively. It is human nature to want a player in your position to do poorly. I have no issue with that, provided the bitching isn't sustained or conducted in public. A rugby player has to have the will to fight. He has to believe in himself, and feel his setbacks deep in his guts. His restlessness shows how badly he wants to do well. It is down to the coach and captain to distil that negative energy.

The All Blacks were merciless. They all had a bit of dog in them. They didn't care how they won, as long as they did so.

They would have kicked the ball until it was square, and lapped up the abuse, if it had meant unsettling us. They would have been content to wait until the 85th minute to stick the knife between our ribs. Their mentality may offend the purists, but all they care about is that W in the record books. That's why they are the best.

They had such brute force in reserve that their coach Graham Henry's controversial decision to dispense with second-row Brad Thorn didn't matter. Thorn is a legend in both codes, and proved Henry wrong by picking up his All Black career in 2008, after returning to the National Rugby League in Australia for three years. He remains the biggest monster I've played against, and is the man I mention whenever I'm asked to recount my favourite tackle.

It was in the 2003 World Cup, my first international at full-back. He popped up from a ruck and just ran straight through it. I realised, immediately, that I was next. I usually attempt to watch the ball and the upper body, because the runner wants you to watch his feet. I try to take control of the situation by shifting my body to offer them an angle. The idea is to get them to go where I want them to go so I get the best out of the contact.

I didn't have to manoeuvre Brad anywhere. There was a whole pitch for him to play with and he just focused on me. I swear to God, there was a smile on his face – a 20-stone beast wanted me for lunch. They don't mention that in the coaching manual, funnily enough. I went down at his shins and tackled him, but there was no way I was going to drive him back. I just held on to his legs, and went along for the ride. I figured that eventually he would trip.

When he did so, it was like a giant redwood crashing to earth. My teammates were priceless as I picked myself up: 'Fucking good tackle, Alfie – great tackle. Now get over there.' That's rugby, in a nutshell. Do your job, get a pat on the back, but get over yourself, quickly. You can't afford to linger in the moment. Get on with it. There's plenty of time to mull over incidents like that when you retire.

Being equally brutal, the third and final Test in Auckland, which we lost 38–19 with barely a whimper, was a suitably low-key end to a disastrous tour. All the wristbands and post-cards in the world couldn't prepare us for the intensity of the opposition. I felt for Clive, because our failure compromised his career. He has since seemed a restless figure, flirting unsuccess-fully with football at Southampton, and as performance director of the GB Olympic team. He has a successful media career, but I sense he would give it up in a heartbeat for another high-profile coaching role.

I valued his confidence in me. It means a lot that he mentions me in the same breath as Martin Johnson, the epitome of the captain who leads by example. When we got home from the tour I visited Clive's home. He was not in, so I pushed a note of thanks under his front door. He had it framed, which is a nice way of returning my compliments.

He made a short speech after that last defeat, and we then

went our separate ways. It was revealing, in its way. We left New Zealand in dribs and drabs, rather than as a team. There were no heartfelt goodbyes, or reaffirmations of faith.

I still cherish my Lions shirt, but it doesn't trigger the warmth of a more significant legacy of the tour, stored in a cabinet in my mum's front room. It's a piece of Prince William's wedding cake.

We met in Wellington. He seemed to be at a loose end so I asked him and his bodyguard if he fancied a coffee. As you do. He seemed pleased to be treated like a normal human being, and was soon talking rugby with me and Tom Shanklin. Shanks and I forgot ourselves, and swore like troopers, but he seemed to enjoy the war stories. He was a big England fan, and remembered our chat a couple of years later, when he became patron of the WRU.

The next thing I knew, I was sitting near David and Victoria Beckham in Westminster Abbey on an unforgettable late spring day in 2011. Elton John was just across the aisle. I was within touching distance of the Royal Family as they filed in for the wedding of the Queen's eldest grandson and Kate Middleton, the soon-to-be Duchess of Cambridge. I cheekily gave my address to a paparazzo, and asked him to send me a photograph of me on the steps, in my hired morning suit.

A Bridgend boy, rubbing shoulders with dignitaries, diplomats, foreign royalty and A-list celebrities? Not the sort of thing you read about in the Court & Social section of the posh papers, is it? I suspect no one else in the Abbey had a timetable for trains back to North Wales in their inside pocket. I was under strict orders to be back for training with the Crusaders, my rugby league team, in Wrexham, that evening. It meant I couldn't accept Elton's invitation to his post-ceremony function.

I made the train, despite giving random interviews to overseas TV crews who stopped me in the street as I searched for a cab to Euston. My welcome back at the Racecourse Ground was muted, to say the least. The Aussies, Republicans to a man, gave me stick for being a social climber, and the local lads seemed more interested in Kate's sister, Pippa. Iestyn Harris, our coach, simply said: 'Fab you went, Alf, but we've got a game on Saturday. I haven't really got time to talk about the royal wedding. Let's talk about the game.'

Chapter Ten

ON THE
EDGE

The third and final miscarriage endured by Jemma followed one
of the most frightening, farcical and commonly misunderstood
sequences of my life. It involved sustained stress, me suffering a
stroke, and the sort of tragi-comic nonsense that tends to define
Welsh rugby in moments of crisis.

I had returned to Cardiff from Toulouse to find myself being
accused of leading a players' revolt against national coach, Mike
Ruddock, who had decided to step down. No one was remotely
interested in the truth that the supposed putsch – a meeting with
WRU chief executive, Steve Lewis – concentrated on issues that
actually threatened the welfare of teammates, and their families.
Put simply, two players were willing to play with existing injuries;
their reward for their commitment was to be told they would not
be insured if they did so.

They were my priority. The team had drifted after the Grand Slam of 2005, when some were a little too keen to claim the credit. Gavin Henson's egocentric behaviour hinted at a deeper issue – the decline in collective standards. I felt Mike hadn't been sufficiently assertive in his leadership, and I had a more productive relationship with Scott Johnson, his assistant, but I respected his coaching credentials and gave him the loyalty he had the right to expect from his captain. It suited others, though, to cast me as a B-movie backstabber.

I was picked up at Bristol airport by my parents, and taken straight to the BBC studios in Cardiff, where they were due to record an edition of *Scrum V*, the weekly magazine show on Welsh rugby. The controversy, inevitably entitled 'Ruddock-gate', had got the creative juices of presenters and producers flowing. Again – in the interests of brevity – I lost it when accused of stabbing Mike in the back without a shred of evidence to back up the allegation, apart from bluster about anonymous so-called 'sources'.

I had spoken to Mike the day before, when he confirmed that he had resigned over contractual issues. When I asked him to put in writing that his departure had nothing to do with perceptions of player power, he readily agreed, but called back five minutes later to tell me he had been advised against doing so by his solicitor. It meant the waters remained muddied, but I understood the note of caution in what was a delicate situation.

The WRU left me alone to deal with the fallout. They knew the search was on for a scapegoat, and ran for cover. If some people had decided that victim would be me, fine. I wasn't going to take a backwards step. It was my duty, as captain, to protect players who had given me everything. They were being treated badly on a number of levels, and I wasn't going to put up with it.

The programme turned out to be an exercise in character assassination, which disturbed Nigel Walker, the former international wing who was BBC Wales's Head of Sport at the time. My parents, who were watching the programme being recorded, heard him tell the presenters: 'Pull out, pull out. You look like you're just bullying him now.'

Time offers an insight into the truth. Early in 2014, I met up again with Eddie Butler, my chief inquisitor during that infamous programme. We had so much in common – Eddie, a former Pontypool number eight, captained Wales in six of his 16 internationals – and we needed to address the issue that had divided us for too long. As we talked, it became clear that each of us had been used by political factions within the WRU. It was important to me that Eddie understood the depth of my distress.

I gave him the story from my perspective. Jemma was pregnant again. I was scared and preoccupied by her welfare. I wanted to scream at the cameras that I was a human being with other priorities, more profound issues to consider. I resented those who were grandly demanding that I live my life on their terms.

It was a cold February night, but I was steaming as I drove home through the Llandaff area of Cardiff and on to St Brides Major, via the M4. Mum and Dad were disgusted by what they had witnessed. Since when did the dealings of the WRU merit

FBI tactics? Jemma was waiting with Compo and Catherine; we had decided to go out for a meal after watching the programme's transmission.

I felt hot and restless, light-headed and pressurised behind my eyes. As the *Scrum V* theme tune flooded into the lounge, I leaned against the fireplace, beginning to feel twinges down my left arm. As I sat down in a corner chair, close to the stairs and diagonally to the TV set, my body began to shut down. I couldn't make a fist. My arm seized up, and I found it increasingly difficult to move my neck.

I felt as if I was falling slowly, inexorably, down a lift shaft. My left side became completely numb. One of my last conscious memories was of trying to shout to my mother, who was sitting directly in front of me, absorbed by the programme's preliminaries. I thought I was saying, 'Mam, Mam, Mam!' Instead it was an unintelligible 'Urrgggghhhh.'

Her first instinct had been to tell me to stock mucking around, but then she saw the panic in my face and recognised the danger signals in my lack of natural movement. She grabbed the telephone to summon an ambulance as I slipped off the chair and onto the floor.

I temporarily lost consciousness, and came round to find Compo blowing gently into my face, because he had been told such an action calms down anyone who is so distressed they are struggling to breathe. I had no idea what was wrong, but I clung to his leg, convinced I was going to die. The recurring thought – 'Rugby has killed you' – echoed around my skull.

My vision was blurred, as if I had been concussed. Tiny worms were attempting to swim across my eyeballs. Still the ambulance hadn't come. Dad called, and was told they hadn't deemed it an emergency. His response was a whip-crack: 'Well, my son could be dying. I think that's an emergency, don't you?' The paramedics were there within ten minutes. They monitored my heart, took a blood sample, and suggested I was suffering from exhaustion.

I was hooked up on to an ECG machine in the closest NHS hospital, the Princess of Wales in Bridgend. The machine had a hypnotic effect and, as I lay there listening to it, I promised myself I would never lace up a pair of rugby boots again. The price of the game was too high. I wasn't prepared to become a martyr. Freeze-frame mental images of every scenario, from paralysis to premature death, haunted me.

The nurse in charge of my treatment concluded I had suffered a severe migraine and sent me home. She was not to know that a bang to the head, sustained in the act of scoring a try for Toulouse against Pau a couple of weeks previously, had caused potentially fatal damage. It was not until Professor John Williams, the Welsh team doctor, insisted I undergo an MRI scan at a private hospital the following day that the extent of my escape became apparent. I had suffered a stroke because an artery in my neck had ruptured during that Toulouse match.

I wasn't seeking sympathy, but when I visited the boys at the next game, against Italy, an incident made me question basic values. A friend of my mother's told me a doctor from the original hospital had been in a bar before the game, seen me on television, and informed anyone who would listen that I was faking the problem.

It was mind-blowing. Why are people so nasty? Why do they lie for effect? A line had been crossed. A supposedly professional man, trying to be big in front of his mates, had obviously decided to belittle me for his own ends. I couldn't work out why for the life of me, but it was not the only example of the way in which prominent athletes are dehumanised.

The insensitivity of strangers, and the national obsession with Ruddockgate, led to me being treated as public property. I was told I couldn't exercise for a minimum of six months, and had to continue to report to the hospital as an out patient. While I accept there's a certain loss of privacy in professional sport, everyone, from ward nurses to canteen workers, demanded minute details of my relationship with Mike. The fact that I was terrified of the consequences of a relapse, and worried about the stress my wife had endured, was ignored.

It came to a head in horrendous circumstances when I took a call from Jemma while I was on a short walk around the village. She had started bleeding. I ran back – against medical advice – and got her to the hospital as soon as possible. We were beyond despair when she miscarried, for the third time. The shining hope in our lives had been snuffed out.

I wandered, in a daze, to a tea-making machine, where a woman started to ask me about my role in the departure of the Wales coach. I'm ashamed to say I exploded: 'My wife has just lost a baby, I've just had a fucking stroke, you work in a hospital and all you want to fucking ask me is what happened with Mike Ruddock? I'm sorry, but if there's ever a time and place to say "Fuck off", this is it.'

We had reached an all-time low. I could have dealt with all the other rubbish – the stroke and the rugby hysteria – if I had known Jemma and the baby were safe. Now that that consolation had been snatched away, and we were tormented by another tragedy, I was in a dark, bitter mood. I felt guilty, resentful and hopelessly compromised.

Had we been blessed with a child, I would not have come out. At the time, I convinced myself a baby was everything my life needed to be complete. It would give me a reason to care for myself, because I had another human being to care for; I would be obliged to start being responsible, instead of reckless. I would take control. Fatherhood would give me the strength to be what everybody else wanted me to be. I believed and still believe, to be honest, that watching a child grow up, giving it unconditional love, and guaranteeing its welfare, would have ensured I would never have done anything to hurt that child.

As usual with me in that phase of my life, there was an unforgivably selfish dimension to the situation. As embarrassed as I am to admit this, I would have regarded a child as confirmation of my masculinity. It would have enabled me to create a false perception of myself. It would have been a way to fight the demons. Being a father would have been my way of showing the world: 'I'm a man and I do what men do – make babies.'

Amidst the mourning for another lost life, there was also that ever-present guilt. I saw what Jemma had gone through, witnessed the loss of an unborn child, and couldn't find solace in the lack of logical medical explanations. I retreated deeper inside myself, and began to believe those three babies had been taken away from me because I wanted to be a father for the wrong reasons. Grief gave me what I thought was clarity. I didn't need doctors to provide answers. The miscarriage was a simple, terrible act of divine retribution for all the bad things I had done. He knew a baby would enable me to escape the punishment of exposure. He knew how little I deserved His mercy. This was his way of saying, 'Mate, you ain't getting out of this that easily. You've got to pay for the lies, the deceit and the hurt.'

I was on the verge of a breakdown. I blamed God for our plight. He was using Jemma to get to me. I would steal away from the house at night, under the pretext of going for a quick walk and some fresh air, and prowl around the graveyard at St Bridget's. I used to scream at the church walls, and beg Him for answers to frenzied questions: 'Why the fuck is this happening? What more can I do? What are you trying to tell me?'

It was a powerful feeling, being in the presence of something I couldn't quite define, but I felt lost. I was raging. It was amazing that no one noticed, since the church is at the end of a lane, and overlooked by a row of houses which lead to a smallholding on a hillock.

I occasionally sat on a bench in the churchyard, and studied the silhouettes of the tombstones and ceremonial crosses. I harboured dark thoughts, of what it would feel like to be in one of the graves that surrounded me. I took to imagining that there was a spectral figure sitting beside me. He taunted me: 'Just keep asking, just keep those questions coming. The more you ask, the less likely it is that I'm going to give you the answer. You're just going to have to figure it out for yourself.'

Life around me was a disaster. The media were all over us, as a family. I felt powerless. Yet I was still Gareth Thomas, Welsh rugby icon. For every fan who thought I had done the dirty, there was another who thought the sun shone out of my backside. Being an exalted figure was a sick joke, given the problems I was causing and the depression that consumed those closest to me.

I took to taking long coastal walks, in stages, for up to six hours at a stretch. I would pass Nash Point lighthouse, which has protected shipping from local sandbanks since 1832. I meandered through woods, and across the pebble beach at Tresilian Bay, which is supposedly haunted. I skirted steep cliffs, pitted by a series of small caves, by walking along the coastal path, towards the outskirts of Llantwit Major.

It was here that a plan began to form. I noticed a small path, down towards a promontory. The grass was soft, and ridges had been formed where the northerly winds had whipped across the Bristol Channel. I lay down to consider my options. The more I thought, the more self-loathing I generated, the more attractive suicide seemed.

It took me several clandestine visits before I plucked up the courage to return to that ridge, which was no more than two feet high, and set back from the cliff edge. I leaned into it, undressing slowly and deliberately. My boots, muddy but presentable, were the first to go. I peeled off a woolly jumper, work shirt and jeans, and folded them neatly where I had been lying.

I didn't feel the cold, though the wind muffled my apologies to my grandparents. I had let them down, too, and wanted to make my peace with them before I leaped the 200 feet or so, onto rocks. Instinctively I curled my toes, and felt them dig into the shallow, stony soil in which local geologists still find fossils.

I walked five paces forward, and took a long stride down towards what I had envisaged as my final stage: a smooth, white rock, roughly three feet square, on a shelf at the cliff edge.

I stood there for fully 20 minutes in my underpants, protected from prying eyes by the contours of the land.

The sea was grey and merged with the horizon. Standing there, on the edge of the cliff, it all seemed so easy. A single step and I'd walk off, into the sky. No more pain. No more loneliness. No more lies. No more causing chaos for people that I loved.

I deserved to be there. I needed to make amends. I craved tranquility. This place – bleak, inhospitable but starkly beautiful with a blue-grey beach littered with eroded layers of limestone and shale – was another sanctuary. It was seductive, simple. I had nowhere to go but over. I would close my eyes, and never have to open them again.

Something stopped me. Something from those anguished hours under cover of darkness in the churchyard close to home suddenly made sense. They weren't prayers, in the conventional sense. They were streams of consciousness. But they were answered. I hated myself, but I couldn't kill myself. God didn't want to let me off the hook. I had penance to pay.

I felt the wind change. There were times when it seemed as if I was staring into a void. Nothing bounced back at me. Quietly, at first, something or someone, a voice, was telling me: 'I'm not going to give you the answers. You'll have to discover them for yourself. You, and only you, can find the solution.' I needed to ask the central question – 'Why?' – countless times. The more I posed it, the more, subconsciously, I was beginning to answer it.

I don't believe you have to go to church every Sunday to be a religious person, and you don't have to know the Bible inside out to do good works. I learned that submission is good for the soul. I had to wait. There was a master plan. I, as someone who had been identified as a leader of men, had to learn to be a follower. Maybe my calling was to help others by sharing my deeper feelings, my most intimate experiences. I don't consider myself a flag bearer for the gay community, but standing there, I thought that maybe it was pre-ordained that I should help, in any way I could.

I know that sounds mad, but how else do I make sense of everything I've gone through? All I know is that something happened on that windblown cliff top.

Honesty made a long-overdue appearance.

Chapter Eleven

TRUTH

I was between coaching sessions at one of my rugby academies in the village of Treforest, just south-east of Pontypridd. Such days are usually a joy, because I feed off the kids' enthusiasm for the game I love, but this was so, so different. I was in turmoil, and determined to push myself beyond the point of no return. I called my wife from the car, just before she left for work. 'Look,' I said, praying my voice wouldn't break because of a mixture of dread and panic. 'I need to tell you something tonight.'

Jemma asked, 'What is it?' immediately, inevitably and understandably. In my befuddled state, I didn't have a convincing response, other than to say it was something we needed to discuss, face to face. 'Why?' she demanded.

Since I was evasive and feeble, she knew something was up. Her alarm was building into anger when I cut the conversation short with an unconvincing excuse that I needed to be out on the training field.

I sat there, closed my eyes, and cursed my lack of courage and common decency. I felt constricted and was suddenly aware of the speed and shallowness of my breathing. I had to open the door, to let in the fresh air and stem a mounting tide of anxiety and remorse. I looked out at the kids, messing around, and envied their innocence. What a mess.

If I didn't care about myself, the least I could do was care about those who cared for me. The weaker I was, the more pain I inflicted on them; the deeper my deception, the shallower my motives became; the more intimate the secret, the more remote were the chances of their love being repaid. It was my responsibility to change, to be big enough to stop belittling those around me with a cancerous lie.

The truth didn't come easily. It arrived in instalments. The priority was to use it to free Jemma. That morning, going through the motions of coaching the kids, I renewed my private promise to release her from fear, confusion and uncertainty. It would be distressing, but she would never again have to wonder who that hastily deleted text was from, or where I really was during those increasingly regular absences. It was time to live up to that oft-overlooked marriage vow to honour her.

After my wife, I would give my parents their rightful peace of mind. I'd give them no more reason to worry, in those endless, wakeful hours before dawn, about what sort of trouble I was getting myself into.

My teammates couldn't be denied their due, either. They needed to know everything about the guy who expected everything of them. It wasn't going to be easy, and it wouldn't provide instant salvation, but I had run out of options.

The third miscarriage and the realisation, on that cliff top, that things were destined to become irredeemably worse, had penetrated the nuclear bunker in which I had hidden from myself. It took me a month from my suicidal episode to tell Jemma, because I foolishly waited for the perfect opportunity, the most suitable setting. Tomorrow was always more convenient. Ultimately, my honesty was impulsive and imperfect.

It took half an hour to drive back to our home, that evening. It was a familiar journey, down the Cardiff road through Taff Valley villages like Tongwynlais and Upper Boat, before a four-junction sprint westward, along the M4. Truth be told, I was on autopilot. I could only think of Jemma and the ordeal ahead. My mouth was dry as I revised my lines like a desperate student on the eve of a life-changing examination.

I sat Jemma down in the living room. Instead of the measured, sensitive speech I had replayed over and over in my head, I just blurted out: 'I'm gay, and I don't know how long I can carry on doing this.'

Jemma recoiled, almost as if the words had a physical impact. She became justifiably upset and started to sob. God knows, I deserved to feel the full force of her fury. Her tears flowed through hurt and indignation; mine were shed through contrition and shame. My heart felt heavy and inert; it was almost an out-of-body experience.

Once she calmed down, she tried to rationalise our situation. 'If you'd told me that you've been sleeping with another woman

I'd have gone mad, but there's nothing I can do,' she said. 'I can't compete with another man if this is how you feel.'

I was humbled by her compassion in a crisis. 'You have to understand,' I replied, 'I am in love with you. I don't love you any less than the day I married you, or the day that I fell in love with you. But this is who I am.'

We were like shipwreck survivors, clinging to the same piece of driftwood. We decided, over the course of a couple of days, to try to snatch at one last chance of shared happiness. Going back to France would free us from prying eyes, whispered rumours, and those who were trying to snoop into our business. It would lend distance, literally and metaphorically, to the grieving process for our unborn child.

In retrospect, it was never going to work. We managed to maintain the fiction that our destinies were somehow inter-twined for the best part of three months before Jemma returned to Wales and I succumbed to drink-fuelled madness. We went through an awful lot together, but she was always the strong one. Where I was happy to conspire in an illusion, she had always had the guts to face the truth. It was best she didn't say goodbye.

My decision to sell the house in Toulouse and flee France some months later was equally predictable. If I was going to sit alone in my bedroom, crying regretfully, it was better I did so in Sarn. My home there has a million memories, good and bad, and it is the place in which I most feel comfortable. Not in the sense of being able to sink into a favourite armchair, but in the knowledge that when I walk through the door, my emotions are equalised. They don't melt away; they remain vivid and affecting, but home is where I have the freedom to do whatever necessary to deal with them. It doesn't matter if that involves crying, laughing, kicking or screaming. I'm taken at face value. There is always a shoulder to lean on, or an ear to bash.

It's strange, then, that I never formally told my parents that I was gay.

I suppose the hardest people with whom to share a secret are those who mean most to you. That doesn't make a great deal of sense, until you realise just how insecure I was at that stage of my life. How could I have any self-worth when I was denying the very fibre of my being? Lying about who you are is not something that can easily be undone.

Rejection by my family would have been almost impossible to bear. One of the many horror stories I've been told involves a son who was denounced by his father, a soldier, when he came out. He became an alcoholic and although they were reconciled, it was not until just before his premature death from cirrhosis of the liver.

This was not a little white lie that I'd been telling for a couple of days – I had been persistently deceiving the people closest to me for more than a decade. And it wasn't just me lying. My family, unintentionally, had been lying for me; their friends were guilty by association with that lie. I tried to put myself in their position. If I had been subjected to that level of disrespect, I would have been livid. I would have felt betrayed.

My parents deny they knew why Jemma left me, but I know they would do anything to protect me. It was far more likely they decided there was nothing malicious in my deceit. They avoided broaching the subject, and trusted me to tell them when I was ready.

I've been similarly fortunate with my friends. They have an almost parental form of unqualified love for me. If they had pushed me on the reasons for our split, I would have freaked. I was paranoid in any case. I'd be out having a coffee, and notice a group on the nearest table leaning forward. They'd just be gossiping, complaining about the weather for all I knew. But I'd convince myself they were reliving my life, scene by scene. They were sitting there in judgement, and I wasn't coming out of it at all well.

Their condemnation might have been a product of my imagination, but it was fully deserved.

I was at my lowest ebb when I made my international comeback, after an eight-month absence following my stroke, against Australia in the Millennium Stadium in November 2006. I have no conscious memory of the game. We drew 29–29, and the record books tell me I reclaimed the captaincy when fly-half Stephen Jones twisted a knee after 23 minutes, and was substituted. I was an embarrassment, about as dynamic as a sloth and as weak as a kitten. The journalist who gave me six out of ten in this summary – 'Given little space to show his wares on his return to the side' – must have been on a different planet.

I was a wreck. I had lost 14 kilograms from my normal playing weight of 103 kilograms, and couldn't bear to look at my skeletal frame in the dressing room mirror. The crowd was happy because of the inferiority complex that demands we celebrate moral victories and honourable draws against the Southern Hemisphere sides, instead of making an objective judgement on the quality of the opposition, but I was beyond consolation. Sitting at my locker, I was ready to admit defeat. The lunacy of repeated suicide attempts and self-destructive drinking had overwhelmed me. Shame hung limply around me, like a shroud. I had let my country down.

Fate, though, decided just then to grant the biggest favour of my life. Karma, in the loose-limbed, long-haired form of Scott 'Jonno' Johnson, wandered in through the double doors. I was about to discover he was a true friend.

In an international career that spans 100 matches, you are not going to play well all the time. You will have the occasional minger of a game, where a succession of errors tends to be played in sequence in a debrief DVD from Hell. But this was different: I was so shot to pieces, mentally and physically, that I was unable even to go through the motions of trying my best. I was a fraud, who deserved to be cast aside by my tribe. There was no way any selector worth his blazer could pick me for Wales again. I slumped back in that familiar corner seat and began to cry, bitterly but silently.

Jonno, Wales assistant coach in that Grand Slam season, had moved on to coach the Aussies. Convention demanded he did his tour of duty. He circulated, shaking hands with the guys in turn, sharing jokes and dispensing praise. My vision was blurred, but I glimpsed him heading down the row in my direction. I couldn't stop weeping; it was taking all my remaining strength and self-control to avoid bawling loudly. Tears were coursing down my cheeks. I prayed he would pass me by, but I looked up, and there he was, standing above me.

He had his hand out, ready to shake. I recoiled, like a maltreated dog waiting to be battered into submission. His eyes locked onto mine. They bored through my skull, seemingly threatening to drill the whitewashed wall behind my head. 'Mate,' he said. 'What's the matter?'

There was something mesmerising about his body language, which demanded the truth, and I couldn't help exclaiming, through gulps of air: 'She's left me – Jemma's left me.'

'Why?' he said, before thinking better of it. 'No, you don't have to tell me why. It's one of two reasons.' By this time I was under his spell. 'One of you has been shagging around, or there's a second reason. By the look of you, it's the second reason.'

I didn't have to tell him the details. He knew. I didn't know how, or why, but he knew.

He instinctively took control of the situation. 'Dry up and sort your face out so the boys don't see,' he ordered, quietly. 'We're getting out of here.'

He motioned to my left, towards the warm-up area. I walked diagonally, precisely 27 paces, until I found myself in the corner of the open-plan room, which was bare except for a single plastic-backed chair and a series of five rectangular mirrors. It was the scariest, most haunted, journey of my life. I tried to make it appear a natural act of reacquaintance between long-time rugby friends, but I was amazed I was able to place one foot in front of the other.

I squatted against the wall in the corner, closest to the door, and cried like a baby for about five minutes. I had never been so vulnerable. Jonno stood there, his taut shoulders defying anyone to intervene. 'We need to sort this out,' he said tenderly. He let me finish weeping before he added, in sterner tones: 'You've got to pull yourself together. You've got a team. You're their captain. Get back in there, have a shower, and do your shit with the boys. Meet me in the medical room and we're going to sort this out.'

I gathered he was not judging me, personally or professionally. I was terrified, but relieved. I had hit rock bottom. My rugby was contaminated by chaos, and had Jonno not been there, to identify and protect the private me I shudder to think what would have occurred when I was alone later that night. I'm not sure whether he saved my life, because the confusion created by repeated suicide attempts made that incalculable, but he certainly stopped me from going any lower.

I loved Jonno, absolutely adored him. He was a mixture of priest, father and brother. He was heaven-sent, but he wasn't going to give me an easy ride. He was waiting in the medical room – the hub of any professional sports team – with two chairs, four cans of lager and an open mind.

The place was a mess – muddied, with bloodied bandages littering the floor. Swabs and stitches were ready for disposal. The physio couches were pushed back. The low ceiling added to the sense of claustrophobia. A film of water, from steadily melting icepacks, covered the floor. The room was filled with that rugby smell of stale sweat and spent tension.

Jonno locked the door, periodically telling those attempting to enter to fuck off. It was surreal; I sat there in my tuxedo, with a bow tie in the pocket, ready for the ceremonial chore of the post-match dinner, as Jonno faced me, expecting me to share the secret I had never wanted to divulge.

Everyone knows Jonno. He's honest – too honest for some – and he gets people, understands individuality. He had long ago sensed I was gay. His was a simple challenge – 'Tell me every-thing' – which cut through the complications of a life that had veered way out of control. In return for my trust, he gave me the freedom to reconnect with myself. He was my satellite naviga-tion system, who helped me get to where I am today.

We'd gone beyond nuance. I confessed that I was lost. The situation was killing me. I held nothing back. I needed absolu-tion, a new direction.

Jonno was measured, firm yet compassionate. He told me to get back to basics. That involved standing on my own two feet, getting my weight back on, and trying to concentrate on rugby. The bluntness of the delivery belied the affection which under-pinned his message. It was a short speech, which is seared onto my brain: 'You've cared so much about everyone else you've forgotten to care about yourself. You can no longer live with this on your own. I've decided, whether you like it or not, to choose the two most senior, most mature, players and tell them what has been going on. Trust me. These boys fucking love you. You need people around you to protect you. This is an environment in which you can be yourself. Get back to the hotel and wait for us.' Jonno's parting shot was his choice of confidants: Stephen Jones, who had initially led the side that afternoon, and Martyn Williams, universally known by his nickname, "Nugget", who was my long-time roommate.

I was freefalling. My destiny was no longer in my own hands, and my imagination was running riot. Part of me expected the worst, and sought consolation. At least I wouldn't be there to see their horror, and hear them tell Jonno how much they hated me. My inner optimist told me, in a faint, reedy voice, everything would be OK. These guys had been in the trenches with me. They would watch my back.

It was surreal. Later, I sat in the bar for several hours with the rest of the boys. I was whacking back the pints as if there was no tomorrow – who knew, there might not be – and in a revealing reflex action, chain smoking. Everyone was wondering where the other two were. Someone said, 'Oh, they're with Jonno,' in a throwaway manner which offered hope, but others were mumbling, 'Something has got to be wrong.'

I was trying to convince myself that this was not as big a deal as I thought. It was a ridiculous process, because I reduced them to stereotypes: 'Jonesy. He's from Llanelli. Played in France, he's been around a bit. Do you know what? I'm pretty confident he's going to be OK. But Nugget? He's from Pontypridd. A real man's man, hard worker, tough fucker as a rugby player. Face it, *butt*, he's exactly the type of person who will despise you for who you are.'

I felt like a teenager waiting for my date to show. The difference was that being stood up would have come as blessed relief. I took an involuntary intake of breath when Steve walked in, scanned the bar, and headed straight towards me. He offered his hand and wasted no time in confirming: 'Mate, it's cool.' We had a nice little chat about it, as though it was as inconsequential as the choice of holiday destination.

Nugget arrived soon after, and was determined not to make a fuss. He walked past, put his hand on my shoulder, and said: 'Bud, don't worry about it. Let's have a beer.' He didn't even want to talk about it because it wasn't an issue for him. That was him, expressing friendship and respect, but it completely messed with my head.

I should have been ecstatic, but all I could do was gabble: 'What? Is that it? Fucking hell, this has been 30 years of my life and you don't even want to have a discussion about it?'

Nugget grinned. 'There's fuck-all to talk about. You're Alfie, you're Gareth Thomas, you're a rugby player. As a person, it means nothing – don't worry about it. Do you want us to tell the others?'

I just laughed at the absurdity of how casual it seemed. This was my nightmare scenario, and I surprised myself with how easy it was to succumb to fate. 'Look, *butt*,' I said, with what I hoped was a gentle chuckle, instead of a manic laugh, 'I wasn't ready for *you* to be told. I don't know if I can handle you telling every fucker else. But you know what? It's your decision. Do what you feel is best.'

I glanced around. The world had not stopped turning. The rest of the boys were oblivious to my little psycho-drama. I felt strangely fulfilled, though I knew that, in such a small bubble, it wasn't going to take long for word to spread. Jonesy and Nugget would tell a couple of the lads, who'd tell a couple more. Nothing was certain, but I felt pretty safe, so long as my story remained in the rugby environment. Jonno had seen my vulnerability, and realised I needed my people around me.

Compo surprised me that night, turning up out of the blue. He had caught me at a low point while I was in France, preparing to come over for the match. I had been so down during our telephone conversation I could barely string a sentence together. When he said, 'Don't worry, Alfie, I'll bring you home,' to fill one of the interminable silences, I had broken down and bawled.

'You OK?' he asked now. 'You were in fucking bits back there.'

I exhaled deeply, and filled him in on the sequence of events, but without sharing my suicidal tendencies. He had my trust, respect and gratitude. 'You've got to let a few people know,' I said, knowing that his first call would be to Glen.

I was in good hands, though it was amazing to think it would be more than two years before I officially came out.

My sexuality became the worst-kept secret in Welsh rugby, but it was still *my* secret. I was protective of it, especially when people whispered, 'Well, we knew anyway,' when I eventually made my announcement. They might have been 99.99 per cent sure, but not many were 100 per cent certain. That fraction makes a huge difference. It implies a reassuring sense of control over a daunting situation.

The consequences of that night were overwhelming. I had been endorsed by people who really meant something to me. They formed a tight network. They enclosed me, gave me love. I felt the full force of their care. At times it was too much, and I had to ask for room to breathe, but mostly words were super-fluous. People would ask, 'OK?' with a knowing look. I'd nod, and they'd say something like, 'That's all we need to know, *butt*.' There was so much support and understanding. It was the perfect scenario.

Rugby is a harsh world, a stereotypically macho envi-ronment. I realised how much I owed the game – not in the financial sense, despite the material rewards it had given me, but from a philosophical standpoint. Rugby allowed me to define who I am. It is a team game, which requires mutual trust and understanding. Unless you have the backing of the boys, you're going nowhere, fast.

Jonno was responsible for my rebirth. Those who mattered finally knew. I had friends to fall back on. It was something much more subtle than having a shoulder on which to cry, if the need arose. The knowledge that I'd be sharing a dressing room with people who knew I was gay, and were OK with it, was, liter-ally, a life-changer. I would find out soon enough that the world was imperfect, but, inside the bubble, there were no barriers, no doubts. I had been accepted for who I was.

I had been picked for the following week's game against Samoa, but in a typically sensitive gesture, our coach, Gareth Jenkins, decided to quietly use the squad rotation system to give me more space. I started to sleep well, eat properly, and train assiduously. Life was no longer abnormal. I could focus on the mechanics of my game, the responsibilities of my role. And I was treated as a rugby player, rather than a freak of nature. That empowered me to a degree that I had feared would be forever denied me.

I felt strong. Not strong enough to confront strangers with the truth, but sufficiently resilient to deal with anyone close to me who might feel alienated because I was gay. Finally, I'd learned the impossibility of pleasing all of the people, all of the time. It made the next stage of the process of renewal easier to deal with, even if that involved coping with some low-grade human beings.

I wasn't daft. I knew Chinese whispers were doing the rounds – Jemma's return to Wales had meant another small circle of knowledge had been created. I had no issue with that, because someone in my position couldn't argue against the impression that a problem shared is a problem halved. But the rumours flew and dislodged some rocks. And I didn't like what crawled out from underneath.

Jemma and I initially continued to live together, while she organised her new life, and the sad formalities of our divorce were completed. We began to be embarrassed by the unwelcome attention we were receiving. Reporters started to turn up in the pub across the road, where we were very good friends with the girl who managed it. They asked leading questions about our personal lives, and generally made themselves unwelcome.

It got worse. They began knocking on our neighbours' doors, asking whether they had seen 'strange men going in and out of Gareth's house'. It was insidious, and reached a new level when Jemma moved out. She found the atmosphere in the village oppressive, and had to get away.

We tried to remain friends, and I went over to help her settle into her new place as best as I could. It was a cosy home, with a small garden that faced on to a road. One night I was there, I noticed a black van sitting outside. There was a guy with a camera, shooting straight through the window at the pair of us having a conversation in the front room. It was blatant, obviously designed to intimidate or provoke. It was all I could do to stop myself pulling him out and giving him a right-hander when the van duly turned up outside our house in St Brides.

My neighbours were elderly and understandably bemused by what was going on. I've generally had a decent relationship with the media over the years. While I understand the rugby guys have a job to do – even if I sometimes don't appreciate the conclusions they reach – these news reporters were feral. They didn't care who they hurt, what they did. They sensed blood, my blood, in the water. They were circling, closing in for the kill.

It came to a head the night before our final Six Nations match against England in Cardiff in 2007. The WRU assigned a security guard to me because news reporters had checked into the team hotel, and were on the prowl. I had a solicitor on speed-dial. It was unreal. On the Friday, the night before the game, I was summoned to see Gareth Jenkins and Alan Phillips, our team manager.

One look at their faces set the alarm bells ringing. 'Look, mate,' said Gareth. 'They're running with your story on Sunday. Do you want to play tomorrow, or what?'

My pursuers didn't realise it, but they had made a fundamental mistake. I knew I was in a weak position, but was enraged by their audacity and callousness. How dare they disrespect the jersey I was going to wear the following day? What gave them the right to deny me the honour of leading players I trusted, on behalf of my country?

I had a two-word response: 'Fuck 'em.' If they were going to run the story, it would be about me as the captain of a winning Wales team, in the aftermath of a fantastic occasion. That took some imagining, because I had endured a wretched time with a three match suspension, unfairly imposed in the aftermath of the Heineken Cup match against Ulster, and we had not won a Six Nations contest that season. But I was determined to take control of the situation.

There's a photograph of me, taken immediately after that 27–18 win over England. I'm screaming exultantly into the lens. My eyes are sunken, but alive; my mouth is wide open, revealing a dental nightmare of missing teeth and bloodied gums. There's a blood blister on my lips, a sheen of sweat on my bald head. Privately, I was convinced I had played my last game for Wales. Publicly, though, I wanted to exude defiance.

In essence, I was telling the tabloids: 'Come and have a go, if you think you're hard enough!' They weren't. Nothing appeared the next day. They had decided to bide their time for the next great opportunity: the World Cup, six months later.

I made a point, at the official dinner following the game, of saluting Stephen Jones as 'our captain'. I was speaking in the sort of code which teammates tend to understand. Jonesy was injured, but I wanted to imply I would never forget the ties that bound us, as a group.

That culture of inter-dependence was tested to destruction during the World Cup, which was staged mainly in France but, bizarrely, included a smattering of fixtures in Wales and Scotland. We trailed for 50 minutes before overhauling Canada, before returning to Cardiff to lose 32–20 to Australia.

We then faced a winner-takes-all qualifying game against Fiji at the Stade de la Beaujoire in Nantes. I knew, realistically, that defeat would signal the end of an era. A new four-year World Cup cycle would begin, and would be unlikely to require my services. Right on cue, the hyenas returned. They threatened to take advantage of our plight – we were playing poorly, and Gareth's limitations as a coach were becoming apparent – by running my story on the day of the game, when I was due to be the first player to win 100 Welsh caps. Again, I invited them to do their worst. Again, they relented. The only difference from the England scenario was in the quality of our performance.

We were 25–3 down after 26 minutes, recovered to lead 29–25, and were still 34–31 ahead with six minutes to play. But we couldn't close the deal. Fiji scored a late try, validated by a TV referee, and before we knew it, we were conducting a desultory lap of appreciation at walking pace.

We were out, and my international career was over. My final team talk, amidst the human debris in the dressing room, was heartfelt: 'We are going home to people who love us. Life goes on.'

I missed representing Wales immensely, yet settled back into club rugby with Cardiff Blues. I'd had 12 great years in the international game, and my focus had shifted. I was still not entirely comfortable with myself, but I was coming round to the prospect of coming out. I was tired of being in the shadows. I wanted to go to London without having to gravitate to the lonely side of the pub. I wanted to stand with my friends in the light.

I sat down with Emanuele Palladino, my friend and business manager. I had tried to shield him from most of the external pressure, though he knew I'd been hounded, and that I'd grown to hate what the press represented. We spoke about taking control of the situation, telling my story in a positive fashion. The tipping point came when I spoke to his wife, who was working for the charity, Childline.

It is a fantastic organisation, which provides advice, without presumption or prejudice, to young people. It deals with relationship issues, questions of sexuality, body image problems, and a range of social concerns from discrimination to drug abuse. They were looking for a male role model to challenge homosexual stereotypes, and address the resistance of adolescent boys to seek answers for perfectly understandable questions.

It was a lightbulb moment. Finally, I could see a way to share the benefit of my experience. Statistics showed there was an 80-20 split in the number of girls and boys seeking reassurance and information on their sexual identity. Coming out was an intimidating prospect, but the compensations could be very special. The central campaign message – 'Be yourself, rather than what society expects you to be' – was inspiring, and so personally relevant.

I told Emanuele that I would go for it, in the knowledge that the best way to make my statement was to use a national newspaper. I loathed them at the time, but I needed the platform the press provided. I was ready to demand the right to live my life, in the way I chose, without fear or favour. I wanted the freedom to walk down Old Compton Street, holding hands with another man.

I sought succour at the graves of my grandparents down the hill in Sarn. I have always had a sense of them watching over me. They supported me without question, watching every game I played until the exertion became too onerous. I wanted to share my thoughts with them formally, as mad as that might sound.

The churchyard was deserted. It was December, in the twilight of mid-afternoon. The skies were slate grey and carried the threat of sleet. There was a side of me that found it easy to speak to them beyond the grave, on which I placed some fresh flowers from the supermarket. They would have appreciated my practicality, and my honesty. It helped that I couldn't see their eyes as I outlined my plans, and apologised for not sharing my secret, but I could feel their presence.

I sat there for about ten minutes, talking through it all: 'This is the scenario. This is what has happened. The press are doing this, Jemma's done this, my life's going this way. I just needed to tell you why.' I told them about being gay, and asked for their forgiveness that I had not been as candid when they were alive. It doesn't take much for me to cry, and the tears were soon streaming down my face. But I felt this strange serenity, and gained a quiet strength.

It would be OK.

I wanted to use the *Daily Mail,* unaware then of the negativity it aroused in the gay community. It might have been unconventional, in that sense, but it was an understandable choice, because my dad read it, every day. I was obsessed with how my story was going to be perceived, because my entire family was coming out with me. I wasn't ready, but it was one of those moments when the stabilisers were off the bike, and I was accelerating down the hill. It was a little too late for circumspection.

I met the journalist who was assigned to the story in a hotel. Her questions were a blur, because I was still a little in awe of what I had become embroiled in, but I will always remember my final words to her, after the interviews had been completed. 'I'm just asking you one thing, as a parent,' I said. 'When you finish writing this story, read it to yourself. If I was your son and you read it, would you be proud of me? Do me that service, please. That is all I care about.'

She gave me her word, which was good enough for me, until panic set in 24 hours before publication. My imagination ran riot: I had been hopelessly naïve; I would be an object of idle curiosity, branded for the rest of my days. I called Emanuele and begged him to pull the story. He refused, as we had agreed beforehand that he had ultimate responsibility to do what was best, rather than what I demanded. 'You've told me you're doing it, and you're doing it,' he said. 'You've got to do this, for the sake of the rest of your life.'

I was beside myself when I called again, 12 hours later. 'You've got to fucking stop it!' I shrieked. 'I can't do it, I can't take it.'

Again, he stayed calm: 'No, it is going, it's going.'

It didn't feel like it at the time, but it was a unique, unequalled act of friendship. Emanuele remembered what I had said to him, word for word, when we decided to take the plunge: 'You have to take control, because I can't.'

Judgement Day, when my story became common knowledge, wasn't the best day of my life, but it was the biggest occasion. I will always be indebted to Emanuele for his strength of will. He knew what I had been through. He had my back. We had pored over proofs of the article. My parents read them as well. The headlines were daunting, but it was one line that registered most vividly: 'The only openly gay professional athlete in a team sport.'

That's some status. It triggered conflicting emotions. I dreaded the paper hitting the streets and setting the news agenda, but in a strange way I felt a warrior's sense of expectation. It was eerie, like waiting for the first artillery shell in a decisive battle to explode. The questions formed a starburst in my brain:

What will Dai down the rugby club think of this? What will the neighbours say? What would my beloved grandparents have said, had they been alive to see the day? What will my brothers do? What reaction will Dad get in the sorting office? What will Mum find, when she reports for work on Monday morning? What will people think about us?

Forget me, *butt*. What had I done to my own flesh and blood?

Chapter Twelve

OUT

Gary Powell ambled over, threw his arms around me, and wouldn't let go. No words were said, because prop-forwards are a distinctive breed, bigger on actions than words. I couldn't speak, because he was squeezing me so hard I could barely breathe. He was in imminent danger of splintering my rib cage.

Props look like dockside gangsters, but occasionally behave like doting granddads. If you want to see their softer side, ask them to share the romance of a rolling maul, the spirituality of a disrupted scrum, or the poetry of a blindside punch. They're an emotional bunch of galahs, who love the mythology of their trade. They also never let down their mates.

Gary was one of the best, though he narrowly failed to make the senior Wales team after breaking through at under-21 level. He learned his trade at Treherbert and was playing for Cardiff Blues at Toulouse on Saturday, 19 December 2009, the first day of the rest of my life. He would eventually be forced to retire with a torn Achilles tendon, sustained against Leinster four months later but, to me, he is one of the immortals.

I've played with some great forwards down the years, but Gary's response that morning meant more than anything. I had told the boys what to expect on the flight over, the previous evening. This was not going to be an ordinary rugby match. I apologised in advance, because it was going to be momentous, utterly mad. They said, 'That's fine, we don't mind,' but, like me, didn't have a clue about what was about to unfold.

I hadn't slept well, and my first instinct that Saturday morning, after checking my text messages and calling home to gauge the mood, was to switch on the wall-mounted TV in my hotel room. There, on the BBC feed, was my story. People were using phrases like 'ground breaking'. They were using words like 'brave' and 'pioneer'. It was surreal. There was my secret, recycled as a talking point for millions over the cornflakes.

I had a sudden sense of being in the dock. The presenters who used such words and phrases didn't really know me, yet they had leaped to some important conclusions. I only hoped they knew their audience. The public are judge and jury. They decide whether you are worthy of support or scorn. My immediate consolation was my faith in my teammates, but there was still the tightest of knots in my stomach as I entered the breakfast room.

The boys had been brilliant to my face, the night before, telling me not to worry. Yet now that the world was involved in the conversation, a pulse of paranoia seized me: they would surely have had second thoughts, wouldn't they? They didn't deserve to be part of a circus.

The room was large and airy, until I walked in, at least. It looked like I was one of the last down to eat. I was expected. Everyone looked in my direction, though some disguised their interest in the overnight soap-star better than others.

Gary broke the spell. When he was eventually prised loose, I found I was surrounded by teammates, physios, rub-a-dub men, coaches and team officials. It was amazing. Some shook my hand, others wanted a hug. Still more squeezed me, silently, on the arms or shoulders. Then Xavier Rush, the All Black number eight, shook my hand. When he finished, he slowly stroked my palm with his thumb. It was a tiny gesture, but so affecting. I was in serious danger of losing it.

I knew what it all meant. In a single word, on a day when words were pretty superfluous, it signalled acceptance. People in teams have a special kind of connection. My mind set changed at that moment. I knew my boys were with me. I became insanely confident I could get through whatever the day threw at me. It was such a relief.

And then we left the hotel.

Whoa. It was only a short walk to the bus, but we had to file through an entirely different type of scrum. Cameras were waved in my face. Flashbulbs exploded like huge fireflies. Reporters were babbling at me in what seemed like Esperanto. I was not ready for the frenzy. How on earth had my news travelled so far, so fast? I was probably naïve, but I had no idea of the magnitude of the story.

In my cosy world, I had imagined the whole business of my coming out would be a ten-second wonder. People would read the paper, watch the TV, and move on to something altogether more important. By the time the sun was over the yardarm, I'd be free to concentrate on my rugby and my old club. I'd have the boots on, and be back in the old routine.

It wasn't to be so simple, obviously. I felt disorientated as I made that familiar journey to the Stadium Municipal, which staged Toulouse's biggest games. I wondered what to expect. I had shared some fantastic moments with them, such as winning the European Cup in extra time, against Stade Français at Murrayfield in 2005.

French rugby considers itself inherently superior to the rest of the world. It doesn't accept outsiders easily. Toulouse, typically, regard the club as an extended family. Hierarchies are well established, and traditional loyalties are cherished. Respect is a two-way process. Rugby isn't a game; it is a symbol of belonging. The emotions it arouses are extraordinary.

I thought I had seen it all until we went into the additional 20 minutes in that European final. National pride was obviously at stake, because of the familiarity of the opposition, but there was something almost spiritual about the mood in the huddle. Everyone – coaches, replacements and injured players – was on the verge of hysteria. I couldn't understand most of what was being shouted, but it convinced me that defeat was not an option.

A penalty and a drop goal by Freddy Michalak in extra time ensured Toulouse became the first club to win Europe's biggest prize three times. It is a matter of enduring regret that I had to miss the homecoming parade, because I was required to report to a Lions warm-up Test match against Argentina in Cardiff. Toulouse had apparently come to a standstill during the match, when thousands congregated in the main square to watch on giant screens.

I had been accepted as one of their own. I had felt their love and valued their desire to protect me when I had had to deal with long-standing and utterly unjust assault charges, arising out of a nightclub brawl which followed a Bridgend game in Pau. Added to this, I was still ashamed of the messy nature of my exit from the club, and understood the ferocity of the club's mentality.

If they wanted to make my life hell, it would be second nature. Toulouse fans are mad for it. If you are wearing the red and black they will elevate you to the Gods; if you dare to challenge the tribe, you are treated as a scabby, heinous mongrel.

As fate would have it, that day, the home team's bus pulled into the forecourt just before ours. We hung back while their players walked through a tunnel of love, formed by fans who had enjoyed a sumptuous liquid breakfast and were in the mood for raw meat. Their oaths of allegiance were guttural, frenzied and beyond rational translation.

I hid in the middle of the group when we disembarked, jamming my beanie hat over my forehead and staring hard at the ground. It was the child inside; I figured that if I could see none of my foes, they couldn't see me. But, as we approached the door to the changing-room area, I realised something was missing.

We were being watched silently, almost reverently. It was as if the fans had turned out to pay respects to a funeral cortège.

Normally, they pride themselves on the antagonism of the environment they create. Again, I felt a strange sense of guilt. I knew these people, or thought I did. Why were they acting so out of character? There was nothing – none of the usual booing and pantomime hissing. No name-calling. It was as if the exceptional circumstances had tipped their world off its axis. The Cardiff boys were also bemused. Once we'd got into the changing room, the consensus was, 'Wow, that was fucking weird.'

It *was* weird, and we would need the light relief of seeing our jerseys hung out on the pegs. They were a deep pink, our change colour. Nugget, Martyn Williams, shouted: 'Oh, fuck, Alf! They must have known today was the day. Look, they've got your fucking colour for you!' It was perfect. Everyone broke up. That was the moment I knew all would be well. What world did I think I lived in?

The release of being able to laugh at myself, in the company of people who meant everything to me, was indescribable. I had feared that I would spend the day in a vacuum, created by the uncertainties of the situation. The boys were obeying the conventions of the trade, and acting naturally. When in doubt, take the piss.

It had been the same on the bus. I'm still not sure whether this was a set up, but a music video of Queen's 'I Want to Break Free' had suddenly appeared on the TV screens. It features Freddie Mercury dressed as a mini-skirted maid, hoovering the house while singing. A disembodied voice had piped up: 'Look, lads. Alf's on the telly …'

That's why I never feel alone, playing rugby.

I'd better qualify that. Few players actually admit this, but we all feel utterly alone, for a few seconds, when we are waiting for our names to be announced over the tannoy, before the start of a match. This ritual had a special resonance at Toulouse, where the names of their players are regarded as war cries. I knew, or thought I knew, what was coming when the public address announcer cleared his throat and got to work on us.

Sure enough, the names of the visiting players were drowned out in orchestrated abuse from a 30,000-strong crowd. I was going through the motions of warming up on a bitterly cold afternoon, dreading the response when it was my turn to be introduced. Let's face it, I deserved some stick. I was not only a former player, an ungrateful wretch returning to the bosom of the mother club, but I had disrespected the tribe and challenged the game's machismo.

Ben Blair and Leigh Halfpenny, the two players closest to me on the team sheet, got the treatment: *BOOOOOOO!!* Then my name was screamed, rather than spat out, as is traditional. I tried hard not to flinch in that millisecond before my turn came.

They gave me a standing ovation. The applause was respectful, rather than raucous, but time stood still. I was frozen to the spot, unable to take in the magnitude of the compliment I was being paid.

The tears didn't flow immediately, though the memory of the moment is so special I cannot recall it with dry eyes. I had never experienced a feeling like it. It was the first time I had been presented as *me*. People were judging me on who I was, rather than as a character I had created to cover up my differences. It was the first time I had been honest with them, and they were acknowledging me for that honesty. They were saluting me for being normal.

As we filed off, the Toulouse coach, Guy Novès, a local legend, gave me another of those silent hugs which are so eloquent. I was nervous about making eye contact. He is a rugby man, versed in its lore of courage under duress. He is a hard taskmaster, whose players are expected to shake the hand of each teammate as they enter the dressing room. His eyes shone when finally he pulled away from me to take stock. He stood back and saluted me with the gravity of a general taking a parade.

Dai Young, Cardiff's director of rugby, fronted up to the media, while I sat on the toilet and cried undiluted tears of joy. He asked the journalists: 'Why are we making a big deal of this? We are 100 per cent behind Gareth, totally supportive of him. He is a top man. It has taken a lot of courage to talk about his sexuality, but that's his call. Let's not forget what he has done for the game, what he is continuing to do for the game, and what he is like as a bloke.'

That meant more to me than the trinkets of fame – the trophies, caps and mementoes. It was simply overwhelming. I had thought everything was stacked against me that day. I had feared I would be treated as a leper. The nature of my confession, and its timing, given that I was playing against the club from which I had fled, had been ominous. But the reception signalled that everything was, in fact, working in my favour.

The match itself is a blur, but it was reassuringly routine. I came off the bench and couldn't prevent a 23–7 defeat. The mundane nature of proceedings was joyous, because I didn't want it to be about me. I wanted a proper rugby match to break out. It did so, and the fuss it generated underlined the fact that I was involved in something bigger than me, bigger than the game. When it was over, I gave my jersey to Albert, the ancient Toulouse kit man who slept in the dressing rooms and, to all intents and purposes, lived in the clubhouse.

It was a moment of epiphany for me. I realised that the rest of my career, probably the rest of my life, would be dictated by what sort of environment others created for me. That day gave me a unique peace of mind. I have always prided myself on my patriotism. I will shed blood for my team. I like to think I'm pretty good at rugby. But the realisation that people were supporting me above and beyond loyalty to a club or a country, because of a simple act of sincerity, changed everything. I had touched a nerve, without consciously trying to do so.

We flew back that evening, taking off through a snowstorm, and I got back to my parents' house very late. I was obviously worried about how they had found the furore. As I've said before, no one comes out on their own: my entire family had come out with me. Our bonds, already strong, had been tightened.

Mum was accustomed to questions from her workmates. They usually went along the lines of, 'Who is your Gareth playing against this weekend?' Now they were tinged with hesitancy. Dad had to go to the sorting office, which is as macho an environment as a rugby changing room. Suddenly, he had to hear people whispering about me behind his back. He's not stupid; if he walks into a room, which suddenly falls silent, he knows they've probably been gossiping about his son, the gay rugby player.

My parents had a bottle of champagne, and three empty flutes, waiting for me. 'How are you feeling, Gar?' Mum said. 'How did it go? No need to worry – everything's been fine here.'

Dad made a toast: 'To the start of the rest of your life.' Everything, and nothing, had changed. Those closest to me, those who gave me life itself, had come through the process with me. Life carried on, with a greater sense of freedom.

I slept well that night. The Sunday was a family day, and the family were economical with the truth. I didn't discover, until later, that my niece Carys had been bullied after the announcement. All the teenagers in Bridgend were talking about it, and she was their target. Kids can be so cruel. It was kept from me at the time, because they didn't want me to feel guilty. I might well have flipped. Carys is a fantastic girl, and I will never forget she suffered because of me.

The story mushroomed. It was of massive personal importance, but it almost became more relevant to strangers. I was a symbol, a talking point, but I had to think like a professional rugby player. I had a career to extend, and knew cynics were expecting me to shrivel in the spotlight. I had to reinvent myself, answer those who felt I would struggle to deal with the additional attention. I resolved to train harder, for longer. I wouldn't give anyone the satisfaction of showing even momentary weakness.

Within the team, however, it was suddenly a non-issue. Professional sport is about the next match, a new challenge. The media might have still been transfixed by the ramifications of my announcement, but all that really mattered to my mates was me getting over the gain line, if given the opportunity. They didn't care if I was being portrayed as some sort of folk hero; they wanted my help in securing the win bonus.

To be fair, the external response continued to be heartfelt, and supportive. There was the odd wolf-whistle when I played in the New Year's Day derby against the Ospreys at the Liberty Stadium in Swansea, which we lost 26–0, but my name again triggered a wave of applause. The boys were still really tight with me and, with the exception of criticism from a fringe fundamentalist group, I was being judged as a human being.

I've never met Stephen Green, director of Christian Voice, but, as someone who has a strong sense of faith in God, I cannot reconcile his views with the concept of Christian kindness. He insisted I could be cured of my supposedly 'vile affections' with 'sexual healing' by Christian ministries. Bizarrely, he proclaimed: 'Most right-thinking people would be appalled that sex in any form and sodomy in particular is being thrust down small children's throats, yet that is what Gareth Thomas is now promoting.' Thankfully, his was an isolated, discredited voice.

I was Mr Ordinary in Sarn, at least. My neighbours were reso-lutely normal, utterly unfazed by the fuss. All I heard, on those familiar streets, was, 'Morning Alf, you all right? Off training? Good luck – have a good one at the weekend.' Such familiarity gave me stability. I would have been worried if they had acted differently, because that would have signalled a problem.

I was reluctant to share the assumption that, overnight, I had become a role model. That's such an overwrought notion, an over used phrase. Initially, at least, I needed normality in my life. I needed ratification from the postman and the milkman. I needed Compo's benediction. I needed my parents to act as if everything was normal. I needed their strength, their conviction that all was well.

I didn't come out to wave a flag, or validate a movement, though I understood I had dues to pay. The gay community had protected me when I was at my most vulnerable. I was acutely aware I had a responsibility to those who felt unable to make my leap of faith. I was wary of media overkill, but chose to do my most in-depth interview with *Attitude*, a gay lifestyle magazine, because I wanted to reach their constituency.

It took time for the significance of my gesture to register. I began to receive profound, deeply personal feedback from people I would never meet. I was stopped on the street. I never thought my story would transcend my sport, never mind my nation. People with no link to me, no connection to rugby, found personal relevance in my internal struggle.

My learning curve was vertical. Slowly, I saw the chance to redress the balance, to highlight the negativity and stupidity of traditional stereotypes. If, in so doing, I could encourage others to take control of their own lives, and feel the subtle, yet powerful pride that was beginning to wash over me, I would be in a win-win situation. The human spirit doesn't need a licence, or official permission to exist. It doesn't require a passport, or a DNA test, for validity. It just needs a chance to flourish.

Socially, it all went a little Simon Cowell. I was being invited to the sort of celebrity parties that get covered by the magazines you tend to read in the hairdressers. If they were opening an envelope, I was invariably on the guest list. The interest in me, and what I represented, was genuine, but I was wary of appearing false or immodest.

The dilemma hit me when I made my first visit to Soho as an openly gay man. I was with a film crew, doing a documentary on diversity for use in schools. They wanted shots of me walking down Old Compton Street. Nothing special, you'd think, but I was panicked by the attention I received. In my mind, those staring at me were sneering: 'Just look at him. What a prick. He comes out, and now he's waltzing around with a cameraman.'

Just as I thought I was about to die of embarrassment, the director decided he had enough in the can. And that was the cue for people to come up to me – a bit self-consciously at first, but they simply wanted to thank me for highlighting the issue. It had helped them, or those they loved.

Their good wishes were wonderful. I wanted to make a point of sharing them, just in case there was someone watching from a distance, lacking the courage of his convictions. That refugee from reality had been me, some short weeks earlier.

Even today, I can still feel the fear. That will never leave me. Rejection is a silent terror. Guilt has the consistency of superglue. When you lie, if you have a modicum of decency, you have to convince yourself you have a justification for doing so. Speaking to others who have come out, I've been amazed by how many of us created a parallel world, dark and forbidding. It evolves in your imagination as an evil, dangerous place. It is homophobic. You construct an imaginary world in which you are an outcast, where your family will refuse to accept you for who you are. The horror of such a prospect gives you the reason to lie.

The compulsion to protect your secret, at all costs, is addictive. It is a very personal process, and untruths become your ally. I had lied constantly, for longer than I cared to remember. I had lied about stupid things: if someone asked me what I'd done the night before, for instance, I'd tell them I'd been roaring drunk at the local, when in reality I had slobbed out in front of the telly. I can't explain or excuse that; I just did it. It was as if lying was so crucial to me it became a muscle to be exercised in case I needed it. Usually I did it to please other people, and make life easier. It helped me to avoid confrontation or discomfort. In many other cases it was an unthinking, reflex action without logic or substance. It also allowed me to avoid answering questions that were too close to the bone.

I didn't become a different person overnight, by the simple act of issuing a statement about who I was. I still have to stop myself and correct the odd, daft white lie. That's where this book has helped, in peeling away the layers of my personality.

I realise I have a duty to tell the truth, because that truth is universal, and exceptionally powerful. I've been stopped on the street across the world, from Sunderland to San Francisco. They are chance encounters, accidents of fate, but they follow a similar narrative. Strangers make the most of the coincidence to share their stories of how my example helped them, their families or their friends to have a better life.

Or even to have a life at all.

During these conversations, there is a real sense of connection, on a human level. At the risk of sounding trite, I'm humbled by such fleeting relationships. They make me wonder how many others are out there, too shy to take the initiative and make that contact. I'm nothing special, but it seems I am thought of as a special case. Perhaps that is because, as a rugby player, I've challenged the stereotypical perceptions of a gay man.

I've lost eight teeth and broken my nose five times on the rugby field. I've fractured both shoulders, wrecked my hip, and have a vivid scar down one forearm. I've been concussed, on average, three times a year for 20 years. John Inman – a character actor who became a camp cliché – might have risked arthritis in his limp wrist, but there isn't much of a comparison, is there?

I've met so many people who have felt intimidated about coming out because of the examples set in the era of Larry

Grayson & co. I remember sitting with my parents, watching him on prime-time TV, and laughing uneasily at the campness of it all. That stereotype persists, though it is, mercifully, being toned down. It still invites ridicule. As a gay man, you are insulted by the insinuation that you are the punch line to an unfunny joke.

It hurts people, because it establishes a certain status quo. There's still a breeziness, an emptiness, in the portrayal of the average gay guy on TV. People meet me, and can't compute the difference between normality and artificiality. A gay man is the same, in terms of physicality, as a straight guy, in 90 per cent of cases. If individuals are happy to be laughed at for being camp, and can reconcile that with themselves, then good on them; if it leads to fulfilment, then that is brilliant. But it is not how I would like to be accepted. It doesn't help the gay person in Bridgend, Bradford or Brixton to come out. People need to be able to see that if you are gay it doesn't make you intrinsically different. I'm not the sort to lecture, to stamp my feet, but I do believe, passionately, that the media, and all of us, have a responsibility to resist pigeon-holing a significant sector of society.

Why? Let me introduce you to Gareth. He's in his 50s, a single man and a big rugby fan who approached me in the streets in Cardiff. He had come into the city centre on a night out, from a small valley town. His story struck such a chord that we have remained in contact.

He was brought up in that 'Ooh, you are awful, but I like you' era. He felt belittled and daunted by the image of weakness and silliness it presented. The weekend after I came out, he called his family around to his house for dinner. When they assembled, he served drinks, and asked to be excused. He re-emerged after changing into a pink shirt, and sat down at the head of the table. That, inevitably, led to questions. He announced, with as much confidence as he could muster: 'I've got something to tell you. If Gareth Thomas can wear pink and come out as gay, on a rugby field, then I can wear pink in front of my family and come out to my family.'

All those years, all that anguish. Finally, acceptance. Gareth was no longer alone.

Chapter Thirteen

VOICES

Dear Gareth Thomas,

I am not in the habit of writing letters to famous sportsmen. In fact, this is the very first one I have ever written. I am writing to say that by coming out to the world, in my opinion, you did something heroic. Being a public figure you had so much to lose, but you stood up and told the world your secret. I can only imagine what mixed emotions you must have felt: an unburdening, mixed with anxiety about how people might react to the revelations.

I myself have not yet had the courage to do what you did. I live in a small town in South Africa, where everyone knows everyone else's business. For me to come out would be a juicy bit of gossip, and I am not even famous. In this town I have seen what coming out can do. Abuse, beatings and even one killing. Despite this, there is growing pressure inside me to let everyone know.

It is ironic that South Africa has a liberal constitution, on paper. In reality it is still very conservative. The older I get (I am 39) the more important it seems to be to come out. My brother knows, but no one else.

I was amused, just after your news, at the reactions of some people here. They were confused. To them gay people are supposed to be effeminate hairdressers or florists. Not rugby players! You broke that stereotype, for sure. It made the conservatives uncomfortable: 'What if one of them is living next door to me, or coaching my son in football, and I don't know about it? How can we tell now?' Hopefully one day it will not even be an issue worth speculating about. I hope so.

Thanks so much for what you did. I imagine it really has helped many people, given a feeling of hope. One day, when I do unburden myself, it will be partly thanks to the confidence you have given me. All the best for the future.

Yours sincerely,

-------- ------------

I won't share my correspondent's name, out of respect for his privacy. Let's call him Kobus. He's an Afrikaner, but he could be anyone from anywhere. I received thousands of letters in the weeks and months after my announcement. They flooded into my club and to my management team. They were sent from all parts of the globe. Some were simply addressed: 'Gareth Thomas, Wales.' The Royal Mail, my old boys' team, played a blinder.

I read them with a sense of wonder, and kept them all in a set of boxes at my mother's house. Slowly, the magnitude of events started to sink in. I chose to embrace the scale of the response, rather than be intimidated by such overwhelming interest. Maybe, just maybe, something good could come from something that had seemed so irredeemably bad.

The voices within those letters vary in tone, and the languages are diverse, but nationalities merge, because the message is universal: Cut me, and I bleed. Condemn me, and we both suffer.

I feel empowered when I am stopped on the street. People still say things like, 'Through you, my father found the strength at sixty years of age to finally be who he wanted to be. He was able to tell us all and finally be happy.' Others tell me I have proved that sport is not exclusively for stereotypical heterosexual men or women. Occasionally encounters involve deeper conversations, about the contemplation of suicide, and the restoration of life's balance. They generally require greater scope than that offered by a chance meeting.

But I find the letters most humbling. They are uniquely affecting, because I visualise the writer, and imagine his or her circumstances. I try and read between the lines. I appreciate the privilege of their honesty and empathy. It brings the old proverb – 'Before you criticise a man, walk a mile in his shoes' – to life. They are from priests and policemen, teenagers and senior citizens, those who are in or those who are out. Several asked me to destroy their notes after reading them, because they were profoundly personal.

I complied, of course. But the stories contained within the boxes deserve to be told. I promise to do so sensitively, and with the benefit of anonymity. The level of ignorance they reveal is shocking, and by articulating the breadth, intensity and sheer humanity of everyday dilemmas, they serve an invaluable purpose. This isn't about sensationalising the experiences of strangers, or stroking my ego. It is a challenge to take a 360-degree view.

Some are amusing:

I am a Welshman living in Newcastle and am bombarded regularly by English 'friends' making derisory comments about Welsh rugby. When I received the following email from one of them – 'Seen what Gareth Thomas has admitted to?' I was full of apprehension. Imagine how pleased I was when all he was referring to was that you'd said you were gay. 'Thank Christ!' I shouted. 'I thought he'd confessed to being bloody English!

Some are tender:

Growing up in small-town Devon in the seventies and eighties, I feared that life being gay would be lonely and miserable. Luckily I met a much older couple who showed me that love and companionship is not exclusively heterosexual. They have been together happily for almost 60 years now. Incredible.

Some are disturbing: a cricket umpire in the north of England has been blacklisted by several clubs after choosing to be open about his sexuality. One club will not allow him to officiate in junior matches. As he writes: 'The reasons given are laughable, but deep down I know the real reasons. I hope your brave decision helps to raise the issue of homophobia in sport, which is rife.'

Some are unutterably poignant. A former rugby player, now 78, writes from the Basque region. He has repressed his true sexuality throughout his adult life, and will continue to do so 'although I know I do not have long left'. This, he asserts, is out of respect to his late wife. 'I have told no one but you of my deeper feelings, and do not wish her memory to be affected.'

All are relevant. A social worker shares the following case study:

At the age of 16, Paul [not his real name] was a very promising rugby league player. He had been with a professional club since he was 11 and lived for rugby, playing and training almost every day of his life. At 15, he began to feel he was 'different' but was unsure of how he was different. Over the next few months, he began to realise that he didn't relate sexually to women in the same way as his friends seemed to.

By the age of 17 he had decided these feelings made him gay. Around that time, he stopped going to practice, and became an undisciplined nightmare. Eventually, by 18, he had withdrawn from playing rugby altogether. After going off the rails for a couple of years – problems with

205

alcohol and the police – he had what he described as 'a total mental breakdown'. Though now out of that initial crisis, he still, at 23, experiences major bouts of depression.

Your coming out has had a huge impact on him. He has now realised that being gay and being a rugby player are not mutually exclusive. He has told people he played with that he is gay, and had a positive reaction from them. He intends to start playing again. Suddenly, he seems to think that he can resume his life after seven years of what he describes as 'hell'. I have no doubt he can. Your story has struck a huge chord with many people who are stuck in the closet, limiting their potential to be happy.

A trainee nurse from the north-west of England speaks for us all when he reflects:

Coming out is a completely nerve-wracking thing. I remember saying 'I am ...' and finding it so insanely hard to finish that sentence. Being a non-obvious gay man like yourself must make it a million times harder. I went to school with some of the local rugby league team. Some of them look at me like I am not human, and I imagine you have possibly heard homophobic banter in the locker room.

My ex-boyfriend was a bit like you. He was in his mid-30s, a down-to-earth guy who you'd never guess was gay. But he couldn't find the strength to come out. It hurt me, but I had to leave him in the end, because I was always going to be a secret and I knew I deserved more. Coming out is a private battle, but by doing it in the public arena you may begin to break the assumption that gay men have to look and act in a certain way. We come in all shapes and sizes – you prove that!

The sense of isolation is tangible. Another man, let's call him Brian, writes:

I know there must be many thousands of gay men who, for whatever reason, find themselves in marriages or straight relationships, and feel trapped and miserable. I am one of these. I am 42 and have been married for 14 years and have a teenage son.

I have two choices, either to stay or go. Both options have some pros but also some massive cons. Ultimately, it comes down to either what is right for me or what is right for others. I don't know what I'll do. Your actions have motivated me to make this the year I decide on my future. There will no doubt be some fallout from your news, but I hope in the medium to long term it is right for you, and that you are happy. After all, that is what we all want for the time we are on this planet.

I realise I risk appearing self-indulgent, but it is important to remember that 'being gay is about one per cent of who we are'.

That is a line from another letter, which warns against simplistic judgement. It reads, in part:

> I must I admit I didn't know who you were before your news broke. I am not a sports fan and, as an American by birth, I don't understand much about rugby (sorry).
>
> This story brings back many good and bad memories for me. Six years ago, I told my wife of 20 years that I was gay. She has, of course, been very angry with me since (in varying degrees, from absolute hatred to mild repulsion). We have three children. I don't intend to use this letter as some sort of sob story, but these years have been what I guess people would call 'interesting'.
>
> Some friends have abandoned me, my sister thinks I'm perverted and my parents have embraced me for who I am, and that has brought us closer. We have to get on with our lives, but there is a lot going on, personally and emotionally. In my one-to-one relationships with the people closest to me, a lack of understanding of what is a very complicated internal situation leads to conflict and pain.
>
> From my experience, coming out later in life at 39 was, at times, a horrible experience. I didn't know how people were going to react until I told them (you know this, of course). If you were brought up with a religious background as I was, you feel like a bad person, embarrassed by your sexuality and worried about social stigmas.

Six years after coming out, I am still trying to find a fit with an identity I am completely comfortable with. After all, where does a man who was straight, married, had children and is now gay fit in with society?

Receiving a card from a policeman, reminding me that '… until 1997, I could have been sacked and sent to prison for being gay' is sobering. Were we so ignorant, constitutionally, for so long, and until so recently? The moral courage of a priest who admits 'your journey is my journey, and probably the same journey that many people take of whom we know nothing' is awe-inspiring. He speaks of 'trips to London, sitting quietly in the back of a pub, longing for company but always afraid of being recognised'.

Time and again, I'm struck by the contradictory fragility and durability of the human condition. 'Henry' writes from Cornwall that he was:

Married to a girl I met at university. I fell in love with this girl and, 20 years later, we have three wonderful children. During this time, I always thought there was something missing and the more I tried to put it out of my mind, the more it haunted me.

I was attracted to certain men and I could deny it no longer. Like you, I would play away whilst on business, particularly in London. I realised there were a lot of gay men like me, straight acting, straight looking, but who needed sex with men. This continued for a period of years but the guilt of deceit finally caught up with me. I came out to friends and some of the family, including my children.

I set up house on my own and I am pleased to say that my relationships with friends and family have never been better. I do not regret my decision for a moment. I now have a full and interesting life in sports, the arts and just being with friends. I hope you take some comfort from this.

I did, but the problems of self-image and peer pressure are persistent. Another correspondent, from a naturally conservative Welsh-speaking farming community in North Wales, confides:

Being gay is not easy. I have struggled with my sexuality since leaving school with no one to talk to, and trying to hide my feelings. This would lead to me always getting very drunk when out with friends. I would have to drink as much, if not more, than the others to prove my masculinity. That was my way of dealing with being gay!

In the end I was drinking too much and suffered from depression and anxiety. By now, friends know I am gay but they never talk about it with me. They find the subject very awkward. Whenever I am out with them I just feel a bit dejected. It can become a lonely and sad existence. Thus, in order to meet other gay men, I have to travel to England or further afield. I suppose most people in my situation would have moved to England, and got on with life, but my love for Wales and where I live is too strong. As you said, we have to be content and accept who and what we are. I have good and bad days on that one.

Stereotypes add to the stress of an already stressful situation, because they encourage people to live down to others' preconceptions. Listen to 'Donald', who moved to Scotland to refocus:

I have no sob story of how hard it has been for me to be gay, nor have I particularly struggled with my sexuality to any great degree, but what you have done is show the British public a different image of a gay man. An image that you and I know exists, but is so often neglected by popular culture and absent from the eyes of kids dealing with their sexuality.

The only struggle I have had with my sexuality is that I have struggled to mix the different aspects of my personality. I knew I was gay early in my teens and, had a certain opportunity not arisen, it may have taken me many years before I would have been brave enough to come out. I was fortunate to have supportive friends, but what I truly regret to this day was that I abandoned many things that I enjoyed because they didn't fit with my new gay image.

I left behind rugby and outdoor pursuits for more obviously 'gay' activities such as drama etc. I enjoyed these pursuits but I wonder if, had I had a role model like you when I was younger, I would have made the same choices. I have recently started to reclaim my personality and balance my sexuality with the life I want to have. It has taken me a few years of unhappy displacement as I tried to figure out what my personality was, beyond being gay.

What's that old adage, of not judging a book by its cover? 'Malcolm' conforms to macho culture. He is a part-time wrestler, who moonlighted as a nightclub bouncer and works with offenders serving community punishment orders. He was determined that his background – he comes from the sort of mining town with which I am familiar – should not define him. He writes:

I remember dating girls until I was well into my 20s because that was just what was expected. I was always being asked when I was going to settle down and have kids. I tried, but knew at the back of my mind that that wasn't for me. Coming from my family environment, I thought they would disown me.

I met a guy when I was in my mid-20s, a footballer funnily enough, and we saw each other for a while. It was difficult because he wasn't at all comfortable with his sexuality either. It caused a few problems and tension. In the end, I didn't have to tell my family (my mother found my Alan Shearer scrapbook under my bed!!!!). I got the obligatory 'You're going through a phase' speech. I told her it wasn't a phase.

You know what? They were all fine. Further along the line it is not an issue. I now have a partner who was married for 20 years (from a Durham pit village – same issues) and he has two kids as well. It's hard enough when parents split up, but having to tell the kids you're living with another man is even tougher. They're fine with me. My partner thought he had let his family down, and thought that he was worthless. There were countless nights where I had to tell him he shouldn't feel like that.

It was difficult for me too, but now I'm cool. I worked on a nightclub door for two years and when they found out about me they were all fine. It was the same with the wrestling. Straight guys didn't give a toss about wrestling with me. With my job, I deal with a few guys who have confided they are attracted to other men. They ask me what they should do. I always say honesty is the best policy and always be yourself.

If people judge you and suddenly don't want to know you, I figure they are not worth knowing in the first place. I see a lot of guys having a tough time, though. One told me his brother was gay. They live in a dodgy part of Manchester and every time he comes out of the house the local hoods throw stones at him.

It is a quantum leap from some of the rougher council estates of England to the gilded playgrounds of the Hollywood elite, but my story bridged the social divide. I visited Los Angeles soon after my announcement, and couldn't get over how small the global village really is.

We've all had our visions of Tinseltown sharpened in the local cinema or the gossip columns. There is a sense that its stars are somehow detached from real life. I found those I met reassuringly human.

The highlight of a whirlwind week of meetings, interviews and social functions was my appearance on the *Ellen* chat show. Ellen DeGeneres and her partner, Portia de Rossi, are among Hollywood's most respected power couples, but I was struck by how naturally she empathised with my situation.

Being on her show was a big deal. I dressed with calculated casualness – lilac, open-necked shirt, fawn waistcoat, smart jeans – and made a point of presenting her with a Wales jersey.

My introduction involved a short film sequence, which attempted to explain rugby to an American audience. The voiceover man likened me to Peyton Manning, the legendary quarterback who has been named the most valuable player in the National Football League five times. Manning described my sport as 'a bone-breaking, extreme version of football played without helmets or pads'. What was that about two nations divided by a common language?

Ellen's journey, which involved coming out on the Oprah Winfrey show, had so many echoes with mine. She told me:

'I give you so much credit for deciding to live your life, your truth. That is such a big deal.' The studio audience whooped and hollered.

I might have appeared calm on the outside, but inside I was churning with pride. Here was someone who had used her prominence positively, as a trailblazer for gay rights. She highlights fundamental subjects, such as depression and AIDS awareness. When she exclaimed, 'What a cool dad,' as I explained the strength my father had given me, I nearly lost it.

Elton John and his partner, David Furnish, invited me to their LA apartment. He's known for his football affiliations with Watford, but is a huge sports fan. Again, he was just so natural, warm and supportive. He invites me every year to his White Tie and Tiara ball, at his home in Windsor, but I've never had the courage to attend. Strange, I know, because he is so grounded, but I find the scale of such occasions unnerving.

Elton understands the sporting landscape, and the obligations of being identified as a role model for the gay community. I regard that as a huge responsibility, but, as I explained to him, that was an unintended consequence of my actions. I didn't come out because I wanted to be a role model; I came out because if I had not done so I would have died.

He asked about the reactions of fans, teammates, and the wider rugby community. It was a concerned chat. How had my parents and family dealt with it all? Had the opposition given me much grief? He remembered one occasion, in his early days as Watford chairman, when he sat in the front row of the directors' box at Rochdale, a small club then in the old Fourth Division. There were not more than 3,000 people in the rather ramshackle ground, but they all joined in a chorus of 'Elton John's a homosexual'. He laughed, rose from his seat, and gave them all a wave.

I loved that. He understood the trauma I had been through, and was checking whether I was OK. He asked about my future plans, and asked after Jemma. He understood the symbolism of my situation and impressed upon me the importance of ensuring I had a constructive story to tell. 'Let's not give some people what they want, which is a car crash,' he said. 'Let's move forward positively, and show that others can gain spirit from what you have done.'

I have never tried deliberately to hurt anyone, with the exception of that player I pursued for several years around the playing fields of Wales, but I am not naïve. I still feel hugely guilty for the pain I inflicted on Jemma. As I told Ellen: 'We were addicted to each other, best friends as well as lovers. Emotionally, I tied her up in chains. I had to set her free.'

Jemma's voice, too, deserves to be heard. She did it most eloquently through a CD she sent me, by British singer-songwriter, Lucie Silvas, as we were going through our divorce. The stand-out track, 'What You're Made Of', has such personal relevance it is almost unbearable for me to listen to, but I still keep it on my phone.

It is a beautiful song of love and loss, which could have been written for us. I can almost hear Jemma singing these lines to me:

If it's not what you're made of
You're not what I'm looking for
You were willing but unable to give me any more

The last time I listened to that song, through tears, I was lying on the floor in the front room of my mother's house. I had been rummaging through some bits and pieces I was intending to take to my flat in London, and couldn't stop myself playing the YouTube version. Everyone told me to move on, in my own time, but it was not easy. The pain I inflicted on others saw to that.

For a year, in 2010, while my life stabilised, I took refuge in what was literally a halfway house, living in a Georgian hotel that was equidistant between Wrexham and Chester. It was to be a strange setting, since it specialised in wedding receptions. There was I, a gay divorced rugby player, surrounded by soft-focus images of domestic bliss, photographs of newly married couples exuding love and happiness.

I'd look at those pictures and drift away. I'd mentally transplant my face, and that of Jemma, on to those of the couples whose devotion was frozen in time. There was a reception every Saturday night. I'd hear the music, see the guests spilling out from the bar and into the lobby, and be transported back to our wedding. The laughter of our friends, the light in Jemma's dark eyes, her love of our life together.

I'd feel helplessly, hopelessly sad. I would go back to my room on my own and look out over the gardens. I'd feel the thump of the music, and detect the rhythm of the disco lights.

I'd turn the TV up a little too loudly, in case I'd hear a peal of laughter from below. I'd look around the room and linger on the few personal possessions, family photos, I had, and wonder where my life had gone. It was hard, having everything I valued thrust into my face.

Ironically, I had moved there because I felt I couldn't be on my own. Living in a hotel gave me simplicity and a sense of belonging. I could have saved money by renting a house in the transitional period I changed codes to rugby league, but I craved human contact. The little things, the daily greetings from the receptionists and the rugby banter with the boys in the restaurant, meant a lot. It represented acceptance, of a sort. I would buy the girls tokens of appreciation, flowers and chocolates, and make small talk when they were bored. They were a surrogate family, who unwittingly helped when waves of loneliness washed over me. I still missed Jemma, who had moved to Spain to start a new life. As difficult as it was for me to admit it, we were both in the right place.

If only ... Those two little words still taunted me. Logically, as I came to terms with divorce, I knew our split was for the best. But love and logic are uneasy bedfellows. I was still grieving; tears would come suddenly and irresistibly. They could be triggered by a fleeting memory, vivid and intense, or by an idle thought as simple as, 'I wonder what Jemma is doing today.'

We had reached a crossroads and taken different paths. That didn't stop me imagining where an alternative route would have led. Those wedding photographs of strangers, lining the walls in

Signing autographs after my Toulouse debut. It is a wonderful community club, a rugby institution that welcomed me with unforgettable warmth and respect. The haircut, a remnant of my initiation ritual, didn't last long.

With Trevor Brennan, after Toulouse had beaten Stade Français in the 2005 Heineken Cup final at Murrayfield. A giant of a man who dispensed tough love in hard times.

Rugby League is the hardest game. My body took a complete pummelling, but my spirit soared when I was given one last chance to captain my country.

Bridging the generation gap: passing on my experience to the youngsters at my rugby academy. We need to nurture their love of the game in a changing world.

At Number 10 with my friend and business manager, Emanuele Palladino. His wisdom and strength of will sustained me when panic set in, just before I came out.

Compo Greenslade, my old captain, is now head coach at my rugby academy. He was my best man, and my fairy godfather. He watched my back, whether I knew about it or not, on countless occasions.

A huge honour: named Hero of the Year by Stonewall, the gay rights charity
and campaign group. The real heroes are those you never hear about,
who have the quiet courage to be themselves.

'I give you so much credit for deciding to live your life, your truth.
That is such a big deal.' Those words to me from Ellen DeGeneres
on her TV chat show meant so much.

A Bridgend boy with a buddy in Hollywood. Mickey Rourke
is a fine actor, a force of nature, and a fearsome friend.

It took me two years to wean myself off rugby. *Dancing on Ice* was a perfect release, like learning a new body language. I couldn't have done it without my professional partner, Robin Johnstone.

Yvonne and Barrie, the best Mam and Dad in the world. Everything I've done has been for them. I hope I've made them proud.

Finally, after all those years, the freedom to be myself. It means so much to my partner Ian and me that we are accepted as a couple.

My life story, as body
art. These tattoos
have tales to tell. They
remind me to take
something from every
day, every experience.

the hotel lobby, reminded me of what I had lost: contentment and companionship.

There was also a temptation to go wild, and revel in my freedom. Without wishing to be crude, there were opportunities. There are always people who want to be associated with you, because they've seen your face on the front page of the newspaper or your chest on the cover of a gay magazine. But I didn't want to be defined as the world's most popular gay athlete, or some sort of trophy companion. I still wanted to be defined as a rugby player. I needed to focus on what I had gained.

Chapter Fourteen

WELCOME TO THE JUNGLE

It was only my second game of rugby league. I shouldn't have played, as I had been concussed in my debut for the Crusaders a week previously, but I was determined to defy the doubters. This was a symbolic introduction to my new sport's heartland, Castleford, and the Tigers' atmospheric ground, the Jungle.

Rugby was the constant. It has nearly killed me, but has given me a life. Coming out had been everything I'd thought it would be, but I needed an additional challenge. The decision to change codes was a conscious attempt to stretch myself. I cared what the rugby fraternity, union and league, thought about me. I wanted their respect and understanding. I trained like a demon, worked harder than I thought possible. Failure, at this stage of my life, was not an option.

The pace of the match was relentless – I couldn't catch my breath. And then I couldn't believe my ears:

'Gareth Thomas takes it up the arse.'

It was the manifestation of my worst nightmare. This wasn't 'banter'. It wasn't the ranting of an isolated homophobe. It was an abusive chant, taken up by a couple of hundred people in a crowd of just under 6,000, who stood on the steeply banked terraces and had decided to belittle me and everything I stood for. It didn't happen once, but three times.

Castleford officials would later claim two of the chants were drowned out by public address announcements. They weren't – they were replayed on a tape loop in my brain for the rest of the match, and for months afterwards. Even today, I need only close my eyes to recall the braying ignorance of those cowards, who sought refuge in anonymity and sheer weight of numbers. It was a form of mass bullying which made bile rise to my throat.

As the game raged around me, I found it increasingly difficult to concentrate on anything but an anguished internal conversation that went to the heart of what being a professional athlete is all about. Where are the acceptable limits of criticism? What entitlements come with a ticket to a sporting occasion? Who do these folk think they are?

Fuelled by fear and anger, I played with a madman's intensity that night. We lost 22–16, but it seemed incidental. As I took off my boots in the dressing room, I doubted I would ever lace them up again. It remains the only time I, as a rugby player and as a man, regretted coming out. My story had been so positive, but now I felt powerless in the face of such a sudden show of collective prejudice.

I had never before felt such contempt for spectators. I never did so again. No sportsman should forget the privilege of the position. People pay money to come and watch you play sport. That's pretty amazing, if you think about it. If you play poorly, or perform listlessly, they have the right to criticise and berate because they've paid money to judge you as an athlete. But out there, in the Jungle, they crossed the line. It became painfully personal. They hadn't parted with their hard-earned cash to judge me on how I live my life. They had no right to do so. If that came with my job, I didn't want to do the job anymore.

I knew I could not win in those circumstances. Those people – who, to be fair, were challenged by fellow fans and shamed into eventual silence – didn't know me. They didn't understand what I had been through. They couldn't conceive of what it takes to run out into the arena and put your body on the line. They weren't aware of how proud I was of my achievements, and the way I had handled a fundamental challenge.

Fortunately, my teammates did. I had not thought about walking off, because I didn't want to give the bigots the satisfaction of knowing they had got through to me, but as I had returned to the changing room, my thoughts had been dark and toxic: 'Why the fuck am I wasting my life? Why the fuck am I pushing myself to the limit, learning a new sport? Why the fuck have I gone through everything to be in this position?'

Nick Youngquest, who became my closest friend on the Crusaders team, read those thoughts. He sat down next to me and let things settle for several seconds, before touching me lightly on the shoulder. He simply said: 'That was fucking disgusting.' It wasn't so much what he said, but how he said it that was so affecting. He spoke with a quiet passion, an earthy dignity. It was one of those intimate moments that recur in team environments, usually in stressful situations.

His response reinforced the reasons I found my outlet in team games. While the bonds are special and the rituals private, they mean everything. Simple gestures of fellowship and demonstrations of shared humanity make even the bad times good.

It wasn't the time for florid speeches and dramatic gestures. None of the boys needed to broach the subject, but they let me know they were with me. Messages are sent in different ways in a dressing room, with a wink, a touch or a tap. As we were dressing, a couple of guys came across to me and said something similar: 'We heard it. You know what? You're our teammate. You'll do for us.'

Talk about taking the positives. Some of the Castleford players even popped in to apologise. They were embarrassed by their own. I still doubted whether I had a future, but I felt perversely empowered, walking back through the crowd to an upstairs dining room in the clubhouse. I was eager to see if anyone had the balls to say anything to my face. No one said a word. A few fans even asked for my autograph.

It was probably a good job they weren't reading my mind, because I was raging inside. This wasn't a ten-minute wonder: it had taken 20 years to summon the courage to get to that point. I had put myself through hell. I know the noble thing is to forgive, and excuse the nuances of human nature, but if anyone had chosen to challenge me on that walk to the post-match meal, I would probably have given them a slap.

I wasn't a reality TV star, offering myself up for public consumption by inviting the TV cameras into my house for 24 hours a day. If I had done so, I was fair game for judgement. I had worked my bollocks off to be on that team, that night. I gave up my childhood and wasted my education to be a rugby player. That was all I ever wanted to be.

When I looked at those faces, expectantly pushing their books at me, I wondered if their respect was a charade. That inner voice was emphatic: 'I don't mind signing, but remember this. You don't pay 15 quid to come and sit in my living room and watch me in my own home. You pay 15 quid to sit in a fucking stand on a Friday night and watch me play rugby. Judge me on what you see. I'm not a creature in a freak show. I'm giving this a go. It's not my game, but I will give it everything I have.'

The reports the next morning carried no mention of the abuse. The narrative involved the importance of the Tigers' win, and the doomed defiance of our late comeback.

But then, suddenly, the story was taken out of my hands. Overnight, someone, somewhere – I still do not know who, or why – reported the incidents to the Rugby Football League.

It was not me, despite the enduring suspicions of Castleford fans; nor was it my club, as far as I am aware. Perhaps it was an individual who understood the wider implications of narrow-mindedness. Maybe that person was going through the existential crisis of preparing to come out. I made a conscious decision never to try to find out.

It became a corporate crisis for the code, but all I could do was be honest about the impact on me, and point out the implications for society, and the sport. When I was approached officially, I couldn't go into denial and suggest everything be quietly brushed under an appropriate carpet. I had a responsibility to deal with the issue head on, even though I had effectively moved on in my own world – the dressing room. I told the truth about what I had heard, and what I had felt. It was emotionally draining, but here was an obvious opportunity to shape the outcome. I wasn't on a soapbox, and I wasn't on the back foot.

As events unfolded, support grew. There was a general acknowledgement this sort of thing has no place in a civilised society in the 21st century, and Castleford were eventually fined £40,000. To this day, their supporters insist, through social media, that I should get over myself. They don't understand the dynamics of professional sport; in such a competitive, confrontational environment, there is no point holding a grudge.

I had no respect for those who hid behind the crowd, but they ultimately bolstered my self-belief. The fact that no one was willing to repeat the slander to my face was a source of strength. From that day, I had a new mindset: if you, my accuser, are not willing to stand in front of me and explain yourself, then you are the weaker man. You no longer matter to me.

Despite the Castleford incident I realised, over time, that others' opinion of me was not dictated by my private life. My sexuality simply didn't matter to the vast majority of people with whom I came into contact. I had sacrificed my secret, and it wasn't necessarily a big deal. That was my starting point, my release. I was liberated from a permanent state of anxiety. I could be proud of who I was, instead of being afraid of arbitrary judgement.

Sport is a microcosm of life: just because you are good at it, it doesn't mean that you are necessarily a good person. The star system distorts, because it conditions people to see you differently. Though my circle of acquaintances grew when I came out, some were thrown by my determination to behave normally, irrespective of my installation as a so-called celebrity. I did what I had been taught to do as a kid: I respected others, I said please and thank you, I opened doors, gave others space.

My reward was to have them say, 'You're nicer than I thought.' Why, because I smiled when they gave me a pot of tea, or said good morning? Manners cost nothing, my mum always told me. Be polite. Do unto others as you would have them do to you. I hadn't changed core beliefs, or abandoned basic values. Wherever life takes me, I will still have the same roots. I'll be the same person, even if I'm going in a different direction.

The chance, in March 2010, to join the Crusaders, a recently established Super League club transplanted from Bridgend to Wrexham, was perfectly timed. I had interest from the 13-man code throughout my career, but never really took it seriously.

I still cringe at memories of agreeing to meet Warrington officials, with a view to joining them in 2000. I travelled north with Compo Greenslade and Leigh Davies, my old running mate at Cardiff.

At the time, it made some sense: Warrington had a history of recruiting Welsh players, like Jonathan Davies, Allan Bateman, Rowland Phillips and Kevin Ellis. Kevin, a Bridgend boy, was known to everyone at Wilderspool, Warrington's home for more than a century until they moved to the Halliwell Jones Stadium in 2003, as 'Champ'. He suggested we watched the match from behind one of the goals before going in for our meeting.

Our vantage point just happened to be beside the bar. It was game over. We were hopelessly drunk on cider and blackcurrant when we tottered into the clubhouse to meet Darryl van de Velde, the Warrington coach at the time. He took one look at us behaving like idiots, smiled and said, 'Boys, do me a favour. Bugger off and come back when you're serious.' We weren't, and we didn't. We didn't understand what we were missing.

Dai Young did. As my coach at Cardiff Blues, he sensed my growing alienation from rugby union in the immediate aftermath of my coming out. My contract had a couple of months to run. He had unrivalled insight into both codes, having won 51 caps in union, a record for a prop, and captained Wales in the 1995 Rugby League World Cup. He excelled for Leeds and Salford, and was the perfect sounding board.

'This is a crazy time in my life,' I told him. 'Things are changing and this is the last change, the last challenge. I've always wanted to give rugby league a go, although I've had a funny way of showing it. I've got my hundred caps, and I've retired from international rugby. Nothing against you, *butt*, but I might as well not be on the fucking field these days. I touch the ball maybe three or four times a game. I'm training like crazy six days a week to not even break sweat. The sport has changed around me. Everyone is kicking the ball away, constantly. All I do is just chase, like a dog running after a stick.' That drew a wry smile. Dai gave me his blessing, but warned it would not be an easy ride.

Rugby union is a game ruled by the laws, even though I've never claimed to know all of them, as they're complex and ever-changing. I learned – the hard way – that rugby league is a game ruled by the game. If you master the laws of rugby union you can be a good player, but to excel in rugby league, you have to be able to play. It is not as simple as it looks.

Though professionalism has broken down barriers, there are still those in either code who want to fight battles that have already been won. Union snobs caricature league as crude and one-dimensional. League's class warriors remain enraged by injustices from another generation, when players were banned for playing the 13-man code. In an age in which the supply lines between the codes are well established, such attitudes don't make a lot of sense. Quite simply, both are brilliant sports.

I knew some were desperate for me to fail, because of my rugby union background rather than my sexuality, but I had bigger things to worry about at the Crusaders than outdated prejudice – like surviving my first training session. I had never, in all my union career, been as physically shattered as I was by my first fitness test in league. It was horrendous. I threw up several times before I reached the point of no return. That's when you've run so hard, and for so long, that you are too tired to control your stomach muscles. There's a real and ever-present danger of shitting yourself.

Nothing prepared me for that. I thought I was a decent specimen – I'd done my time in the gym, and prided myself on my resilience as a professional athlete, but I had nothing left to give. My cosy theory that I'd train for a week to get up to speed before my Crusaders debut was hopelessly unrealistic. These boys were something else. They occasionally drank like demons – I was told to expect three-day benders at convenient stages in the season – but they did their work.

At the end of the first week there was no way I was ready to play. We staged a mock game and I was gasping for breath within minutes. I knew I had to take drastic measures. For the next week, I trained really hard in the morning, lapsed into a coma for a couple of hours in the afternoon, and then spent the evening in the gym. Athletes are proud people who don't respond well to confirmation of weakness. I didn't tell anyone what I was up to, because proving I was fit for purpose was a deeply personal process.

The intensity of league is constant and unforgiving. I tried to recreate game situations by doing intervals on a running machine. Twenty repetitions, 30 seconds on, 30 seconds off, got the heart rate up. I augmented that exercise by doing more squat thrusts than I could count. The sports scientist would probably have had kittens, but I know my own body. When I train hard, and focus on recovery, I can build my fitness really quickly. I can live with the tiredness, the burning legs and the acidic stomach.

The parallel challenge, in league, is dealing with its technical and physical demands while someone is trying to do you harm. The violent intent is more potent because of its subtlety. Watching on television, where the play-the-ball process looks relatively simple, only reveals a fraction of the picture. Tackling, and the subsequent sequence of what looks like choreographed scuffling, is a black art that literally takes the breath away.

The initial tackler envelops you and tries to strip you of the ball. He and his mates then make a couple of seconds on the ground feel like an eternity. It's a dangerous place in which to linger. They try to turn your body the wrong way, to wrestle you onto your back to delay recycling of possession. They wrench your head sideways to further disorientate you, and pin you down to ensure you are never first to your feet.

All that is pretty easy to spot, with a modicum of understanding of the game. The more insidious things are not as simple to detect. Tacklers use martial arts techniques to squeeze the life out of you, applying pressure up and under your rib cage. They pinch you under the armpits, and on the temple. I thought the scrum in union was evil, but in league they think nothing of sticking their fingers in your eye, or giving you the sort of physical examination that prompts doctors to don a rubber glove. It's savage stuff.

I was trying to forget everything I had learned in nearly 30 years of playing union, where my thought process was to draw the tackle and, if caught, turn my body on the ground so that I could feed the ball back to supporting teammates. Train as you play is one of the great maxims in sport, so I had to endure multiple moments of truth, where my brain and my body were often at odds.

My teammates knew the only way to prepare me for the nefarious antics of opposition tacklers was to give me a taste of what they would do, but under controlled circumstances. They were gentle with me in training, but only up to a point. It was obvious I had a lot to learn, and little time in which to do so.

My debut was a fait accompli. The club, understandably, wanted to cash in on the interest stimulated by my signing. I'd had a fortnight's training, and we were due to play the French team, Catalan Dragons, live on Sky, in front of a big Friday night crowd at Wrexham. They were a serious unit – big lads with a reputation for getting their retaliation in first. The script had been written, and it was my job to ensure it wasn't a comedy. Some hope.

Foolishly, I couldn't resist a look at the fan forums, to gauge the mood. The following post, submitted by the appropriately named Mr Badvibes, summed it up rather well: 'He will be in hospital before the month is out. He's 35, which is too old for RL. No disrespect to a man who has served Welsh Union with distinction, but he's way out of his league (no pun intended).'

I have a great affinity with North Wales. It is quiet and unprepossessing; I love the landscape and the down-to-earth nature of its inhabitants. My rugby academies, which are designed to pass on my skills and experience to the next generation, flourish there, and I consciously choose to try to balance the geographical bias towards the south. The locals turned up at the Racecourse Ground with balloons and banners on a wet March night, ready to acclaim me as a hero.

I've long since forgiven the critic who concluded my debut was worthy of an episode of *Only Fools and Horses*. He had a point. I came in off the right wing for my first carry from dummy half, less than 30 seconds into the match, and suddenly felt like I'd been hit by a truck. I learned later that the initial tackler took my legs, the second assailant wrestled me to the ground, and the third elbowed me in the face on the way down. So much for the *Entente Cordiale*.

I lost consciousness for a split second, and though I struggled to my feet, my vision was blurred and my legs had the consistency of softly whipped ice cream. I was hopelessly uncoordinated and dropped the ball at my feet. The farce was compounded because I happened to be facing the wrong way at the time, towards my teammates. They knew, better than I, just how much trouble I was in. I was a space cadet.

I wouldn't do the sensible thing, and allow myself to be helped off after my first touch of the ball. Concussion is one of the preoccupations of modern rugby, but instinct ordered me not to succumb. The commentators would have had a field day.

The reputation I had worked so hard to develop in union would have been shredded. I would have spent my life as the subject of one of those Bateman cartoons: The Weakling Who Tried Rugby League. I had to continue to put myself in harm's way, like a crash-test dummy.

I ran into a succession of brick walls, disguised as defenders who loved the taste of fresh meat. Inevitably, after another heavy tackle, I left the field arm-in-arm with the doctor and the physio. The 'Gay Rugby Icon' who had featured in the pre-match advertising had lasted less than half an hour – he was now a spectator who would need a scan the following day.

I felt empty as I sat hunched on the bench, underneath the hood of an unzipped waterproof jacket. My self-esteem had taken a huge hit. I thought I had let everybody down. In retrospect, though, it was the best thing that could have happened, because it literally knocked me into shape. Had it been one of those schoolboy fantasy evenings, featuring a hat-trick of tries and Man of the Match champagne, I could so easily have been influenced by premature perceptions of my status as a marquee player.

Brian Noble, the coach, was brilliant. He praised my application, made diplomatic noises about my need to better protect the ball in the tackle, and kept a sense of proportion. We won the game 14–6, but the response from my teammates meant more than the win bonus. They had seen I was willing to give it a shot; they understood I didn't have a clue about what was going on around me, but gave me professional credit for hanging in there for as long as possible.

There was, though, a pink elephant in the room. My team-mates had been coy, unsure how to react. It wasn't until my debut was out of the way that anyone felt confident to use the 'G' word.

One morning our captain, Ryan O'Hara, a top bloke with an Aussie's subtlety, was holding court with seven of us in the treatment room, when he suddenly blurted out, 'Hey, what about that Ricky Martin coming out as being gay in the papers?'

I could see glances being exchanged as an awkward silence descended. A taboo subject had been raised. Someone dived in and asked, 'Are we doing rugby this afternoon?' It was a well-intentioned intervention but the purpose of such a banal, rushed question was obvious. I understood, as well as anyone, that it contravened the code of raw honesty that operates in and around the treatment benches and physio equipment. I felt so uncomfortable I slipped away as soon as I could, without giving offence.

It was perverse. The guys were unintentionally unsettling me because they respected me. No one wanted to mention my sexuality until I broached it, and I was hardly going to walk into the changing rooms and announce: 'Ta da, boys! Here I am and by the way I'm gay! Let's talk about it.' There was a barrier between us, because they were desperate not to offend.

Ryan was obviously mortified, and took it upon himself to redress the balance over a beer. The boys were up for a few slurps, and we were sitting around a group of tables. 'Mate,' he asked me, just loud enough to command the group's attention, 'obviously the guys know you've come out. Are you OK with us talking about it, or even saying the word gay?'

I let out a whoop: 'Halle-fucking-lujah!', which certainly got the barman's attention. 'Boys,' I said. 'I respect the way you've handled this. It's OK. You can talk about it. We talk about everything else, don't we? You can take the piss. I'm cool with that. Treat me like you'd treat any teammate.'

It was one of the shortest, most important speeches of my life. Judging by the way it stimulated the audience's thirst, it seemed to go down well. Rugby league boys call a session 'going hard'. I worked out why the next day, when my aching head reminded me that I'm a lightweight drinker.

They cared. Not in an extravagant way, for show, but in an understated manner. Just as I had come to terms with the curiosity and compassion of my Cardiff teammates, I became used to my new teammates at Crusaders coming up in quiet moments, and asking how I was coping. They couldn't have realised how valuable it was that my life had become a talking point. By sharing my experiences and emotions, almost on a daily basis, I was able to get so much off my chest. Without knowing it, they had granted me freedom.

My invitation to extract the proverbial was quickly taken up: Nick Youngquest and I were christened 'the girls'. Nick, another Aussie, has become one of the world's leading male models, operating out of New York, where he lives with his American wife, Mira. He's become a leading campaigner for LGBT rights, most vocally on same-sex marriage. He was dabbling as a part-time model when he joined Crusaders and, having posed nude for a players' calendar in aid of breast cancer awareness in Australia, he developed a big following in the gay community.

The boys ripped into him, warning him to be worried by the competition I was providing in the thinking-man's crumpet stakes. It was silly, harmless, brilliant fun. We played up to it, posing shirtless in the dressing room with our arms around one another's shoulders. The photo went viral, but told only half the story. Nick is straight, but intrigued by the instinctive nature of disrespect shown towards gay men.

We had some deep conversations on the bus to and from matches. I could see them shaping his thoughts. His views on same-sex marriage – 'It should be a union of two people in love, why not?' – coincide with mine. Since there are no barriers in functional teams, I found myself having similar chats with other Crusaders players. Some of them were prurient – 'Where do you go to pick up guys?' was a common question – but most dwelled on the human dimension to the issue of acceptance.

I genuinely believe those who joined in the chant, on that day in the Jungle, are not necessarily bad people. Easily led, perhaps; ill-educated, almost certainly. But I never experienced anything like that again in rugby league. I was wolf-whistled when I played at Hull Kingston Rovers, where one fan shouted, 'Thomas, you're gay.' I burst out laughing, because it sounded like something out of the school playground. Was that really his best shot? Was it the worst slur he could throw at me? Give me a break, *butt*. That was too immature to be an insult.

'I know I am,' I shouted back. That seemed to end the debate.

I felt strong. I had accepted who I was. I had faced the unknown, and refused to back down. I've always prided myself in my self-sufficiency, and my inner peace signalled that I had passed the ultimate test. The vast majority of fans were on my side, instead of being on my case. The guys around me finally knew the real Gareth Thomas. I was the mate who would put the hard yards in, rather than the soft, simpering stereotype they were conditioned to fear in the shower.

In hindsight, it was good that I lived away from my family and friends in the hotel at that time. I missed them terribly, but drew strength from my isolation. The best and biggest challenges are overcome on your own. I had done with deceit; I no longer had the inclination to hide. I was an open book. Satisfying the understandable curiosity of my teammates was another indication of normality.

I was learning so much about myself, because I was obliged to explore. I began to consider what I truly wanted from life. This may sound weird, but I suddenly understood how an astronaut feels on a spacewalk. They speak of feeling utterly alone out there in the vacuum of space, but feel uniquely connected with Earth revolving away below them. They can't indulge themselves, because there is important work to be done before they return to the mother ship.

I had been given the gift of clarity and honesty. I was able to rationalise my ambitions, personally as much as professionally. Did I want to find love, and settle down in a picket-fenced paradise? Or did I want to take advantage of my profile and availability, and go crazy for a couple of years? I was the master of my own destiny, after being afraid of my own shadow for far, far too long.

Fate, though, was to provide a devilish twist. Nick Youngquest's prowess, as a brave, fast winger, got him a move at the end of the season … to Castleford Tigers. He scored 29 tries in 40 matches for them before retirement. Karma demanded that his most memorable game was to be against the Crusaders, in March 2011. It was not the most straightforward of occasions, given the nature of our individual stories.

Castleford, to their eternal credit and my enduring gratitude, had responded impeccably to the previous season's problems, and were at pains to make my return there for a match a positive experience. It was designated a family day, designed to enshrine the RFL's Respect campaign. Advertising hoardings and a succession of public announcements championed the cause of equality and understanding, and I was made to feel hugely welcome – until the match kicked off.

Cue carnage. Most of the controversy swirled around Nick, who had left Crusaders in bitter circumstances: he had complained of not having been paid for the final two months of his season in North Wales. Frustration had spilled out into social media, where he had used his Twitter feed to question the professionalism of some of his former teammates.

We were, in essence, a new team, but tribal loyalties had been offended. The mass brawl that erupted 17 minutes into the match was an inevitable purging of the soul. It was sparked by Crusaders half-back, Michael Witt, another Aussie import who had – ironically – also posed nude with Nick on that NRL calendar. He punched the Castleford full-back, Richie Mathers, who had objected to being tackled dangerously when he was on one leg having taken a high ball. Witt was sent to the sin bin along with Vince Mellars, our Kiwi centre and also Nick, who had shown an impressive turn of speed in rushing to get involved in the handbag swinging.

We were all over the place. Clinton Schifcofske, our new captain, was also sent to the sin bin for attempting to slow the pace of the game by tossing a spare ball onto the pitch. We were 22–0 down at half time, and Nick evidently enjoyed scoring one of six more tries run in by the Tigers during the second half.

The crowd were generous towards me, but let's just say this final sentence, from a match report in the *Guardian*, was uncannily accurate: 'Despite the warm welcome he received on his return to this atmospheric old ground, Alfie, who turns 37 in July, will be relieved that he may never again have to play in Castleford.'

I had been conscripted into the second row because we had run out of serviceable players. We lost 56–16, and I was too tired to care.

Chapter Fifteen

A MEMORY

The end effectively came at just after 4.15 p.m. on Saturday, 9 July 2011, at the Racecourse Ground in Wrexham. It was a warm afternoon, softened by a rain shower soon after half-time. A crowd of 2,820 were watching Crusaders' seventh successive defeat.

I threw myself into a tackle on Australian second-row forward, Ben Galea, who was in the process of scoring three tries in Hull Kingston Rovers' 38–10 victory. He saw me coming, and dropped to one knee in an entirely unexpected submissive gesture.

Though his progress had been stalled, it was my job to ensure he didn't get up in a hurry. My left arm was extended, and made heavy contact with the top of his skull. I rolled slowly away from him and thought nothing of the occupational hazard – a sudden burst of pain. It was only when it grew in intensity, and developed into a deep, relentless ache that I realised something was amiss.

There were about 20 minutes left. I was one of the few senior players in a team stripped of seven regulars, who were serving a one-match club suspension for 'going hard', or breaking curfew, to use the more formal term.

My instinct was to slink off, to save myself. The risk of sustaining further damage was too great. But the home truths, first relayed to me as a boy at Pencoed, kicked in. We had no more bodies to throw into the breach. Three of the guys were part-time players, recruited from the South Wales Scorpions on an emergency basis. We were being talked about as Super League's worst team. It was daft, but I resolved to hang around for as long as I could. No guts, no glory.

An X-ray, taken immediately after the game, confirmed the arm was broken. I made optimistic noises about making the final match of the season, against Wigan in early September, but suspected the Four Nations tournament in the autumn was a more realistic target. I had signed a contract extension with Crusaders covering the 2012 season, but the situation at the club was bleak. The wages were already late.

The attempt to establish a community-focused Super League club in North Wales expired 18 days later. Iestyn Harris, the former dual-code international who was Wales and Crusaders coach, called a team meeting at training. He warned us to expect an imminent announcement that the club were withdrawing their licence and pulling out of Super League for the following season.

Logically, it made sense. Crowds were declining and results were poor. The business plan didn't stack up. We had already resolved to play without guarantee of payment for two matches but, emotionally, it was a huge blow. A league table doesn't chart friendships formed in the heat of battle; a balance sheet cannot hope to record the intrinsic value of loyalty to a collective cause.

Those are the sorts of days when the realities of professional sport become onerous and forbidding. I could see my teammates drifting off mentally, preparing themselves for private scenarios laced with anxiety. They all had bills to pay, families to support. The collapse of a club might be a public spectacle, but the most affecting dramas are played out behind closed doors. That first phone call home is a uniformly wretched experience. You want to sweeten the pill, but know it is laced with cyanide.

In the short term, the players resolved to see out the final five games of the season. The uninitiated might struggle to understand that, but the team ethic is bombproof. We got on well as a group of human beings. Our characters were disparate and our backgrounds diverse, but we were rugby men with a shared faith in the shield of unity in adversity. We were survivors, eking out a fragile existence. We would stand up for one another, and give the fans their money's worth.

Inevitably, there was a sense of betrayal. I was in plaster, but had agreed to alleviate the boredom of rehabilitation by doing some community coaching sessions. Seeing the unrequited enthusiasm of the boys recruited from local schools took me back to the Ogmore Valley, and the contracting communities that could offer their young no future. Now, another set of boys would be denied an outlet for their dream, a chance to represent their people.

The situation became increasingly complicated when it transpired our insurance premiums had not been paid. I was without medical cover, and my arm was taking longer than expected to heal. The RFL, to their credit, offered to help, but everything pointed towards cutting my losses and walking away from a sport I had come to love.

It's the hardest game. If I'm generous, I made an average of about five carries and four tackles in a high-quality union match, such as an international or a Heineken Cup tie; in a Super League game, I'd be aiming to attempt 25 runs and make around 30 tackles. The body takes a more complete pummelling. I was 37 and thought, 'Enough is enough.'

The problem was that to protect myself, I had to let my country down. It's an understatement to say that didn't sit easily with me. I took fantastic pride from the four Welsh caps I won in league, during a hectic spell in October 2010. I scored our try in a 13–6 loss to Italy on my debut, a warm-up match before the European Cup series.

I scored one of the 11 tries we ran in during an opening 60–22 victory over Scotland, and after squeezing past Ireland 31–30, we faced a winner-takes-all match against France, the hosts and favourites, before a capacity crowd in Albi. The prize, a place in the 2011 Four Nations against England, Australia and New Zealand, represented a momentous opportunity.

This chance to play against the sport's dominant nations was complemented by an honour I never considered possible: Iestyn asked me to captain my country for one more time, because of an injury sustained by Lee Briers, the usual skipper.

The city of Albi, in the Tarn region, is a rugby hotbed, in both codes. The raucous, colourful crowd in the Stade Municipal reminded me of some fabled afternoons 60 miles away along the A68 motorway, in Toulouse.

I may have been the new boy, but the old instincts kicked in. Lessons learned on the Devil's Chair were recounted, and I asked those around me to stand up and be counted.

Though I put us ahead by completing a four-man passing move on the hour, France were leading 11–10 with four minutes remaining before Lloyd White, my Crusaders teammate, ignored a cascade of booing to convert the winning penalty from 40 metres. It was an inspirational demonstration of nerve, which went a long way to earning him a move to Widnes, and the Wales Player of the Year award. Lloyd deserved individual recognition, but collective pride in the shirt pulled us through.

Afterwards, the dressing room was its usual cross between a party tent and an accident and emergency department. Joy shone from scarred faces, florid through exertion. We replayed snippets of the game in the sporting equivalent of a post-coital glow. I told anyone who would listen that this compensated for one of the biggest disappointments of my career, that of being eliminated from the 2007 Rugby Union World Cup by Fiji in Nantes, in my final game for Wales.

These boys were not household names. They were honest, hard-working pros. There would be no welcoming committee at Cardiff airport, no herograms from dignitaries or lavish praise spread across the sports supplements. The Welsh papers barely bothered to give credit where it was massively due. But we didn't need external confirmation of what we had achieved. We knew. My subsequent dilemma was fiendishly difficult, but the choice was fairly simple: play in the Four Nations, against the biggest teams, with a weak arm, or accept that no mercy would be shown and there was every chance of sustaining long-term damage. I spoke to my parents, and tried hard not to listen too intently to my heart. I missed a warm-up match against Ireland because I was uncertain of what to do, and appreciated I owed the lads and the coaching staff an honest decision.

It was too messy. On 25 October 2011, four days before the tournament was due to begin, I announced my immediate retirement from all forms of rugby. If I couldn't guarantee giving 100 per cent, I'd be a danger to myself and a liability to my teammates. I thanked my family and friends, and walked off into the mists, like a second-rate Humphrey Bogart. Here's looking at you, kids.

Iestyn issued a statement that read: 'I've worked with Gareth for just under two years and the work and desire that he put into his transition from union to league was testament to his supreme professionalism. Even though he switched at a mature age, his enthusiasm for information made his switch a huge success. Gareth's honesty and reasoning behind his decision were unselfish. It would have been easy for him to play the Wales internationals for his personal gain, but he didn't want to take an opportunity off somebody else in our squad.'

A newly retired athlete stumbles into a vacuum of sudden indifference and unfamiliar ignorance. There are two elements of paying for the privilege of playing professional sport, as the physical aspects are suddenly matched by the mental challenge of rationalising the fact that you can no longer define yourself by your commitment to your craft. Focus shifts, and many stumble.

Your career remains with you, of course. It's almost an extra body part. People become accustomed to sharing your life, so it is natural that they should remain curious. I'm often asked to describe my greatest achievement; there's an understand-able yearning to know what it feels like to win a Grand Slam or a European Cup. Sport stimulates the imagination, so it is reasonable for a supporter to wonder about what goes through your mind when the anthem strikes up before an international. They'd give everything to be standing alongside you.

I worry about being regarded as a bit of a fraud when I admit that, in moments of supreme achievement, I felt numb. I didn't feel anything because I was just doing my job. As a player you are programmed to concentrate on the next challenge, rather than what you have just achieved. There's no time to bask in the spotlight. It's only retirement that eases that restriction because you have earned the right to indulge yourself, and channel the emotions of the day.

GARETH THOMAS

It was not until very recently that I took time to sift through the mementoes of my career, which have been stored, lovingly, by my mother. It was a surreal version of the Christmas morning ritual of opening my presents when I was young: I had a good idea of what I was about to see, but couldn't be certain. Little things stood out: the ornate stitching on my collection of caps, and the slightly musty smell of my first Wales shirt when I took it from a pile and unfolded it gently, as if it would disintegrate under my clumsy touch.

I looked at it and thought, 'Fucking hell.' Nearly 20 years gone in an instant. All those games, and all that heartbreak, that lay ahead. I didn't know it at the time, but that jersey was my chainmail on the day I came of age as a rugby player. My forefathers were watching over me. People were telling me what playing for Wales meant, but I didn't have the emotional maturity to understand. It is only now, when the pipe and slippers are out, metaphorically, that the truth manifests itself. Enjoy it while you can.

I would have liked to have been given a formal opportunity to pass on my knowledge, but in Wales we have a bad habit of turning leading players into ghosts of the game. I look back at some of the stellar players I've played with, or been captained by: Scott Gibbs, Scott Quinnell, Garin Jenkins, Robert Jones, Mike Hall, Ieuan Evans; hard men, distinctive characters, all essentially lost to the game in the hospitality lounge or the commentary booth.

They endured. They mattered. They proved themselves worthy of the term 'great'. A great player, to me, is someone who is willing to stand at the head of the line when the shit is down. That's when the pretenders are found out. They think they can find subtle ways to burrow their way out of trouble but they can't. The boys who've been there, the boys who've done the knowledge, *know*. They just know.

Occasionally, fate blindsides you and sport is put into proper perspective. One such moment came before Wales's defeat by South Africa in Cardiff in November 2013, when I renewed acquaintances with Joost van der Westhuizen. As a player he embodied the culturally ingrained arrogance of the Springboks; as a man suffering from a terminal motor neurone disease characterised by slurred speech, breathing problems and creeping paralysis, he redefined heroism.

He was barely intelligible, but amazingly expressive. It was difficult to reconcile this physically diminished, spiritually dynamic human being with the scrum-half who once stood over me, when I had missed a tackle, and boasted: 'I am fucking better than you.' He brought a boxer's mentality to the Test match arena; his aggression was barely refined and he loved to dominate. Now he was in a wheelchair.

Joost wanted no one's pity. He had a haunting serenity. 'I've got no financial worries now because I don't need money for anything,' he told me, slowly and deliberately. 'I can't walk anywhere. I can't really do anything. Other people are worrying about me, but I've got fewer worries than I've ever had. I'm just getting on with whatever life I've got left. You're the one walking around, but inside your head you've probably got more worries than me.'

He was right, even though I was not one of those who stopped playing and suddenly wondered, 'Who am I?' My self-awareness, though painfully acquired, was sharp. Having made the transition to supposedly normal life, I can relate to the decidedly minor problem of people identifying me with something other than rugby. I've had to come to terms with a younger, broader generation knowing me more for my involvement in projects like *Big Brother* and *Dancing on Ice*. That's strange, since I gave infinitely more of myself to my sport, but understandable given the power of television.

It's crazy shit, television, and it can create freaks. I had no identity crisis to deal with. I was pretty secure in myself, because I wasn't going through a mourning process for my sporting career, which had reached a natural conclusion. Some of the people around me in the *Big Brother* house didn't have that certainty. They wanted something, but couldn't define what it was. They loved the idea of fame, but didn't have a clue what it entailed. They were lost in space. I kept my head down to be honest. It seemed to work because I finished third, and I was deemed to be a popular participant.

When I'm out in the supermarket these days, I'm just as likely to get stopped in the aisle and asked about *Dancing on Ice*. I found it a release. I loved the ritual of getting up before dawn, and travelling to the rink before the world awoke. I fell over three times a day, at least. My hips, in particular, became painful and swollen. I was bruised from shoulder to toe, because I was determined not to be timid. I rejected the chance to wear padding, to get the most out of the experience.

It was like learning another body language. Skating is a technical sport, which leaves me physically shattered and mentally stretched. It is the opposite of rugby, where if you mess up, you can let the anger out by being confrontational. It demands the same type of commitment, but you must remain patient, graceful and in control of your emotions. Sod's law being as it is, I was eventually beaten in week eight by a form of motion sickness; I'm no Superman when asked to fly through the air with the greatest of ease. That meant I had to drop out of the series; I felt for Robin Johnstone, my professional partner, because we gelled so well, and were considered to be one of the best pairs.

The world of a newly retired sportsman is tipped off its axis. You reach a plateau in your life, and fear that decline is inevitable. It grates that the career trajectories of your mates are still on an upward curve. They have the comfort of relative certainty and well-established ambition. You are adrift, and find yourself struggling to have a relevant conversation with them. In life's game of snakes and ladders, you have slipped from 99 to 1.

I was fortunate in that coming out partially prepared me for the mourning process, but it was still a shock to the system. Most immediately, you miss the adrenaline rush of competition, the endorphin high of conquering yourself. More profoundly, you miss what you once considered the mundane rituals of athletic life. You yearn for the alarm call which summons you to training. You fret about filling your day. You search for that elusive buzz, which you once took for granted. You look for a reason to get out of bed.

There's a sense of nothingness, and it is easy to be sucked into the void. Two former Wales teammates have had nervous breakdowns because they failed to come to terms with the sudden sense of inadequacy. It wouldn't be fair to name them, but they each have a handful of caps. They gave everything of themselves to their rugby, sacrificed their time and their bodies without becoming household names. They are fine men, who have admirable values, ethics and principles, but the world outside sport sees them as somehow less worthy.

They have been treated terribly, as nobodies, because they don't have the protection of instant recognition. The brutality of potential employers can be remarkable. One thought it was entirely logical, and perfectly acceptable within the boundaries of the workplace, to dismiss one of my former international teammates with the words: 'I don't really know who you are. If I don't know you, my customers aren't going to, either. What use are you to my business?'

Allow that to sink in for a second. Then consider this: what would your life feel like if it changed overnight? What would that sort of rejection do to your self-esteem? All the old certainties are gone. One day you have everyone's undivided attention, the telephone never stops ringing and you are nestled comfortably at the centre of the universe. The next day you are an afterthought; no one calls, and you are left to fend for yourself. You have to swallow your pride and get out there, knocking on people's doors.

Your value was as a professional athlete, not an institution-alised individual in early middle age. It is rather like being a teenager again. You have to lower your sights and accept you have to work your way up from the bottom. The problem is you have adult responsibilities: the need to pay for food, family and a roof over your head. The knowledge that the money you have saved from your career will not last for ever gnaws away at you.

My initial instinct was to train harder than I had ever done. I would push myself through punishing sessions in the gym twice or even three times a day. That might seem purposeless, because I had no realistic outlet for my fitness other than to look and feel good, but it retained my link with what I had come to regard as a normal life. I felt I had to maintain the mindset of a professional sportsman, as an emotional bridgehead. My satis-faction came in the familiarity of the pain, and the fulfilment of achieving private targets.

I have been lucky. Physically, I do not face the ordeal of former teammates who are much worse off than I. Those who have gone through knee reconstruction surgery find temporary relief before the onset of premature arthritis in the joints. Weakness ambushes you: several of my mates have suffered a dislocated shoulder simply from rolling over in bed. I sleep well, but my back has taken a bit of a bashing. I have to sit for regular periods, and can't walk around for more than half an hour without taking a break. I'm not like many, though, who live on anti-inflamma-tory tablets.

Psychologically, the world is a scary place. Rugby, like all sports, is a closely knit environment. Suddenly, no one has your back. I can understand why so many seek to renew the bonds, by entering coaching or other related disciplines, such as strength and conditioning training. I didn't feel lonely, because I'd rationalised that emotion, but I did feel that part of me was missing. I was incomplete. I had to come to terms with those dreaded words of 'former' and 'ex'.

I felt the presence of spectres, mates who were usually to the right and left of me on the rugby field. I could no longer afford to be sceptical about the significance of the huddle, because I was no longer in that sacred circle. I had left a space in the dressing room that had been taken immediately by someone else. The world had moved on without me. I was a memory.

It took me two years to wean myself off the game. I resolved to train my brain in the way I used to prepare my body. I learned to challenge myself in a new way, using deeply ingrained instincts. I'm still massively ambitious, but in a different context. Now, I put as much into my commercial projects or charitable initiatives as I did into my rugby. I seek out best practice, look for marginal advantage and leave nothing to chance. I duplicate the dedica-tion that made me a decent rugby player to become a better, more effective individual than my rivals.

This book completes the process of tying up the loose ends of my life. My old teachers will be amazed to discover that, to do so, I drew inspiration from William Shakespeare. He had a way with words, which never quite managed to pierce my consciousness as a stroppy schoolboy. Having come through a period in my life when I questioned everything about myself and tested those closest to me, his definition of a friend as someone, 'that knows you as you are, understands where you have been, accepts what you have become, and still gently, allows you to grow' strikes a chord.

It is only since I retired, and have become more comfortable in my own skin, that I've been able to appreciate I'm blessed. But for my own peace of mind, I wanted the perspective of Compo Greenslade and Glen Webbe, my closest friends. I needed to know what they knew and thought during all that time that I was in denial.

We met up in a quiet corner of a pub in Cardiff to reminisce and ponder the meaning of life, on a bright winter's afternoon in early 2014. I've found over the years that the best way of sharing their wisdom is to let them speak for themselves as often as possible.

Glen, typically, cut to the chase once the drinks were in: 'I'm just thinking about you coming out, Alf,' he said. 'You reach a point in your story where everyone can relate to it because it is just like being bullied. When you are growing up, it seems so important to protect your reputation and keep your name. You don't want to go to school, because you know the bully will be waiting at the gate. You don't want a packed lunch because you know he will steal it from you. When you get home, and your parents want to know why you are so subdued, you say nothing. But you're thinking, "He's going to get me, he's going to get me."

'Eventually, he finds out where you live. You're thinking, "Right, it's five o'clock, I've escaped him again," but when you get home, the bully's there. He gets hold of you and punches you right in the face. Whack. It hurts, and you ask him, "Are you going to get me again tomorrow?" He says, "No, I've punched you now." You think, "That's it?" It's over. It's done. You had built it up into the worst thing in the world. When it happens you deal with the pain, walk away, and go live the rest of your life. You've taken off the overcoat of fear.'

Compo reinforced the point, in a seamless manner that underlined just how tight the emotional bonds are between us: 'Fear is pretty pointless. You worry so much that it really gets to you, but even if the worst happens, it's usually just an anti-climax. It helps that rugby allows you to know a man as he really is. Nobody wants to be on the outside, when it comes to rugby. So people who haven't played at the top end of the sport think that internationals are great men, with great lives. But it's a front. We know they aren't different. We understand their lives aren't necessarily great.

'They're normal people, with everyday problems and anxieties. They're either good at what they do, or have people around them, teammates, who make them look good. Ultimately, they're no different to someone walking down the road, the bloke who plays on the parks on a Saturday. Where rugby makes things special is the set of rules we follow, on and off the paddock. The code of respect is huge. It's changed a bit, mind. When we were young boys, what went on, on tour, stayed on tour. Now what goes on, on tour, goes on Facebook. It is home before you, isn't it?'

Glen's knowing laughter prompted drinkers on the other side of the bar to look away from the TV in the corner, which was droning out the daily digest of sports news. He has been close to Compo since persuading him to leave Cardiff for Bridgend back in the day, and it is fair to say that they have closed a fair few pubs in their time. They are rugby's Yin and Yang, the prop and the wing who somehow hit it off.

'The rugby animal doesn't change,' Glen continued. 'When you meet someone who plays the game, you've got something in common. It doesn't matter that you've never met them before. It doesn't matter what level you play at, or where you are from. You just talk about the rugby. I think what makes our game unique is that, as in life, it takes all sorts. Front-row forwards when we were kids all used to look the same: they were big, fat and dirty. They couldn't do anything else. You had those little racer things on the wing. They couldn't do anything else, either. But you'd hoof them the ball and they'd do the job. Although the wings and the props were different people, they were there to achieve a common goal.

'The team thing just works. You're playing together to achieve, to get on – to win. And I think that's what makes the game of rugby so appealing. It's like life. We've all got to get on, haven't we? That's what makes it work for me, without taking it too serious, like. I remember I was once up by Gwent, and got talking with this guy. It turns out he's a leading surgeon, saving lives, doing operations. And he played rugby as well. I asked who he played for and he said Aberavon thirds. He's boasting about saving lives and saving the world and he only played for Aberavon thirds? Pah, what's special about that?'

Don't take him seriously. He was acting as a light-hearted spokesman for the Brotherhood. When you retire, you miss the little things about the big occasions. Compo spoke evocatively about running out with me and Glen, smelling the cigarette smoke rising from the densely packed crowd, and feeling the ground vibrate when supporters shifted and swayed in unison. Everything magnified by the tribal undercurrents; everything in its proper place. Instead of a schedule shaped by the whims of the TV schedulers, the week revolved around matches on Wednesday at 7 p.m. and Saturday at 3 p.m. Those days will never return.

There was a darker side to the game, though. I asked Glen, for the first time, about the experience of having bananas thrown at him in a match against Maesteg. 'It was odd,' he said, with a tranquility which surprised me. 'I used to hide behind humour. I'd laugh at it, to make it trivial. Verbal insults will never bother me. If they lay a hand on me, well, then that's something different. But if you change the way you think it defuses everything. I know what I'm feeling. I know what I'm thinking. You don't. That gives me an advantage.

'Remember, we were only seven or eight miles away from Bridgend. The better players from Maesteg seemed to migrate to Bridgend and the people who couldn't quite make the grade at Bridgend would just go the other way. In those days there was one band, 19 teams and that was it. No relegation, no promotion, just first-class rugby. The proximity made it even more of a derby. Everybody there had an axe to grind. They hated Bridgend, and I didn't like playing up there, anyway. It was cold, and I really couldn't stand the place.

'That's why I identify with you, Alf. An insult is something to be aimed, like any missile. If it is thrown at you because you are different, and you let on that it has hit its target, you're the loser. If you don't get upset or affected by it, well, they've missed the target, haven't they? They've failed. Every time they've tried to offend me by saying things, or doing things, I try to show that it really doesn't affect me. If they can see that they've failed to wind me up, they know they aren't going to get anywhere. And you can see they hate it.

'Why do they do it, though? Why? It affects other people around them, rather than the person they're aiming at. So, if anything, I get concerned about the people around the bloke who's saying, "You black bastard".' I see them squirming. I'm feeling embarrassed for everyone – not for me, because I give as good as I get most of the time. It's like Sally, my wife, being in the crowd. She is white, and some people have said things, and they've not known she's my wife. And she'll say, "I'm married to him. You can't say things like that." Then they say they're sorry.

Does that make it all right? Does it make them not feel that way any more? No.'

He was unwittingly expounding on one of the truths of my own life. In my experience, if you confront someone expressing prejudice, whether it is racist, homophobic or anything similarly offensive or irrational, they simply clam up. They lack either the intellect or the courage to justify their beliefs and feelings. They are belittled by their ignorance. Education is the key to everything.

Glen's logic, in resisting invitations to be involved in formal anti-racism campaigns, is challenging, yet revealing: 'I won't because you can't make people feel a certain way just because it's the law. All it will do is send it underground, where it will be recycled in what they consider to be safer circles. Can you really legislate against hate? It's irrational. Normally it's passed down the generations, from parents to sons and daughters. You learn to be racist, you learn to be sexist, you learn to be homophobic.'

This was my chance to have one of my few outstanding questions answered. This was my chance for closure. I took a deep breath, and asked: 'So, when did you realise I was gay? I knew you were protecting me, but why didn't you say anything?'

Glen was typically thoughtful, and forthright: 'It was such a secret, wasn't it? One that grows. Because you're in the public arena, the bigger that secret got. The more people that knew you, every time you met someone, every time you were in the press, it was getting bigger and bigger, and bigger and bigger. Something had to give.

'Remember at the end of that season, after our last game at Ebbw Vale? We all went out in Cardiff. We went to the Green-down, where there was a meal called the Ultimate Meal. Eat it all, and you had it for free. We polished that off, went around town, and at the end of the night we went to a little bar called Minsky's. It was a gay bar, so all the boys were in there, thinking, "Oh, fucking hell, stick together." It was such a good night. All the drag queens, all the acts, were fantastic. I told Sally about it when I got home. She wanted to go the following Saturday. When we turned up, we looked across the bar, and there you were, having a good night.

'I asked who you were with and you went, "Oh, just mates." I went, "Right, OK," and that was it until the Monday. You know how we'd have a pow-wow in the changing room, and talk about what we'd been up to at the weekend? I was talking to Compo and told him I saw you in the gay bar again. He said, "Alfie? Alfie's gay? He's never said that." So not thinking at all, not knowing, we started doing the rumours thing. You know, starting a whisper to see where it ends up. Someone soon came to us and asked, "Alfie's gay, is he?" We were like, "Don't say anything, don't say anything at all."'

Suddenly, memories began to stir. Strange things, the furtive whispers and unguarded glances I'd notice when I'd walk into a room, or down the street, began to make sense.

Compo took up the tale: 'You'd get the boys in, wanting to have their *craic*. They'd be saying, "Alfie's bent, isn't he? Alfie's bent." The next thing Glen and I know, we're going to watch

Wales together and people in the crowd are pointing you out and are telling us, "He's gay he is, he's gay." And we're going, "This is ridiculous. We've created a monster here. We need to fucking stop this."'

I'm grinning now. I can see the funny side of their dilemma.

'Neither of us had said anything outside the club, but the rumour had legs. It did make me think, though. You were living next door at the time. We were living in each other's pockets, and that's when things weren't ringing true. You were telling me you were at such and such a place, and I'd find out you had been there, but not for the length of time you told me.'

Then he looked at me, with that mischievous smile I knew so well: 'It was my jet-ski that blew your cover.'

'You were desperate to borrow it, with that white Jeep I had. Someone mentioned to me that he'd seen them in a car park near where I trained. I'd seen blokes down there, and knew it was a meeting place for gay fellas. Remember I asked where you'd been that day? You told me you'd been down to the beach at Port Talbot to have a go on the jet-ski. I had a little look that night and licked the propellers. There was no salt water on them at all, nothing. I wasn't going to say anything. It was up to you to say it. I knew what was going on, though. You'd been having a bit of afternoon delight.'

Poirot lives! I was bang to rights in the grand tradition. Glen completed the jigsaw: 'Around that time, because Compo had his suspicions, and I thought it had just got out of hand, I started to say to people, "Look, I know Alfie. There is no way he's gay.

He's just not." Time passed, and then one day Compo came to me, and said, "Alfie wants you to know that he's coming out." I went "Whaaat?" And Compo said, "Yeah, he really has – he's come out to some of the boys."

'It was weird. I'd been worrying about how we were going to get you back in! Race, size, gender, anything at all, people will take the piss in rugby. But nothing changed when I knew your truth, Alf. It wasn't like, *Oh God, all this time you've been lying.* Nothing, nothing like that. I just thought, "OK, well, it's still Alfie. It's still exactly the same bloke I've known all this time." It wasn't about what happens behind closed doors. And because I knew you, and was able to make a first-hand judgement, I began to consider what happens to gay people.

'What did you fear about coming out, then? Was it what people would say or think? I could see how you would be worried about the family, or Jemma. Coming out is a thought process, isn't it? You have to accept where you are, and who you are. So you think about it, and it affects you. You're not going to change everybody, but you can always change yourself. And the only way you can do that is to change the way you think, and make sure you are proud of who you are. That's the way I deal with any shit, really. Just change the way you think about a problem. That's easier to do.'

I can't tell you how good that chat made me feel. I felt secure and loved. I was a man on a mission.

Chapter Sixteen

LEAP OF FAITH

The telephone call ripped my heart out. It was from a footballer, so frightened and depressed he was on the verge of premature retirement. Life without sport to him was not a life, yet he saw no alternative. Listening to him rationalising the loss of something central to his existence, and agonising over the ramifications of surrender to his situation, was a reality check.

He faced the nightmare scenario of sacrificing something to which he had dedicated himself, not because of his inability or lack of professionalism, but because of the cultural and religious connotations of his preferred lifestyle. His faith demonises homosexuality. He was convinced his family would disown him if he came out. I shared his despair and had a sense of dread when the contact between us became more haphazard.

I will be there for him, if required, but understand his reluctance to unleash the hounds of Hell. I do not expect him to come out. It is easier to take cover, suffer self-loathing and sustain the deception. As heartening as it was when such footballers as Thomas Hitzlsperger and Robbie Rogers cited my example when they revealed their sexuality, we are all fortunate compared to my anonymous acquaintance. His plight triggers both guilt and gratitude in me. I veer from optimism that we are on the cusp of profound change, to apprehension.

It is the athletes like him – those who disappear off the radar after calling and contemplating their options – who worry me. I value their trust, protect their identity and comprehend their distress. They consider themselves isolated, pressurised and vulnerable. They lack the luxury of logic and the comfort of certainty. They feel friendless. The world seems forbiddingly bleak and hostile.

Those calls are a privilege to take, because they are a precursor of potential change, but they carry no guarantees. Several of the sportsmen I have counselled on an informal basis have subsequently come out. They remain steadfast friends. Many more have retreated back into the shadows. My faith in them is undiminished.

Every story is so individual but, in essence, it is the same. Coming out is as terrifying as plunging over Niagara Falls in a barrel. There is that same dislocated sense of terror and helplessness. It is a dangerous gamble. You cannot see the crowds watching and waiting, but you are painfully aware of their presence. There is a natural affinity with anyone who survives the ordeal.

I would never climb into someone's head uninvited, because fear is an individual emotion. However quickly we sense the world is changing, and however candid our conversations, fear will never be eliminated. The prospect of public judgement and private remorse is intimidating. I see my role as being a critical friend.

I am a sounding board. I know the unwritten rules of the game from personal experience. When athletes ask for advice, I try to act as a satellite navigation system: if you are at position X on your personal journey to self-expression, I have a good idea of your direction of travel. I know the potential dead ends and diversions.

I try to be a good listener, and get to the crux of the issue. People tell me their story, but tend to find it more healing to cross-reference their story against mine. It's unofficial therapy. I can't give answers, only share experiences. I would never be so presumptuous as to tell anyone when to come out, though I understand why they wish me to do so. They will know when the time is right, if it is right. It is a subtle process, which is rarely quick or straightforward. It can take years, from initial contact to ultimate decision.

Suicidal thoughts are common. Research suggests a gay man is four times more likely to take his own life than his heterosexual equivalent. When someone tells me: 'Do you know what? Life just isn't worth living any more,' I can offer more than saccharine sympathy. I've been there. I've looked into the chasm. I'm not someone in a white coat, a professional counsellor offering coping strategies. I'm a fellow athlete, a similar product of an industry that has an unnerving habit of eating its young.

It's ironic, given that many gay people grow up being told that God hates them, but I occasionally feel like a priest taking confession. The most poignant but satisfying moment usually occurs when I have sent someone down the right path. The conversation goes along the lines of, 'Wow. You said that would happen. Where are we going now?' Trust is established, so I can tell them what to expect next.

Football remains the final frontier for the gay sportsman. Justin Fashanu, the first openly gay player, was a shy, vulnerable man who hanged himself because he could not deal with social rejection and alienation from a game which cherishes its macho culture. The acceptance of other pioneers, like Sweden's Anton Hysen and Robbie Rogers, who has returned to the United States to play for LA Galaxy, is long overdue.

An anonymous poll in May 2014, organised by Stonewall, the leading equality charity, and Football Addicts, a Swedish initiative, asked 30,000 fans in 29 countries if they would be comfortable with a player in their national team coming out as gay.

Scandanavian supporters were the most tolerant, with 79 per cent of respondents in Sweden and Denmark suggesting they would be at ease with such a scenario. Fans in the UK, where 73 per cent were sanguine about being represented by a gay footballer, were markedly more liberal than the Dutch, 65 per cent of whom were fine with the prospect. Fans in Germany (53 per cent) and the United States (52 per cent) were more reactionary.

Progress is being made but what, fundamentally, has changed? I can fully understand the magnitude of a player's dilemma. In a sense, it is harder for someone to be honest now than it was a generation ago, because the game itself is so much bigger. The interest has intensified with the rewards. Footballers are fashion icons, global celebrities and, occasionally, media punch-bags. It is all too easy to become a victim of your own success.

The Football v Homophobia campaign, run by far-sighted volunteers, is an admirable initiative but the fate of the Rainbow Laces campaign mounted by Stonewall is more instructive. Introduced in the right spirit, it seemed to offend corporate sensitivities, and be deemed impertinent by certain clubs, who complained of inadequate warning. Despite strong support from players, most notably Joey Barton, it failed to make an appropriate impact.

Solidarity is the key that can help unlock closed minds. In Australia, the heads of the five main sports – rugby league, rugby union, football, cricket and Aussie Rules – made the unprecedented public statement of combining to support the launch of the 2014 Bingham Cup, the biannual gay world rugby championship. They share a commitment to tackling discrimination based on sexual orientation.

Leaders have an obligation to lead. Cesare Prandelli, who resigned as manager of the Italian national team when they were eliminated from the 2014 World Cup, wrote the following in a foreword to a book by gay-rights campaigner, Alessandro Cecchi Paone: 'In the world of football and of sport in general, there is still a taboo around homosexuality. Everyone ought to live freely with themselves, their desires and their sentiments. We must all work for a sporting culture that respects the individual in every manifestation of his truth and freedom. Hopefully soon players will come out.'

The Football Association and the Premier League have a responsibility to create a better environment. Progress has been made in the area of anti-racism, but what makes racism any different to homophobia, or any other form of bullying? There should not be a scale of seriousness. This is not about demanding special treatment. Abuse is pernicious, however it is triggered and whatever it concerns.

As an athlete, all I wanted was an environment where I could concentrate and do justice to the thousands of hours of practice I put in. I received great support from the authorities in both rugby codes, without easing my sense of loneliness. I can't be at that footballer's side when he runs out in front of 60,000 fans at an away game. I can't circulate in the crowd and plead his case if they choose to be cruel. There's a time where you've got to stand on your own two feet, and it's scary.

One misjudgement of mood, a solitary thoughtless action, and a person's life in football can be made a misery. I'd love to be more optimistic about it, but the people I've spoken to in that world dampen my expectations. Progress will be limited until leading figures are more outspoken as to why it is so wrong to judge somebody on their private life. The game needs more open-minded men like Joey Barton. I know he is ridiculed for some of his pronouncements, but I found him a fascinating and intuitive guy. He's straight, but willing to stand up for gay rights. He's provocative, but there is an underlying sensitivity to his comments. People judge him on preconceptions rather than personal experience.

Footballers do have access to a shallow, superficial world. They are lionised, and the temptation to take advantage of their celebrity status is immense. They have the power to create their own scenarios, for better or for worse. I have heard of some who go to extraordinary measures to disguise their sexuality and give themselves a laddish legitimacy.

The subterfuge is relatively simple to arrange, but it involves playing with fire. The threat of being burned is very real. I know of people who use women as arm candy when they know they are going to be in the limelight, at something like a nightclub or restaurant – it doesn't take much to create some conveniently deceptive headlines. The girls are fragrant props in photographs that provide the camouflage of supposed love interest. Perception is more important than reality. All of a sudden you've got a new girlfriend, or you're assumed, in tabloid lore, to be playing the field. I'm sure the papers are wise to it all, but they get what they want while allowing the subject of their story to generate sexual and social credibility. But all these people are doing is making it harder, ultimately, to be true to themselves. They are digging a bigger hole than is wise, or necessary.

The counterpoint to such cynical manipulation of public perception is the very real fear that innocence offers inadequate protection. One of the first athletes to contact me after I came out was Australian swimmer, Daniel Kowalski. He envied my sense of liberation, and admitted to being angry at what he considered his lack of moral courage. He, too, wanted to set an example.

He had retired as a world and Olympic champion, acclaimed as one of his country's finest freestyle swimmers. Yet his greatest fear was exposure, not as a gay man, but as a supposed threat to the children he was then coaching. He was cowed by the power of myth and mischief.

My first reaction was utter disbelief. It was implausible to think that anyone could consider he was anything other than an expert, passing on his knowledge. But when I forced myself to think through the dilemma, I realised that he probably had a point, as crazy as it seemed. I understood why the ignorant minority would see him in his bathers and wantonly jump to the wrong conclusion. For some deep-seated reason, whether they admit it or not, some people connect bad things, like paedophilia, to gay stereotypes. It is irrational and demeaning, but Daniel's fear made sense. I felt similarly uncomfortable about the potential reaction of some observers when I was asked to put on some coaching sessions for the kids at Pencoed, in addition to my academy programme.

Fortunately, Daniel was brilliantly received when he came out. He has his problems, like everyone, but he is fulfilled. I couldn't guarantee him that happiness, but he found the process of coming to terms with his place in the world instructive.

Intriguingly, he also feels he could have achieved even more had he revealed his sexuality during his career: 'Things pop into my head that make me realise that I clearly suppressed these thoughts of being gay because it was "wrong" as a male, and even more "wrong" as an elite athlete. I always knew that I lacked confidence when I stood up on the blocks, and I do wonder sometimes if that lack of confidence was fear, fear of not really knowing who I am. I lost to some amazing champions, so I'm not for one second saying that this is the reason I didn't win, but I often wonder if the lack of self-confidence and lack of identity held me back.'

As general manager of the Australian Swimmers' Association, Daniel is using his renewed sense of self-awareness to help rebuild the sport after a terrible London Olympics, in which the culture of the Australian squad was said to be 'toxic'. The team lacked leadership, and splintered into conflicting factions. The inquiry highlighted issues with the abuse of prescription drugs.

I'm proud of his response. He has acted on the principles that framed our discussions. Daniel is advocating progress through 'open and honest dialogue'. He has acted on our shared belief in the importance of mentors: former swimmers who will share life lessons, in addition to offering guidance on the requirements of elite competition. He is a role model, in the best sense of the term.

The duty of care in aquatic sports is a delicate area. Its athletes tend to be young and impressionable. Coaches have been known to take advantage, but biological age can be deceptive. I spoke with Tom Daley, the Olympic diver, before he came out. His maturity and clarity of thought was hugely impressive for someone aged 19, but his sport, and the loss of his beloved father to cancer, had taught him self-sufficiency.

I felt so proud of the young man speaking from his heart to the watching world, through a YouTube video, about love and life. I'm not ashamed to admit that part of me was also jealous. I would have loved to have been 19, at the top of my game, and been able to take control of my destiny in such a manner. It is wonderful that the world has skipped a beat between generations, so that his candour was so well received.

Acceptance will never be universal in an imperfect world. It is one thing for a well-balanced, secure person to say, 'Well done, Tom. But it really doesn't matter, does it?' but for every individual who thinks that way, there are others to whom it does matter. They might not have a loving family or a fulfilling relationship. They may be insecure, not necessarily with their sexuality, but with the minutiae of their life. They are resistant to new beginnings and happy endings.

To understand those who oppose change, it is essential to relate to their angst and anger. This is not a simple issue. It can be cultural, political, and can have a religious connotation. Dogma diminishes the humanity of us all.

According to official Government figures, six per cent of Britain's population is gay, lesbian or bisexual. Stonewall places the figure at somewhere between five and seven per cent. Are we too complacent that homosexuality is still illegal in 80 per cent of Commonwealth countries? Persecution is endemic in what we are asked to regard as civilised nations. While I can now marry my partner, my peers, across the world, fear for their lives.

The temptation for the casual observer is to judge my impact on the number of prominent athletes who followed my lead. That misses the point. Its value, if it has one, lies in the effect it has had on the everyday lives of those who are rarely considered – like Gareth, the man who wore a pink shirt in my honour. If Tom's influence enriches the life of a single stranger, his gesture has been worthwhile.

The rest of us must keep our side of the bargain. Tom must be allowed the concessions of his youth: he has a lot of living to do, and must be given the freedom to make the mistakes of a 19-year-old. He must not be long-lens cannon fodder. He has the right to privacy and a right to a life beyond his sport, which will hopefully involve winning a gold medal at the Rio Olympics in 2016.

In time, he will realise the enormity of his opportunity to make a difference. He has the support of a strong, loving family. It helps that he has grown up in elite sport. He has learned to develop a thick hide, because you've got to expect stick. If you can't take it you'll get even more, and deny yourself the chance to give it back.

You have to set your own standards, and ensure that those around you differentiate between banter and unacceptable insult. Intent is the key. As far as my rugby friends are concerned, they are in no danger of crossing the line. We've been through a lot together, so they've carte blanche to chuck in a throwaway line about me being a gay boy. There's no malice. But if something similar is said by a random guy in the street, with a different tone, I would find it offensive.

I'm not inclined to preach, despite my concerns, and it is dangerous to be too proactive. The grapevine buzzes with half-formed theories and inaccurate case studies. I consciously wait until I am approached for advice. I believe in the value of a quiet word, an understated anecdote. I spoke to cricketer, Steven Davies, the former England wicketkeeper, about the anxieties that had preceded my announcement, but he seemed pretty sorted, and at ease with what he wanted to achieve when he came out in February 2011.

He had told his parents about his sexuality when he was 19, and waited five years before Andy Flower and Andrew Strauss, respectively his England coach and captain, shared the knowledge with his teammates. His subsequent experience mirrors my own. He is respected within his sport, and seen as a role model by those whose lives he has touched.

The overall aim is to minimise the issue, so that it has comforting normality. When you complete the process of coming out, you really feel like you're the only person in the world ever to go through it. You live it on a daily basis, and are unafraid of the bittersweet elements of the process when you are asked to share. There is a sense of community and identity, a feeling that if you have come through your darkest times, then so can the person seeking reassurance.

There is a hint of sadness in everybody's story, but that is more than neutralised by the sentiment that something significant has been overcome. From feeling so alone, you become part of a global network of people whose lives have the same foundation stones. Secrecy and discretion are valued, but once the story is in the public domain, there is almost a duty to instruct others on its importance. It becomes an affirmative process.

I stress to those who seek perspective that they do not necessarily have to come out. I try to reassure them that the secret doesn't have to seize control. There is no need to create a dark world as punishment for their reluctance to acknowledge their sexuality. If I can offer them a survival strategy, by talking through how best to live the rest of their lives, I will do so. I understand the fear that grips them; they are a kid again, with their toes curling over the edge of a 10-metre diving board. They're suffering from emotional vertigo. In their imagination, the water shimmering below them has the consistency of concrete. If they make the leap of faith, they will be hurt.

For me, the objective is not to recruit another foot soldier in the war against prejudice; it is to help the individual to create a context which makes living worthwhile and productive. If that is a lifetime commitment on my part, as an ear to be bashed now and again, bring it on.

The reality is that my story had only just begun when I stood on that field in Toulouse, in trepidation of how I was about to be received. That day was merely the tipping point. My strength has been derived from the strength I have subsequently given others.

My announcement wasn't an ultimatum: 'I'm gay, end of.' It was a mission statement: 'I'm gay, and I'm going to make sure that my life is a successful life.'

I believe attitudes are changing, slowly. There was something refreshing about the feel-good factor generated by the marriage of Kate Walsh and Helen Richardson, who were in Great Britain's bronze medal-winning hockey team at the London Games. They celebrated their hen night at the European Championships in September 2013 in a hotel corridor, eating fast food forbidden by their nutritionist, in one of those team-bonding sessions that transcend sport.

Thomas Hitzlsperger, the German footballer who came out in January 2014, summed up the next phase of the debate very well: 'You hear the word "courage" a lot,' he said, in an interview with the *Guardian* newspaper. 'That's nice to hear, but it's part of the problem, of course. That's something that should change. I sincerely hope that we'll see the day when nobody mentions courage in these circumstances anymore, because it will be seen as totally normal that a sports person will speak about his homosexuality, the way others talk about their wives and girlfriends. It won't be easy for the next person to be truly the first in that regard, but maybe I've been able to help them a tiny bit.'

Intolerance needs to be challenged, because it causes damage if unchecked. I was appalled by the ill-educated wittering of Neil Francis, the former Ireland lock-forward, who used a TV interview to suggest that gay people had 'no interest' in such a manly enterprise as sport. Perhaps he should test that theory on Orlando Cruz, the Puerto Rican boxer whose sexuality is a striking challenge to his culture. Or he might wish to ask Darren Young, the WWE superstar wrestler who goes under the moniker Mr No Days Off, to demonstrate his signature move, the Gut Check. Stone Cold Steve Austin, a strident supporter of same-sex marriage, would surely offer to form a tag team.

Francis dredged the depths when he went on to recommend his host did 'a survey of the hairdressing industry and find out how many heterosexuals work in that'. He spoke about ballet in derogatory terms and insisted, ludicrously, that rugby dressing rooms were inherently homophobic in nature. He vomited further bile on Michael Sam, the first player to preface his NFL career with an explanation of his homosexuality.

Francis, who had seen him play as a star defensive end in college football for the University of Missouri, called Sam 'very flamboyant', before bizarrely likening his coming out to Jimi Hendrix regarding Janis Joplin's death as a 'great career move'. He did not dwell on Sam's athleticism: watched by 30 scouts at his school's open day, the NFL prospect completed 19 consecutive lifts of 225 pounds, ran the 40-yard dash in 4.69 seconds and made a standing vertical jump of 30 inches.

It was infantile and unbecoming of Francis, a player I once respected. He apologised, but not before smearing a brave and intelligent young man who has the power to help engineer significant social change. A poll of NFL players, in the immediate aftermath of Sam coming out in February 2014, revealed that 86 per cent would support an openly gay teammate. When that question was last posed, in 2006, only 57 per cent had promised to back their colleague.

The positivity, when Sam was drafted by the St Louis Rams in the 2014 Draft, was marked. Since the NFL is a prime example of market-driven economics, it was also appropriate that acceptance had a commercial dimension. His shirt quickly became the second highest selling in the League.

Jason Collins, who became the first openly gay player in the National Basketball Association when he joined the Brooklyn Nets as a free agent in February 2014, has received similar support, despite one opponent – a 'knucklehead' whom he chose not to name – subsequently abusing him on court. He attended the State of the Union address as a guest of First Lady Michelle Obama, and has become a powerful symbol of progress. *Time* magazine named him as one of the world's 100 most influential people.

He has received standing ovations in major cities, but it is in the Bible-belt states where his impact has been most profound. Even his jersey, which has become the bestseller in the NBA, is an invitation for spectators to examine their conscience. Collins wears the number 98 as a tribute to gay college student, Matthew Shepard, who was pistol-whipped, tortured, tied to a fence and left to die in an attack near the town of Laramie, Wyoming, in October 1998.

Derrick Gordon, an NBA prospect playing for the University of Massachusetts, was inspired to come out by the example set by Collins. I understood perfectly his sentiments when he made his announcement, in April 2014: 'It was torture. I was just going around faking my whole life, being someone I'm not. It's like wearing a mask because everyone else was wearing that mask. Now that I'm taking the mask off, people can finally see who I really am.

'People think gay men are soft. I'm not. Especially with my background growing up, I was never a soft kid and I'll never be a soft kid. People think gays are very delicate. That's not the case at all. I know Michael Sam and Jason Collins aren't delicate. My strength coach compares me to a pit bull. There's no softness in this body.'

Anyone who spends time in the United States, as I have in the last couple of years, understands the social importance of sport in North America. The college system produces local heroes, whose names may be unfamiliar, but whose experiences have inordinate impact. When someone like Mitch Eby, a junior defensive end on the Chapman University football team in Orange, California, comes out, he relates to a tightly drawn community. This is the speech in which he shared his sexuality with his teammates:

'I came up here today to talk to you guys about something that I've been dealing with for quite a while. It's something personal that I've always thought I could just bury away, but I can't. We live life so worried about how other people view us that we forget about ourselves. I can no longer go on living in fear, repressing myself because of how society may view me. I can no longer lie to my friends, family and teammates. It's time I lived life for myself for a change.

'With that being said, I am ready to share with you all that I am gay. It has taken me years to accept myself for who I truly am, so it's irrational to expect everybody to unconditionally accept me right away. However, the one thing that I hope that I can count on from each of you, my teammates, is your respect. Your respect as a friend, your respect as a teammate, and your respect as a man.

'Being gay may be something that defines me, but it does not limit me. It is such a small part of who I am. I am the same person you all know, no different than before. I'm still the kid that is obsessed with pretty much anything having to do with sports, I'm still the kid that some of you love to call stupid nicknames like "Mom" and "Hot Dog", and I'm still someone who will continue to go out there every day and push myself and push my teammates to be the best football team around. I am your teammate, I am your classmate and I am your brother. And I know that my brothers will continue to stand by my side, no matter what.'

Those words move me to tears. They prove every story is distinctive, nuanced and unique. Athletes have been defying social mores and political systems for years. I was particularly struck by the example of Marcus Urban, an East German youth international, who gave up football in order to live as an openly gay man. As he explained to CNN: 'Constantly hearing "gay" used as a curse word like "shit" made me think, "Of course, I'm shit." I realised that if I became a professional footballer, I would suffer as a man. I chose freedom over a constructed prison.'

These athletes represent a common thread, a golden cord that stretches across sport. Each individual deserves to be defined by their talent, because ability is more important than sexuality. I feel lucky to be a Welshman. I'm fortunate to know Nigel Owens as both a fellow countryman and as one of the finest rugby referees on the planet. He is, in the opinion of many better judges than me, the world's best. He uses humour to great effect, and is universally respected for his calmness and common sense. He came out two years before me, in 2007, and our stories are similar because of our shared experience of the deepest depression.

My crisis points came beside a swimming pool in Toulouse, and on the edge of a cliff near Llantwit Major; Nigel's moment of truth arrived one April morning in 1996, when he left his parents' house at 3.30 a.m. and walked to the top of Bancyddraenen Mountain, overlooking Mynyddcerrig, the West Wales village in which he had lived all his life. He left a note saying: 'I've reached the end of my tether. The only solution for me now is to take my own life.'

His self-esteem was shredded. Hooked on steroids and suffering from bulimia, he was ashamed of his homosexuality. His secret was suffocating him. He took a shotgun with him, but chose to swallow a bottle of sleeping tablets. He was found by chance. But for the prompt action of paramedics and the provision of a police helicopter, he would have died.

He recovered in hospital, and understands now the importance of bearing witness. Like me, he is haunted by the pain he inflicted on his parents. He was an only son, but we both survived because of the strength of those closest to us. Helping other people come to terms with who they are is our way of marking the good fortune of being allowed a second chance in life. To do so to the best of my ability, I had to understand myself.

Chapter Seventeen

BODY TALK

What, then, is real? What do I stand for? What made me who I am?

The answers are indelible and etched across my body. My tattoos are a throwback to ancient cultures, but a strikingly modern form of self-expression. They are an illustration of who I was, at the time I had them done, and must be read in the context of what I have become. They are living history, symbols of deeply personal experiences. Each speaks for itself, creates and tells its own story. Viewed together, they are a timeline, a mind map. They represent rites of passage.

I've never cared to explain them before, but I've seen the quizzical looks and instant assumptions that I am some sort of hooligan. On the contrary, I would not have had them done had I not been sensitive to my most intimate feelings. They helped me get through a number of profound private crises. When I study them in the mirror, or in photographs, they stimulate the imagination. I remember the basics: who, what, where, when and why.

They are manifestations of memory, which mean a lot to me. I will take them to my grave. Every one of them denotes a detail in my character. They are an abridged life story; most were done when I was repressing my sexuality. The most obvious ones, on my hands, were done soon after I came out, when I was in the United States. They were statements of intent which might seem ridiculous to you, but have perfect clarity to me. The images will, I hope, help you to understand me. They offer a guided tour of my psyche.

Having them done was a distinctive, intensely personal process. The pain was strangely addictive. The major tattoos took a couple of weeks to heal, so I couldn't have them done during the rugby season, but were worth the discomfort because I felt compelled to express myself.

The fingers on my left hand spell out the word LIFE. The sentiments may seem pretty obvious, but they are linked to an accompanying tattoo of a dice, which has landed on the number four. In essence, this was me conceding that, at the time, my life was a matter of random chance, like a roll of the dice. I had subjugated myself to the luck of the draw. The significance of the number is that I had vowed to do everything for/four life itself.

The swallow on my right hand is linked to the traditions of long-distance sailing. Sailors would have a swallow tattoo to signify multiples of 5,000 nautical miles served before the mast. They would also signify faith in the folklore that, in the event of their being lost at sea, their soul would be transported to heaven by the bird. In England, the swallow is also seen as the trademark of a working-class hero.

I chose to link it to its migratory patterns. A swallow returns each year to its nesting site. It is a home bird, like me. It is depicted on my right hand, because this is the one that asks for your trust in a handshake. The swallow also represents love, care and affection towards my family and friends. They are assured of my loyalty. I will always seek to return to them. The bird represents freedom and hope. The word VIVA across my knuckles is pretty self-explanatory, referring to the term 'Long live' in Spanish. If we are going to be around for a long time, we might as well make it a good time.

The Chinese dragon on my left forearm was inked in during a time of real insecurity, when the fear of discovery was pernicious. I had read somewhere that it is a sign of power and strength, but also of good luck, for those who deserve a favour from fate. It fitted my mindset perfectly. I felt I needed all the help I could get. The dragon is also associated with the number nine in China, which is regarded as a harbinger of better fortune. That tattoo was part of an emotional insurance policy.

The only other one I've had since coming out is across my chest. It reads 'DEO NON FORTUNA', or 'From God, Not From Chance'. It is my article of faith. My belief in God has strengthened since I came to terms with myself, as has my conviction that I'm alive because a higher being helped me to survive. I'm bearing witness to my gratitude. I wanted to illustrate the Latin version of the phrase, rather than the English, because I wanted people to ask me what it meant rather than just read it and feel that that was enough to satisfy their curiosity.

My most deeply personal tattoos are on my elbows. These hold the key to the most intimate passages in my life.

I had a star ascribed on my right elbow during the heart-breaking sequence of miscarriages suffered by Jemma. I was thrashing around blindly, seeking reasons for such devastation. I was at my most fragile, mentally, and decided that those unborn children were not taken away from me, but merely transported straight to heaven. I understand that this sounds bizarre, and hope it will be taken in the right way, but it helped somehow that they were denied a life because of a higher calling. It wasn't a clinical issue, or some kind of retribution for my errant ways. At that point in my life, I took comfort in the fantasy that I could look up at the night sky and see my unborn children, in the guise of stars.

I had the tattoo placed on my elbow because I associated it with reliance. A mother traditionally uses her elbow to test the temperature of the bathwater; the baby will cry if it is too cold, and risks being scalded if it is too hot. It is symbolic of the responsibility we have for the next generation. It also enables me to have a constant reference point for something only Jemma and I can understand: the depth of the grief we shared, and the bitterness of the tears we shed.

The tattoo on my left elbow, a spider's web, is a plea for help and understanding, but also an insight into the extent of my culpability. It represents the web of lies I span for more years than I care to remember. I asked the body artist to make it as intricate as possible, but to pay special attention to its centre. That contains six squiggles, which represent lies in the form of small worms, burrowing beneath the surface of my life. They have faded slightly because of where they are situated, but they remind me to never again allow these creatures to wreak havoc.

The hands clasped in prayer, situated on the left-hand side of my torso, are a warning of my physical vulnerability. They are positioned deliberately, pointing to my neck, where the ruptured artery sustained playing for Toulouse could quite easily have killed me. I didn't know whether I would be able to play again during the rehabilitation period, but once I did so, I got into the habit of praying that I wouldn't die on the pitch. By having that image etched on my skin, I imagined I had an open line to God, imploring him to watch over me.

Whether I deserved such divine intervention is extremely doubtful. I had a scorpion depicted on my shoulder because I needed to be confronted by the consequences of my selfishness and sheer stupidity. It was in response to sleeping with one particular guy. I was completely pissed off with myself for doing so despite the risks, and I wanted that tattoo to be so menacing it would warn me never to do such a thing again.

The scorpion's sting can be fatal, in some species at least. Its image was the representation of an ever-present threat. It sent a private but unequivocal message: do something wrong, repeat a bad mistake, and you will be in mortal danger. The scorpion is clever, and strikes suddenly. If you forget the toxicity of its venom and relax it will have you. It will do you harm.

The image of an Indian chieftain is much more benign. It symbolises leadership, and the dignity that should accompany authority. It is the least threatening of my tattoos, an indication of how seriously I took my role as captain, and how happy I was to have such a responsibility. It is also an emblem of masculinity and the expression of a warrior's spirit. His gaze is steadfast, and his serenity is reassuring.

The ghoulish figure nearby is a polar opposite in terms of mood and timing. This tattoo was done in a period of self-loathing. I intended to illustrate how ugly I felt, and how I was festering from the inside out. It is a nightmarish mask, designed to be repellent. It came from a dark and depressing place. In a perverse way, it is comforting, because I no longer identify with the monster. He remains as a sentinel, a symbolic warning, but is no longer relevant.

Finally, and perhaps most portentously, I have a cross on my back. I feel its heaviness constantly. When it was first inscribed, it felt ominous, a burden I had to bear on my way to my personal Calvary. I had no real idea where I was going, or what fate had in store for me. The cross represented the mass of guilt that had accumulated over the years of my deception.

I may have been spared crucifixion, but I know that I will be carrying the weight of the cross until my last breath. I'm comfortable with that, because I have reached a place of refuge.

My final duty is to show a frightened young man the way there.

Chapter Eighteen

BE PROUD

Dear Gareth,

Happy 16th birthday. It's 25 July 1990, a warm Wednesday in South Wales. Elton John has just been knocked off the top of the charts after five weeks at number one, but you can't get the chorus of his hit song, 'Sacrifice', out of your mind: 'And it's no sacrifice, just a simple word. It's two hearts living, in two separate worlds.' They'll be playing it on the radio for years.

You don't know me, but I know you. Let's just say we're related. I sense you are seeking something, and I am here to help. It's OK, by the way. Your secret is safe with me. Since we're both curious about our place in the world around us, I did a little research before I wrote to you. Just for a laugh, I decided to study a random astrological profile of people who share our birthday. Our element is fire and we are apparently ruled by the sun.

You probably think horoscopes are mumbo-jumbo, but the summary makes for interesting reading: 'You can, at one level of existence, seem to live only for the enjoyment of the moment.

Having said that, however, you have an inherent deep level of understanding that will assist you as you work your way through the intricacies of human relationships.

'The July 25 pattern in life is one of facing up to continual thresholds that you are required to cross over, and of new horizons of conquest that become offered up to you. As an example, imagine yourself poised on the edge of a precipice and pursued by a dangerous creature. You are faced with the situation whereby you can either put up a fight or take a leap off the precipice.

'Either way, you cannot remain on the edge, so that whatever choice you make, it will change you for ever and extend your sense of who you are. The danger of this path in life is one of charging ahead without thinking or giving due thought to the consequences, resulting in your jumping off a cliff unnecessarily.

'As a July 25, your outlook on life is based upon you expressing your own unique personality. While there will be those times when you will feel that you would just like to blend into your surroundings, and find peace in some anonymity, you will find that generally any such mood will last only a short time. Then you will once again be up and running, to project your own special image onto life.

'As a July 25 birth date, you can often feel very restless and be unsure about your work, career or profession. You can take comfort, however, and rest assured that you are one who has abilities and talents, and that seeking how to best apply those abilities and talents will be a worthwhile endeavour. At your best, you can excel and stand out when it comes to a time of crisis.

'The element of air holds a strong influence on this July 25 birth date and when linked with other influences, it can result in giving you something of a dreamy personality at times. This might indicate that when it comes to the purely practical side of life, you may find that you have some difficulty in keeping organised.

'Other aspects associated with this July 25 birth date indicate a strong link to the ideas of creativity. There is a strong likelihood, therefore, that you will express this aspect of your nature through some sort of visual art. Painting in watercolours might be your forte, or sculpting, pottery or weaving.'

Spooky, huh? They're a mile out with the artistic stuff, but some of the other observations are uncannily accurate. I should know. I appreciate this will be difficult to get your head around, but I am you, aged 40. It has taken me a long time – too long – to work out who I am. The least I can do is share the supposed wisdom of my experience, because I also yearned for answers as I lay awake in our front bedroom of the council house in Sarn.

You are lucky to live in that house, with its natural warmth and its kitchen in which the kettle is rarely cold and the biscuit barrel needs constant replenishment. Trust me, your brothers will look after you when your need is greatest. You will never be able to repay your debt to Mum and Dad. You will put them through the mill, yet their love is unquenchable. Try to take a little more time to tell them you love them. I'd also ask you to tidy your room now and again, but I know that's a waste of breath.

Your dreams will be realised beyond your wildest imaginings, even if your nightmares persist. You are ready to soar as a rugby player, though as a young man you are not yet ready to leave the nest. They may only paint the Pencoed cabin red, white and blue, the club colours, once every 20 years or so, but you will be fondly remembered there and welcomed as a returning hero. You will gag on your first yard of ale in the clubhouse, and impress the people who matter on the pitch. A nation will take you to its heart.

You will have big decisions to make. Some you will get hopelessly wrong. Your life will revolve around the day you tell the world you are gay. There, I've said it. Eventually, you will grow tired of shying away from that word. You will stop hiding from its implications. That will be the hardest thing, because you will lie for years, to yourself and those who hold you dear. Your tears will be bleak and bitter. You will occasionally wonder about your sanity.

Here's the thing, Gareth. That secret is the most precious thing in life to you. It becomes your child, something you hold close, and love with every fibre of your being. You are blind to its faults. You cannot give it away, because that would be like abandoning a son on the cold, hard doorstep of a stranger's house. You created it. It contains your DNA. It is your life force.

It will enslave you, and bring out the worst in you. You will do anything to keep it until it is almost too late. Take care, because it has no conscience, and it takes no prisoners. It is devilish and destructive.

Do not be lured into accepting the easy excuse. People will try to give you undeserved benefit of the doubt, because of what you represent. Acknowledge your faults readily and honestly. To be able to live with yourself, you have to take responsibility for your words and actions. It really is that simple, that sharply defined.

I've got a lot of making up to do and, because of that, I spend a lot of my time these days speaking to boys and girls of your age about things like acceptance and empathy. I call them diversity talks. They are a modern concept, designed to cope with age-old issues. I try to offer an insight into the dangers of pre-judging people. I'm no rocket scientist or psychologist, but I try to dwell on the lessons of my strengths and, more importantly perhaps, my weaknesses.

It is pretty straightforward stuff. I start with my rugby career, because that usually gets the boys' attention. The Wales team is as much national property in my day as it is in yours. The 2014 season was a disappointment, after winning the Six Nations (yes, six – the Five Nations now includes Italy) in the two previous years. We were excellent at home, although the French team we beat at the Millennium was one of the worst I've seen. Away from Cardiff, we failed to counter specific tactical plans England and Ireland had prepared for us.

I'm a bit worried by England, to be honest. I thought they were the best team in the Championship, and they only missed out on the Grand Slam by a bad bounce of a ball in Paris, where they lost late on. They've turned Twickenham into a mini-Millennium Stadium: it used to be a bit dull and corporate, but the old boys in their Barbours are now loud and proud. The place rocks. Stuart Lancaster, the England coach, is developing pride in the shirt. They'll be very difficult to beat when they stage the World Cup in 2015.

In terms of natural talent and quality of coaching, I'd rate Wales as third in the world right now, behind New Zealand and South Africa. But, mentally, there are four or five better teams. That's where we come undone. Sam Warburton, our latest captain, was sent off for a spear tackle in the last World Cup in 2011, when we lost a winnable semi-final against France. Suddenly, that was the only talking point: no one bothered to concentrate on the failure to find a way to win. The All Blacks and Springboks would have done so. We're still a nation that allows defeat. As long as that persists, we will not win consistently.

Anyway, I digress. Rugby is such a distraction, isn't it? I talk to the kids about what the game has given me, my enjoyment of rugby's physicality, and the necessary sacrifices. I examine the importance of dedication and leadership, qualities you are only just discovering you possess. I'm convinced leadership is defined lazily and wrongly: people associate it with it being loud, or big, or strong. That's bullshit. You will find your cause, Gareth, and discover it doesn't require a megaphone for you to wield influence.

I support the No Bystanders campaign organised by Stone-wall, a gay rights group who do so much unseen work. It is aimed at young people like you, who have the right to grow up feeling able to be themselves. It tackles bullying and abuse with a range of educational programmes. My favourite promotional poster features two footballers. The caption: 'One is gay. If that bothers people, our work continues' says it all.

I truly believe everybody is capable of being a leader. They just need to be presented with a certain scenario to discover those qualities, deep within. You've got them although, like any teenager, you're too self-absorbed to know, or care, at the moment. In time you will learn, through self-preservation as much as anything else, to study how people interact. You will be able to spot the bully, the cheat, the dreamer or the alpha male who wants everything his own way. The hard bit is working out into which category you fit.

Sex is a mystery, isn't it? You sense that something is not quite right. Some of your urges don't compute. Your mates boast about the illicit joys of copping a feel in the darkness outside the school disco, and though you play along with the teenage game of blind man's bluff, your heart is not in it. Something is stirring inside you, and it is scaring you to death. I'm tempted to say don't worry, that it is OK to be different. Yet I can't do so. That would be hypocritical, and that is a fault I am trying to eradicate from my own life.

I think about you when I speak to secondary school pupils about homophobic bullying. I try to separate the normal rough and tumble – where you are ribbed for being ginger or thin or spotty – from the more dangerous derision. I know you're going to flinch at this, because it is far too close to home. Already, you regard homosexuality as the sin which dare not speak its name. You constantly think about its consequences.

So many boys, asked to speak sensibly about their feelings, desperately hide behind a façade of aggression. When I want them to describe what they imagine a gay man to be, their body language gives them away. They become taut and defensive. They try to act tough because they fear that showing any sensitivity to the subject will lead to suspicion. The stigma of homosexuality is deeply entrenched, and it needs to be teased out into the open. I try to challenge their perceptions without threatening the conventions of the peer group.

Puberty is kicking in. The boys are starting to talk about girls, and the girls are starting to talk about boys. That's when the lonely individual gets kind of lost. I can usually spot them. They are transfixed by me. They don't talk very much, but their gaze is constant and intense. They are listening, trying to absorb everything I say. I can sense their quiet terror. They are desperate to fit in with what everyone else is doing and saying. It's not difficult to recognise the odd one out, because I am looking at me, or you, to be precise.

I ask the group to describe a gay man. Does he like Kylie Minogue? The brash ones in the group, the ones supposedly certain of their sexuality, laugh and start to strike poses. Their idea of a gay man is someone who wears make-up, talks in a camp manner and uses hairspray. He minces down the street and dresses flamboyantly. That gives me a chance to address the stereotype and turn the tables.

They may do that, I tell the group, but then again, they may not. What if they looked the same as you, liked the same bands and TV programmes? What if they played in your rugby team, or hung around with you after school? What if they wore the same brand names, and lived in the same street? The reality, as you're beginning to realise, Gareth, is that a gay man can blend into the background. He's great at charades. That usually carries a price, but it is not noticeable to the casual observer.

Gradually, I see the group starting to understand the foolishness of judging people without due care and attention. I then give the kids an option. For instance, I ask them whether they would visit a doctor, knowing he was gay, if they were seriously ill. I ask those who say no to explain themselves. They usually suggest something silly like, 'He might touch me if I am unconscious.' I talk about professional ethics, and the importance of taking sexuality out of a situation. I want them to see human beings, rather than gay or straight men and women. When they relax, and reflect on that, there is a tangible change of mood. They get it, Gareth. I don't have to ask whether you get it. You will, in time.

That sudden sense of understanding is liberating. I like to think the kids go home and educate the adults. You're lucky, because Mum and Dad have a broad-minded approach, but other kids learn their prejudice from their parents. That's why I use music as a subject. Most kids tie themselves up in knots, trying to explain why all gay guys love Kylie or Abba (a personal favourite). They look a bit stupid in the end. They're challenged by their peers, who see through the absurdity of the argument. The group begins to educate itself. It's good to talk, as someone once said.

There is nothing to feel dirty or ashamed about, Gareth. A gay person is not unacceptable, or unlovable. I'd like to introduce you to Ian, my partner. We've been together for a year. He comes from an RAF background. He's dotty about his two dogs, Gordon Setters named Amber and Ebony. They take us for regular walks. He makes me laugh, and is a better cook than I will ever be. He's in the hospitality business, so sport is in his social and professional orbit, but he had no real idea of my rugby career when we met. That was important to me, because I didn't trust a relationship with stardust as its mortar.

We're affectionate, happy and respectful of our surroundings. You will discover, as you grow up, that the world is an imperfect place. You will become streetwise, and develop a sixth sense about putting yourself in a compromising situation. I never put myself, or Ian, in harm's way. It is one thing to walk arm-in-arm through Soho, entirely another to do so on the terraces at Hull Kingston Rovers. You will discover special pleasure in unthinking acceptance – we are often stopped in the street and spoken to as a couple.

Value your family and friends. Their love is unconditional. They didn't push me to tell them I was gay, although they read the signs. If they had forced the secret out of me, or been too pressing in their concerns, I would have freaked. I would have been ready to die rather than to have my lies exposed. You have so much to live for. Don't waste a single second.

It frightens me how close I came to ending it all. I still have nightmares about Mum and Dad, weeping over my coffin. Ian finds it difficult to forgive his brother for taking his life, but the process is irrational. It is impossible to comprehend why someone wants to die unless you've been at that ragged edge. I understand why suicide is regarded as the ultimate act of selfishness, but, as crazy as it sounds, I can also appreciate why people push themselves beyond the limits of reason.

I'm not talking about the mindset of a suicide bomber, who sacrifices himself or herself for a religion or an ideology. I was in a different type of bubble, where a better, simpler existence was waiting. Death seemed a terrifyingly plausible means of escape. That's why I ask Ian not to judge his brother too harshly. You can't resent someone because you don't know what he went through before making that final, fatal decision. My suicide attempts were cries for help, because I was unable to follow the procedure to its natural conclusion. I wasn't ready. My guilt will never leave me, but my actions screamed, 'Come and see me, come and find me.'

Do you know what, Gareth? I'm torn about telling you the truth. Instinct tells me to gloss over the reality that if you come out at 19 – when, believe it or not, you are on the verge of playing in the Wales team – your career will shrivel and die. I want to allow you to enjoy the blissful innocence of your dreams. Times will change, but it is wrong for me to give you a false sense of security.

Rugby isn't ready for you yet. It is too conservative, too set in its ways. Tell the truth and you will be a target for the boys who stagger out of the bar, looking for a bit of sport. Denial isn't easy. You will condemn yourself as a coward. You are consumed by the game's promise, pride and passion, and it is easy to forget that being gay is such a relatively small part of who you are. If you lie about your deepest feelings – and you will – the chains around you will tighten until you are so constricted you are gasping for breath.

Girls seem to like you. You are sporty, and mask your shyness by playing the fool. No dare is too dumb for you to accept. One girl in particular will become special to you. She is starting to watch you play at Pencoed. There's no easy way of saying this, but you will hurt her, badly. You will take the blame for that to your grave.

I am sorry, Gareth. I'm ashamed of what you will go through when the lies multiply. You will look into the mirror and recoil at what you have become. For all your many achievements, you will know that you are still a fucking liar. All the virtues associated with you as an athlete – honesty, integrity, valour and indomitability – have been betrayed. I hope you can find it in you to forgive that.

But your life is not without foundation. When you acknowledge our truth you will touch the souls of strangers. They will tell you: 'Because of what you did, I came out and my life is so much better for it.' You have a massive responsibility when your actions dictate those of others. It is mind blowing. I'm still learning, still growing as a human being, so to have people refer to my example in terms of life and death is an extraordinary pressure and privilege. I do what I can, when I can, how I can.

I think that's of much more valuable service to the community than being at the head of a gay pride march. I've obvious sympathy with the sentiments involved there, but I've never been much of a political animal. I am horrified by the broader picture, of lynch mobs led by politicians who profit from prejudice, but my fight involves helping to ensure kids like you don't do as I did, and spend endless nights weeping in the darkness. Education, for me, is more effective than theatrical outrage.

I used to lie to make people like me. I won't lie to make you like me, Gareth. There's no point. I need to cleanse myself with the truth. That's why this letter is so important to me. I realise that some people will read it and think, 'What a prick.' I get that, totally get it. There have been times when I've deserved to be treated with contempt.

This is my recompense. My defences are down. I've unlocked some powerful, painful memories. The events of my life, the reasons for my actions and the consequences of my deceit are literally an open book. I'm ready to be judged, not on fragments of knowledge, as I am now, but on the totality of my being. If someone meets me in the future and says, 'Oh, you are nothing like I thought you were,' I will have failed.

I can't live a lie any more. If people want to goad me with the word 'gay' they are wasting their time, and mine. I'm no longer afraid of that word. I have accepted who I am, so it can no longer hurt me. I won't say that I am super-confident; there is still a side of me that fears what the future holds. But I won't hide from that word, and the conversation it inevitably triggers.

Learn to take something from every day, every experience, Gareth. You never know where life will lead. Many sportsmen find their world implodes when they retire; mine expanded in ways you will not fully understand until scientists solve the riddle of the space-time continuum. I went straight from rugby league to the *Big Brother* house (as bizarre as this will sound to you, that's a TV show in which a bunch of strangers are watched by millions, like animals in a zoo, 24 hours a day).

I don't feel lonely any more, but I do feel there is part of me that's missing. I think it may be you, Gareth. I need to keep you close because you remind me of where I come from, and what I have to lose if I regress, forget the chaos I have caused and succumb to my faults. I can live with myself, but only if you remain with me as I grow old.

Being gay is no excuse for bad behaviour. Using tears and traumas as a crutch fools no one. Just because I have said sorry, and admitted to being out of order, doesn't make it all OK. Apologies ease the pain but they don't erase the hurt caused by such selfishness. I accept blame for my actions. There is no getting away from the fact I did wrong. It took too long for me to summon the strength to end the madness. I was weak, and wanted to take the easy way out with booze and a bottle of pills, or an impulsive plunge from that windy cliff top.

I'm a lucky man. I try to be a decent human being. I occasionally see glimpses of you, Gareth, when I look in the mirror. We share the same skin, even if mine is a little tougher these days. The face is lived in, but it has the same contours. I can't do much about the hair, *butt* – that'll be over the horizon by the time you are 30. But I can tell you the secret of my new life.

When you accept who you are, you will be who you want to be.

Be proud.

Your friend,

Gareth

AFTERWORD AND THANKS

By Michael Calvin

It was a tough day. Gareth and I had spent two hours in a grave-yard, sitting on a bench in intermittent rain discussing death, despair and divinity. We had driven along the coast road, parked in a farmyard on the outskirts of Llantwit Major, and walked for a mile and a half across clay-based, freshly ploughed fields. There, before us, was the ultimate reminder of mortality.

This was where Gareth had resolved to end it all: a promon-tory overlooking the Bristol Channel. We were alone. The only indication of humanity was the silhouette of a container ship sailing eastwards. Looking directly ahead from the cliff edge, it was possible to see the outline of the Exmoor Heritage coast. The resort of Minehead, many miles away to our right, was lost in a fine mist.

There's something unbelievably twee about the craze for selfies. They're a modern form of narcissism that scars social media, but in such a bizarre setting, with such a profound subject to expand upon, we decided to record the moment for posterity. It is a single image, captured by Gareth on my mobile phone.

We are close together. The sea, slate grey and vaguely threatening, intrudes in the small space between our heads. The sky is lighter, but mottled by rain clouds. The wind is pushing my hair back on my scalp, a problem Gareth doesn't need to worry about. His orange hoodie, beneath a navy blue waterproof jacket, is the only flash of colour in the frame.

There is still something haunting about the tape of that afternoon's conversation. It moved us both, because of its context and significance. Our words are occasionally overwhelmed by the howl of an onshore wind, but they retain a special resonance. Their honesty, I hope, is imprinted on every page of this book. This was no vanity project for Gareth, nor was it a job of work for me.

We spoke about closure, on the walk back. Gareth resolved never to return to the scene of one of his greatest trials. We were oblivious to the quizzical stares of the farmer as he passed in his tractor, towing a sileage container, and the mud was so cloying we had no option but to deposit our shoes in a bin bag in the boot of the car. I drove back to his parents' house in my socks.

Barrie Thomas had just returned from his postal round, and was having a snack in front of the television. Yvonne Thomas was looking after the grandchildren, but was soon dispensing tea, biscuits and crisps. Gareth flopped into the reclining leather chair beside his dad and closed his eyes. The emotional toll was etched on his face; it was only later that I discovered he had lost weight and was struggling to sleep because of the strain of reminiscence.

Rugby players are meant to be defined by their bravery and physicality. Gareth is defined by his moral courage and sensitivity. I had warned him, over the course of a year or so before we decided to go for it, that the process of compiling this book would be painful, because we owed it to the reader to be dauntingly honest. He loved the idea of conducting interviews at the places where key events of his life occurred, to make our emotions more authentic, but probably underestimated the impact. I know I did.

It is only right that I should begin my litany of thanks by highlighting the kindness of Gareth's family, who put up with my constant burrowing for another fact, a secondary reflection or confirmation of mood and tone. Ian Baum, Gareth's partner, has been wonderfully understanding of the scope of our intentions. Gareth is blessed also by firm friends and a support network headed by his manager, Emanuele Palladino, who has been hugely supportive of our efforts.

Thanks to the Welsh Rugby Union, for giving us the run of a deserted Millennium Stadium so we could relive the day Scott Johnson divined the truth. It would be remiss of me not to mention an earlier collaboration with Gareth, by Delme Parfitt, which enabled me to double check relevant facts and figures.

My belief that Gareth's story has the power to change lives is shared by Andrew Goodfellow. Without his foresight and tenacity, this book would have remained unwritten. His faith was our inspiration, and his team at Ebury, led by Liz Marvin and Amelia Harvell, has been exceptional. My literary agent, Paul Moreton, has provided invaluable insight and encouragement.

I am indebted to Caroline Flatley, who transcribed endless hours of interviews, and became so emotionally engaged she took to dreaming in a Welsh accent. That's some achievement for someone who rarely ventures further west than Oldham. Thanks also to Chris and Mark Stanley, my next-door neighbours, for allowing me to write in the solitude of their retreat on the edge of the New Forest.

My family, as ever, deserve a medal for living with me as I lived with this book. Lynn, my wife, is a candidate for canonisation and my children, Nicholas, Aaron, William and Lydia are mercifully accustomed to the madness. They give me stability and a much-needed sense of perspective. Thanks for indulging me.

Finally, I want to pay my respects to Gareth, for putting himself on the line. It hasn't been easy. We've shed a few tears and shared a few laughs. I'm proud of you, mate.

Michael Calvin, May 2014

GARETH'S THANKS

I would like to thank everyone for their support over the tough, but very rewarding experience of writing this book.

To Mike: a writer who became a friend. I let you in, trusted you, and gave you my soul to turn into words. I could not have wished to find a better person to allow into my life. Your strength gave me strength.

To my partner Ian: to TRULY love another man is a great feeling. To be loved back makes it feel even better. Xxxx.

To Emanuele: my manager for my whole life. Where would I be without you? Who knows, but I know I'm here, thanks to your direction.

To every coach who has helped me reach my dream, and to every player I played with, or against: you always had my utmost respect.

To every fan of the game who cheered me, or jeered me: you all gave me the drive to want to be better.

To my home town, Bridgend: you will always be my home, my refuge. I will strive in everything I do to give something back to the town that raised me as its own son.

To my family: I love you all. I value my brothers for toughening me up, and simply being 'my brothers' through everything.

The last words of this story of my life must go to my parents. I live and breathe today because you supported me. I am blessed to be able to call you Mam and Dad.

All I ever wanted to do was make you proud. Through your love and support you gave me the one thing I wanted to give you, pride in who I am. The son of Yvonne and Barrie. The PROUD son. I love you Xxxx.

Gareth Thomas, May 2014

PHOTO CREDITS